Native Americans' Sacred and Ceremonial Landscapes

Correlation with Groundwater

Aligning the Three Worlds

By David W. Johnson

New York State Archaeological Association

Former Research Associate, Department of Anthropology

University of Massachusetts, Amherst

24 Manor Dr. W

Poughkeepsie, NY

12603

845-454-1860

globaldj@optonline.net

Epigraph Books

Rhinebeck, New York

Johnson dedicates this book to those who constructed these magnificent monuments to preserve their spiritual and cultural beliefs within the Western Hemisphere.

ISBN 978-1-954744-60-8

Library of Congress Control Number 2022903248

Library and Archival Reference:

National Anthropologic and Archaeological Library, Smithsonian Institution, Washington, D.C.

Archival Reference for Johnson's publications and research reports:

David Johnson: 2018 Papers on Ceremonial Landscapes, No. 2014-14, National Anthropological Archives, Smithsonian Institution, Washington, D.C.

Photographic Credits:

David W. Johnson - throughout text

Richard Michael Gramly - Page 108, Figure 115

Bill Sharp - Page 123, Figure 158

Google Earth - throughout the text

Epigraph Books

22 East Market Street, Suite 304

Rhinebeck, NY 12572

(845) 876-4861

epigraphs.com

Table Of Contents

FORWARD

In this groundbreaking book, David Johnson presents his theory that many archaeological sites and features were deliberately located on top of concentrated flows of ground water by both preliterate and historic peoples. Beginning over 20 years ago with his research in Peru, Johnson has gone on to argue that using his methodology one can locate cultural remains in a wide variety of geographical locations across the globe. These cultural remains include habitation sites, cemeteries, petroglyphs, standing stones (cairns), sacred trees, and a multitude of similar sites and features. This book is focused on remains found in North America, from the plethora of ruins found in the Southwest to historic Native American remains in the Northeast.

It's true that dowsing is a major part of Johnson's methodology, and one might be skeptical about the scientific validity of this technique, as I was, when I first saw David apply it to some of the sites in Peru that I was surveying in 1996. But as one can see by reading the remarks of the dozens of professionals with whom he conducted blind surveys, he has proven to many that his methodology works! Johnson was the first to discover and understand the connection between the concentrated flow of groundwater and its association with human activity. How the ancients were able to trace these subterranean flows and all the reasons why they did so needs more detailed explanation, but the correlation seems valid and Johnson deserves credit for his discovery.

It's amazing to me how widespread this phenomenon seems to be. Johnson feels that it could be a universal characteristic of human societies, perhaps going back to prehistoric times. This should be an objective of future research.

At the very least, this book should alert archaeologists and other scientists to recognize ancient remains as sacred components of the landscape by using Johnson's methodology in conjunction with oral history, mythology, geology and the other techniques outlined in this book. One needs to keep an open mind to the new concepts detailed in this account. It is an eye-opening book that should be read by anyone doing historical or archaeological work in North America.

Donald A. Proulx
Professor of Anthropology, Emeritus
University of Massachusetts, Amherst

Introduction

Throughout the United States there are numerous locations where various stone features, such as cairns and meandering walls, appear to be associated with one another. However, the sites are not characteristic of post 1492 European settlements. Throughout the Northwestern Hemisphere, Native American First Nations associate these sites with their ancestral past as their Ceremonial Landscapes. Unfortunately, many archaeologists and federal governmental agencies have interpreted these sites as historical and not related to Native Americans.

This book discusses the Native Americans' concepts of the Sacred Landscapes, Ceremonial Landscapes and Habitationscapes, features associated with them and their correlation to areas of higher permeability (concentrated flows) within the groundwater. My colleagues and I investigated sites throughout the United States, as well as Peru and Chile, and our research indicates that, in spite of diversity among tribes and environments, as well as, during different historical periods, various aspects of cultural uniformity prevailed which are characteristic of these Native American concepts.

The goal of this research is to develop a more in-depth understanding of the ancestral Native Americans' concepts of the Sacred Landscape, Ceremonial Landscapes and Habitationscapes and assist present-day Native Americans in their efforts to preserve their cultural heritage sites. This discussion summarizes the interdisciplinary collaboration of Native American and non-native researchers during the last twenty years throughout the regions discussed in this book.

Although this research concentrates on North America and Peru and Chile, South America, I have had the opportunity to apply my methodology to archaeological sites in southern England, Carnac, France, Italy, East Africa and the Sahel along the southern boundaries of the Sahara Desert, and the results were the same. In recent years, additional researchers are focusing on the association of areas of higher permeability within the groundwater and important ancient archaeological sites and features. For example, in Central America, Dr. Guillermo de Anda has located caves which conduct concentrated flows of groundwater beneath Mayan temples and ceremonial sites (National Geographic 2017). In England, archaeologist Michael Parker Pearson has also been investigating this correlation. It appears the correlation between ancient archaeological sites and areas of higher permeability within the groundwater is not unique to Native Americans. Since Native Americans remained somewhat isolated from the rest of the world for thousands of years, their spiritual / religious beliefs were not influenced by modern religions such as Judaism, Christianity and Islam, to mention a few. Therefore, their beliefs are more representative of those practiced by humans throughout the world prior to the development of modern religions, and it is possible these concepts were a universal human trait. We may never know who began this concept or how it spread throughout the world.

The book is divided into three parts. Part 1 discusses the concepts related to these issues and establishes the criteria for our interpretation of the various Native American features discussed in Part 2. Part 2 lists and describes the features we have associated with Ceremonial Landscapes and areas of higher permeability within the groundwater throughout the United States, as well as Peru and Chile in South America, and can be used as a field guide. The images in Part 1 are replicated in Part 2; therefore, each part can be used separately. Part 3 discusses my dowsing methodology which I use to locate areas of high permeability within the groundwater.

In addition to this document, the site reports for several of the sites mentioned below are available in my national archival file at Smithsonian Institution's Anthropological and Archaeological Library in Washington, DC. The administrative agencies who issued us permits also archived our reports for their jurisdiction. Prior to reading the reports, it would be beneficial to read this document since it establishes the criteria for each site report. The archival files are listed on page 167.

Photos credits for outsourced images accompany the photos. Those without credit were taken by David Johnson, and he maintains the copyright. Anyone interested in using his photos needs to obtain his written permission. Google Earth satellite images were used throughout the text.

In the figures, the width between the parallel blue lines represents the approximate width of an area of higher permeability. A single blue line represents a narrow concentrated flow.

Please keep in mind - This research is ongoing and new datum is being added on a regular basis. The following data is current as of June 1, 2020.

Part 1

Chapter 1

Research Methodology

During the last twenty years I have had the privilege to investigate Native American cultures and their ancestral archaeological sites throughout North America, as well as Peru and northern Chile in South America. As my colleagues and I compared the data from each culture and region, a degree of cultural uniformity emerged which applies to the Sacred Landscape, Ceremonial Landscape and Habitationscapes. This discussion focuses on two important characteristics of these Native American concepts. First, the degree of cultural uniformity among Native American historical periods and cultures in diverse environments in regard to these concepts, and secondly, the correlation between these concepts and site features with areas of higher permeability within the groundwater.

Although both native and non-native archaeologists have documented the association between the Sacred Landscape, Ceremonial Landscape and Habitationscapes with spiritual and cultural beliefs, my colleagues and I have found very few references associating these topics with areas of higher permeability / concentrated flows within the groundwater. Therefore, the following discussion will focus on our research methodology and the correlations we have been able to establish between Native American archaeological sites and the features associated with them; and areas of higher permeability within the groundwater.

Johnson's Methodology

An issue regarding my research is the use of dowsing, which is not generally accepted within the scientific community. Before I discuss the use of dowsing, it is important to consider the following. When researchers learn that dowsing is included in my methodology, they conclude that this is the only method I use to reach my conclusions. Actually, this is not the case. In addition to dowsing, geological, hydrological, archaeological and ethnographic studies are included. Within each region, Native American First Nation archaeological, spiritual, cultural and elder authorities are consulted and collaborate with this research. All of these diverse disciplines are considered prior to writing a site report or publication. As for dowsing, I have found the most efficient way to determine an archaeological site's correlation to geological and hydrological features is by using this technique. Throughout these investigations the same methodology has been used. Thus, dowsing is discussed next.

This research consists of surveying sites using dowsing rods to determine where areas of higher permeability within the groundwater are located, and if they are aligned with the Native American archaeological sites and the features associated with them. Within the bedrock, groundwater is found in permeable strata. Geological features such as faults, fractures, dikes, contacts and alluvium associated with the permeable strata can create areas of higher permeability which collect groundwater and conduct it along their length. I use two metal L shaped dowsing rods to locate areas of higher permeability. One end is contained in a plastic holder and swings freely, thus my hands do not touch the rods. The metal dowsing rods are held perpendicular to the ground and parallel to one another as I walk. When an area of higher permeability is encountered the rods cross to some extent. If they barely cross, it indicates there is a low rate of flow along the area of higher permeability. If they cross in the middle, it is moderate, and if they cross completely, it indicates a strong rate of flow. The trend and width of the areas of higher permeability are determined by crossing it several times and documenting where the rods cross. Although I admit I don't know how dowsing with metal rods works, by practicing and testing on known groundwater sources, I have come to realize it works for me, as well as others who have surveyed the same sites I have and obtained the same results. Whenever possible, I survey at least two sides of a site to determine if any areas of higher permeability intersect it. Then I follow the area(s) of higher permeability into the site and document the archaeological features associated with them, as well as those which are not. Consistently, our data indicates ancestral Native Americans placed structures and other features along areas of higher permeability. Thus far, our data indicates the ancestral Native Americans who constructed these sites were locating the same subsurface features I am documenting.

I prefer to conduct my survey prior to studying the current interpretation of the geological, hydrological and archaeological data for a region. When I began my investigation in Nasca, Peru, previous interpretations of the western Andean watershed concluded eighty percent of the runoff was through the rivers and twenty percent through the bedrock and alluvium. My investigation, followed by the University of Massachusetts study, concluded the opposite was true. Using dowsing I have been able to locate areas of higher permeability within the groundwater that are not detected by current geological and hydrological techniques. Water tables are determined by averaging the depth of groundwater in a given area using various forms of technology and well data. Narrow areas of higher permeability can go undetected using these scientific methodologies. To confirm the location of the areas of higher permeability, I am collaborating with geologists and hydrologists in each of the regions I am investigating.

When people learn that my methodology includes the use of dowsing rods, they often ask if we have found any evidence that ancient native Americans used this technique. At this point in time, my colleagues and I have not been able to identify any archaeological evidence which indicates ancient ancestral Native Americans used some form of dowsing. However, the evidence could be present and misinterpreted, for example, in petroglyphs. It is also possible they never incorporated it into their oral tradition, and dowsing as a means to locate groundwater was lost due to conflicts, conquest, epidemics or cultural diffusion. During the course of these investigations some tribal leaders have informed me that they use dowsing; however, they did not elaborate on this subject.

I realize this methodology does not follow modern archaeological methods of research, however consider the following. Perhaps ancestral Native Americans, as well as other ancient cultures throughout the world, used methods which are considered unscientific today to locate concentrated flows within the groundwater, and these techniques have been neglected in modern times. Although I use metal dowsing rods, the ancestral Native Americans could have used a variety of techniques to locate areas of higher permeability. For example, for centuries dowsing rods have been made out of forked wood sticks to locate groundwater. During the last forty years I have worked and lived with tribes in remote regions of the world whose lifestyle still resembles that of Native Americans prior to 1492 (Johnson's resumes). Many of these cultures were located in dry regions similar to the southwest. From time to time I have observed alternative techniques to locate areas of higher permeability that could have been used by ancestral Native Americans. For example, at times it is possible to hear groundwater flowing beneath the surface. In the lower Rio Grande de Nasca drainage of Peru at Usaca, residents told my colleagues and I they could hear a waterfall at night when they laid down to sleep; however, the river's surface was dry at that time. At that location, the surface and/or subsurface water flowing down the river intersects a fault which crosses it and extends deeper into the ground. Therefore, some or all of the river's flow can drain downward into the fault and follow a different course. The waterfall the people heard was the transfer of the water from the river into the fault. During the Aja Alto survey near Nasca, Peru, my colleagues and I could hear groundwater flowing beneath us along the fault we were mapping, even through there was no indication of water on the surface within the area (Johnson 2009, Chap. 2).

Northern Burkina Faso is located in the Sahel, one of the driest regions of the Sahara Desert. While working with a United Nations development project in 1992 I observed three productive wells, which were located along a 15 mile stretch of desert. I asked how they located the wells, and they introduced me to an elderly man who lived in the region and had a reputation for locating wells. He said by sitting on the ground at various locations he could sense where concentrations of groundwater are located. In 2009 during a Kenya Red Cross well project, I worked with Mohamed Roba, who told me how he taught himself to locate groundwater sources by observing various forms of vegetation and soils. Over eighty percent of his wells are successful. We tested each other's ability to locate areas of higher permeability on known and unknown water sources and had the same results. This suggests, in addition to observing natural groundwater features such as springs, seeps, blowholes, faults, natural bedrock fractures and mineral veins, the ancestral Native Americans of the Western Hemisphere could have used a variety of methods to identify areas of higher permeability. Then they mapped the location of areas of higher permeability with surface features such as shrines, structures, petroglyphs, cairns and geoglyphs, etc.

In Chile, our data indicates the Chinchorro Culture, which inhabited one of the driest regions of the Atacama Desert as early as 9,000 B.P. (7,000 B.C.), documented areas of high permeability, which provided them with fresh water in an area where the surface water was contaminated with salt and arsenic (Johnson 2009, Chap. 6, Camarones & Chiza).

Blind Surveys

Often critics who have not accompanied me in the field suggest I can see various features from a distance and walk to them while dowsing, thus claiming the rods detected an area of higher permeability which lead me to them. However, blind surveys with other researchers who accompanied me in the field indicate the opposite is true. To test this hypothesis, I have conducted numerous blind surveys with other researchers in all of the regions I have investigated. During these surveys, I am not given any information about the site or its features and location. Once in the area, I apply my methodology to locate areas of higher permeability and then follow them to the site. Within the site, I map the areas of higher permeability and the surface features associated with them, as well as those that are not. During all of the blind surveys we have conducted, I was able to locate the site and features associated with it successfully. The following comments represent a selection of those available regarding the results of the blind surveys we conducted.

In the fall of 2000, Dr. Steve Mabee, Department of Geoscience, University of Massachusetts, and I contacted the Navajo Nation and offered to conduct a blind survey to determine if the methodology we were using in Peru applied to Chaco sites in the southwestern United States. Then, in 2012 I returned to the Navajo Nation and have been collaborating with them since that time. In January 2014, Ronald Maldonado, Acting Tribal Historic Preservation Officer, Department of Historic Preservation, The Navajo Nation, commented:

> I was introduced to Johnson's theory regarding the correlation between areas of higher permeability and archaeological sites in the fall of 2000. He had asked to conduct a preliminary investigation of some Chaco archaeological sites within the Navajo Nation. During his visit Johnson and his colleague, Dr. Steve Mabee, Geoscience Department, University of Massachusetts, presented their data to our department and some sites were investigated. Without knowing anything about the sites, they located what they described as areas of higher permeability and followed them. The areas of higher permeability lead to archaeological features they did not know about or could see in advance.

> In 2012 Johnson contacted us and explained he was interested in changing his study area from Peru and Chile to the southwest and would like to investigate sites within our region. Thus far, permits were issued in 2012 and 2013 and he plans on returning in 2014. Johnson has investigated several sites and submitted detailed reports. His methodology is very scientific even though he incorporates dowsing. He has documented several archaeological sites and features which had not been identified prior to his investigation. In addition to our

department, he is also collaborating with the Navajo Department of Water Resources.

Johnson's research is investigating an area of archaeology which has not been thoroughly studied, and this research is helping the Navajo, as well as other Native American people, develop a more in-depth understanding of their ancient past. Please consider issuing him a permit to continue his research in your jurisdiction (Maldonado 2014).

In 2012 following a blind survey with the Hopi Nation, Max Taylor, Water Resources Technician, Hopi Tribe Water Resources Program, who conducted the blind survey with me, commented in his report:

As we drove down State Route 264 we stopped at one spot where the rods crossed. At this location the mesa is narrow, and I knew there are springs at the base of the slope on each side of the road, however I did not tell him until he completed his test. Johnson located an area of higher permeability crossing the road. I could see what he meant about the position of the rods when on the boundary of area of higher permeability…. At another location I had him survey the area to determine if there was an area of higher permeability since I knew there were cairns located in the area. I did not tell Johnson about this or its location. He located an area of higher permeability and began following it directly to the cairns which he could not see (Note: These cairns are very old and the purposes of the 2 markers are lost to the present day land users which are the Hopi). Along the way he also located an archaeological site I didn't know about (Taylor 2012).

Dr. Curtiss Hoffman, Department of Anthropology, Bridgewater State University, Massachusetts, who is also investigating Ceremonial Landscapes, conducted a blind survey with me in 2012. In his comments he discusses the survey and the results:

He had agreed to attempt to locate an archaeological site I know about and which he knew nothing about by locating an area(s) of higher permeability / concentrated flows using dowsing rods and following it to the site. I led him on a roundabout path through the woods around Great Hill. Actually, I led him to an entrance to the woods distant from the known Native American sacred site and let him find his way from there without guidance from me. He used his dowsing rods to locate several areas of higher permeability running off the hill. We came to the sacred site last, and without my telling him anything about it, he accurately located a concentrated flow whose edge conforms to the orientation of the stone row. He then went off downhill to find the opposite edge, and was visibly startled to discover the large split rock right at that edge! He traced the area of higher permeability on uphill, and it turns out that there are 2 others crossing the solstice sunset line, which are also marked by stones. I would say that this was a good confirmation of his method (Hoffman 2012,).

Richard Friedman, geologist and retired director of the McKinley County, New Mexico, Geographic Information Systems Center, and cultural resource archaeologist with the Chaco Protection Sites Program of the Navajo Nation Historic Preservation Department, has been collaborating with me since he conducted the first blind surveys with me. He describes the results as follows:

> I spent several days in the field with David testing his theories on numerous archaeological sites on the Navajo Reservation in northwestern New Mexico. We tested sites ranging in age from early archaic to mid Pueblo III (approximately 6,000 BC to 1300 AD), with the majority of the sites being Chaco Anasazi (850 – 1125 AD) and late Basketmaker III (600-700/750 AD). I conducted numerous blind tests on locations that have not been recorded, and that are not mentioned in any report or other form of documentation. With the exception of one Chacoan Road alignment (which we now understand there is not a 100% correlation with), he located every site using his methodologies, including an isolated pecked/carved linear groove in sandstone slick rock that only 3-5 archaeologists know about. The methodology employed by David is very scientific, even though he uses dowsing, which typically has less than favorable acceptance in the scientific community. After carefully observing David for several days it became very clear that the results (dowsing rods) are not being manipulated, and that there is a very real correlation between the underground features David is mapping and archaeological site locations. When it comes to his research, I can honestly say that it's hard to fully understand and endorse it unless you have observed it in the field (Friedman 2013).

Kenneth Frye, archeological technician, retired, National Forest Service, who also worked for the BLM through a "service first" agreement, San Luis Valley Field Office, Monte Vista, Colorado, for twenty years, has also been collaborating with me since he conducted blind surveys with me. During the first survey he comments:

> In 2013, I took him to a site northeast of Saguache, on private property, where a very interesting stone wall is located. Some researchers believe the wall is an ancient geoglyph in the shape of a snake or serpent. David had instructed the members of our research team at the site not to provide him with any information regarding the site. He described how he would dowse along the perimeter of the property to determine how many areas of higher permeability intersected it. Then he would follow the areas of higher permeability into the property to determine if they intersect any archaeological sites or features. Within the first half hour he located four areas of higher permeability, determined the direction they crossed the property and

flagged them. All four lead him directly to four important features within the site. They included a spring and snake wall, a boulder shaped like an eagle, the high point of the site where there is a perched boulder and a large boulder which is the head of a long snake wall. Our team was amazed at how fast and accurate his calculations were (Frye 2013).

Using this methodology, I have been able to predict the course of areas of higher permeability by interpreting the surface features at archaeological sites. Consistently, before entering a site I have also been able to predict which features, including petroglyphs, will be found at a site based on the characteristics of the area(s) of higher permeability I am following. During the first blind survey with Richard Henderson, Verde Valley Archaeological Center, Camp Verde, Arizona, I described and predicted the location of petroglyphs before I saw them. Henderson comments:

> While driving to the first of the recommended test areas, Mr. Johnson defined his process at some length and offered a 'blind' demonstration, where I might observe his test in an area he was unlikely to be previously familiar with. The process required that Mr. Johnson hold the dowsing rods pointing to the front and initially in a parallel orientation. When nearing a concentrated flow (cf), the rods would begin oscillating and when at the cf, would cross. I asked if his process would work while in a moving vehicle, and when he said it would, I asked him to 'get out his sticks', knowing a site was not far down the road. He pulled the rods from his pack.

> When Mr. Johnson said the rods were indicating that we were approaching a cf, I stopped and he got out and started walking, following the direction the rods were pointing. After a brief search, he asked that I stand where the rods indicated and again began to follow the rods. Where his rods again crossed, he noted that he was now on the other side of this cf, took GPS readings, made some notes and began a new search perpendicular to his previous line of travel which he indicated would establish a trend line. Moving some thirty meters to the side he again 'followed the rods' to a point where he again asked that I stand while he defined a new cf, perpendicular to the first.

> A new trend line was defined and Mr. Johnson said, "Your site is over there," pointing

Figure 1: Zigzag located during blind survey with Henderson

to the area I knew to have a large sandstone boulder with numerous petroglyph elements. Mr. Johnson predicted that we would find among these elements, some 'squiggly' lines oriented both horizontally and vertically, defining the intersection of the two cfs. We Did! (Figure 1) This symbology has been associated by local researchers with water, lightning or snakes (Henderson 2015).

When people read my reports and hear my presentation they find it difficult to believe the results. However, those who have conducted blind surveys with me have seen it work. This strongly suggests I am documenting the same subsurface features ancestral Native Americans located and mapped with structures and other features.

The function assigned to each feature is based on the combined research from Peru and Chile, as well as the United States and Canada, during the last twenty years. The functions discussed below were derived by comparing stone features and structures with geological and hydrological features. When a correlation is consistent from region to region and different historical periods, it is added to the list. In addition to these features, there are others which have not been associated with geological and hydrological features and are not included in this discussion. As mentioned above, many, if not all, of the features are multifunctional, while others may represent a tribal affiliation. They will be discussed at another time.

In spite of different historical periods and phases, the function of several features have remained the same throughout the sites we have investigated within North America. In Peru and Chile, geometrical shapes were used to document the flow of areas of higher permeability, and many of those found in North America have the same shape and function (Johnson 2009, Chap. 2). This suggests ancestral Native Americans were using the same basic concepts to map the location of areas of higher permeability throughout the Western Hemisphere with structures and stone features. The similarity between various stone features strongly suggests some degree of cultural uniformity existed throughout most, if not all, of the Western Hemisphere.

Interestingly, as complicated as this sounds, it is very simplistic in regard to the number of features used to map the areas of higher permeability since they are replicated from region to region. Once you know the function of several features, you can interpret them to determine the course and width of the areas of higher permeability they are mapping without using any form of dowsing. I have also demonstrated it is possible to teach others how to interpret these features. In 2012 while investigating a site in the Verde Valley in Arizona, I met two local residents, Nelson Avery and Glenn Waltrip. Neither one had a background in archaeology or hydrology, however they were interested in my research and offered to help. In the following comment they discuss the events that followed:

> At the first site we visited we wanted to show David a petroglyph panel which had been shown to us during one of our mineral club's

field trips. When we arrived we wanted to show David where the petroglyphs were, however he said he would find them by following the areas of higher permeability. Our interest was broadened since we had heard of "dowsing" but never had any firsthand experience with it or anyone who performed it before. We watched as David began dowsing the north end of the site and documenting areas of higher permeability within the groundwater which he said lead him to archaeological features that mapped the course of these flows. At that point it looked like he was making it up since you cannot see where the areas of higher permeability flow. Then he told us you don't have to use dowsing to locate the areas of higher permeability if you know the meaning of the various archaeological features. He offered to describe to us what he was finding and their meaning as he investigated the site. Then once we knew the function of various features we would be able to follow the areas of higher permeability by "reading" the features. This sounded intriguing and we agreed to his suggestion. The results were amazing. By that afternoon we were walking ahead of David looking for features and then describing what we thought they meant to determine if we were right. When needed, he would correct us, and we continued on. By the end of the day we couldn't wait to get to the next site to see if we could find and follow the stone features, which looked like a mess of random field stones to us when we began that morning.

The following day, as David located an area of higher permeability in one area, we located small stone cairns and circles in another location. As he followed the area of higher permeability it led him directly to us. From that point on we followed the stone features ahead of David and were able to determine the flow pattern of areas of higher permeability, as well as where they intersect one another. We were amazed at how fast we learned this, and how well it worked. (Waltrip and Avery 2014).

At this point in time, several researchers have learned this methodology and are implementing it successfully to locate Ceremonial Sites and features. For example, in 2016 Dr. Forrest Ketchin commented:

The work we have done includes stone features and what some call "living artifacts" -- Culturally Modified Trees (CMT's) -- in the San Luis Valley of Colorado, USA. The placement of such archaeological features here has always been a bit of a mystery to archaeologists, except, of course, when the reason is unavoidably obvious, such as the presence of flowing springs or trails, or evidence of habitation.

The placement of CMT's often seems random to the Euro-American eye, seeming to do only with the presence of the right kind of tree in the ancient territory of an American Indian Nation. Occasionally, a flowing spring, creek, trail, or habitation site is evident, but not always. I have used dowsing and some of Mr. Johnson's techniques with some interesting results that begin to explain the otherwise seemingly random placements of both stone features and CMT's. The CMT's appear to be placed in reference to underground areas of increased permeability, or 'flows'.

In addition, dowsing these underground areas of increased permeability has led me to stone features that I would have missed otherwise, given that these also do not always occur in association with other obvious archaeological features. These include stone circles, stone spirals, cairns and possible burials, all difficult to spot in the heavily wooded and rocky area I have been investigating (Ketchin 2016).

Don Wells, who has also been investigating culturally modified trees, commented in his January 2016 newsletter:

David Johnson, in late 2015, shared his knowledge about using dowsing rods to locate underground streams that are connected to Indian sites. David has been doing research on Indian sites in North and South America for 40 years. He has learned, over this extensive period of time, that almost all Indian artifacts, including trees, cairns, etc., and sacred sites are connected to underground streams of water. This past summer, he showed our colleague, Dr. Forrest Ketchin, in Colorado, that his techniques could be used to locate Indian Trees. We have since tested that theory on trees in Alabama and Georgia and found it to be true on these east coast trees. We have also tested it at a rock cairn site in Georgia and found it to also be true for that ancient site. The Mountain Stewards have been given permission to do an extensive survey of the Georgia rock cairn site which will begin in late January 2016 (Wells 2016).

Since our first geoscience survey of the Rio Grande de Nasca drainage with the University of Massachusetts, additional investigations have been conducted. In 2018 Dr. David Bethune, Dr. Cathryn Ryan and Ryland Bjorndahl, Department of Geoscience, University of Calgary, Canada, researched the geologic controls on the distribution of springs in the Ica Valley, Peru. (Bjorndahl 2018) They compared my data on one hundred and thirty-four areas of higher permeability and springs, and their association with archaeological sites and geoglyphs within the middle Ica Valley, with their data and concluded:

Johnson et al. (2006) mapped the locations of various springs within the Ica Valley to provide the framework and information required to interpret why the springs are located there. When placed on a geologic map, each spring is located on a geologic contact between a relatively impermeable rock, and the permeable unconsolidated fluvial material of the valley bottom. They are also located on faults running through the impermeable intrusive igneous and volcanic rocks provide the conduits for water from high elevations to reach the valley bottom where it can be discharged as springs. The geologic contact does not control the distribution of the springs as the impermeable rock is located above the permeable. Further research is needed to confirm the permeability of the Pisco Formation underlying the permeable unconsolidated material in order to determine if that impacts the distribution of the springs in the Ica Valley. Geochemical and isotopic data from one of the springs confirmed the high-altitude recharge as when compared to a high elevation sample, both were depleted $\delta^{18}O$ and δ^2H, and the EC and TDS increased as you moved to lower elevations. High altitude recharge shows that water is transported through joints, faults and fractures down to the valley bottom where it is discharged into the permeable fluvial and alluvial material. The low silica content indicates that the water does not circulate very deep as it does not experience an elevated temperature to dissolve more silica.

Knowing the geologic controls on the distribution of these groundwater springs can provide information to the municipality of Ica and allow locals to find these springs and supplement their water usage. Ancient Nazca and Ica people knew of these springs and utilized them as it is evident from the pottery and signs of civilization around them. Other areas of the valley surrounding Ica with similar geology may have similar springs and mapping these may provide further insight into the ground water flow system (Bjorndahl 2018).

Thus far, everyone who has accompanied me in the field, observed and independently tested this methodology, agrees that it works.

Chapter 2

Research Prior To North America

Between 1996 and 2012 I studied the correlation between areas of higher permeability within groundwater and archaeological sites in Peru and Chile. This correlation came about as a result of locating water sources for the community of Nasca, Peru. During the investigation, I located areas of high permeability which intersected the tributaries of the Rio Grande de Nasca drainage from the valley sides. Until that time, these water sources were not well known. While documenting them I realized the Nasca Lines / geoglyphs also mapped them. Habitation, ceremonial and cemetery sites were also located along these water courses. Eventually, by comparing the location of various types of geometric geoglyphs with the geological and hydrological data, I was able to determine the function of these features. For example, along the areas of higher permeability, trapezoids mapped their course, paralleling lines of stone piles the width and spirals indicated where they curved. Collaborating with the University of Massachusetts, Amherst, Peru's Institute of National Culture and other archaeologists, this study eventually included one thousand four hundred miles of Peru and Chile's coast and eastward into the Andes Mountains. Our data indicates inhabitants of the Atacama Desert were mapping areas of higher permeability within the groundwater as early as the Chinchorro culture, dating from 9,000 BP to the fall of the Inca Empire in the 1500's. This research is discussed in detail in my book titled <u>Beneath the Nasca Lines and Other Coastal Geoglyphs of Peru and Chile</u>.

As we disseminated our data, researchers began to contact us regarding similar correlations they observed in North America. Thus, in 2009 I began to apply the same methodology I used in Peru and Chile throughout North America, and the results were the same. Ancestral Native Americans located areas of higher permeability within the groundwater and mapped them with surface features, such as cairns and petroglyphs, and placed their habitation and ceremonial sites along them. By comparing Native American sites, such as Ceremonial Landscapes, from one region to another throughout North America, a common pattern emerged, which is characteristic of all the Native American cultures we investigated as of this publication even though they are associated with different historical periods, environments and regions.

During the course of this research, we realized the Ceremonial Landscape features collectively function as a map of ancestral Native American movement throughout the areas we have surveyed, and very likely serve the same function throughout the Western Hemisphere. In other words, these features function like a modern day road map.

Sacred Landscape, Ceremonial Landscapes And Habitationscapes

During the course of this research, the terms Sacred Landscape, Ceremonial Landscapes and Habitationscapes have become paramount in developing an understanding of the ethnology of ancestral Native Americans. Combining the three terms encompasses the Native Americans' holistic perception of Mother Earth. The following discusses each of these concepts in greater detail.

The Sacred Landscape

The Sacred Landscape is a holistic concept which encompasses the underworld, physical world and the cosmos. Historical evidence strongly suggests the Sacred Landscape concept has continued to endure for hundreds, if not thousands, of years, in spite of tribal diversity and different historical periods.

In Native American Netroots, Ojibwa describes the Sacred Landscape as follows:

> All humans have a cognitive map which provides them with a
> spatial analysis of their world, both natural and human-made.

Traditionally, the cognitive maps of American Indians have been carried in their stories. Indian stories, particularly the spiritual stories and the stories of creation, focus on geography, telling what happened where and describing different places and their associations with each other. When one knows the stories, then one has a map of the traditional tribal territory. Traditionally, this meant that a person could go someplace new and know, because of the stories, not only the route, but also the different geographic features which would be encountered on the trip.

American Indians...tended to be animists who viewed the world around them as a living thing. Sacred places were not created by humans. While the people would sometimes designate a sacred place with a structure of some type - a pile of stones, a circle of stones, a mound or earthwork, or a chamber - often places with great sacred power did not have any human - created indications that they were sacred. People know about these places because of the stories and the songs rather than because of the structures which they had constructed.

One example of the interrelationship of sacred space, cognitive maps, and oral tradition can be seen in the Salt Trail Songs of the Nuwuvi (Southern Paiute) which describe both a physical and spiritual landscape. This includes physical features such as oceans and deserts, and spiritual features including life and death. The songs describe ancient village sites, gathering sites for medicinal plants and salt, historic events, trade routes, and sacred areas. The 142-song cycle assists the deceased in their sacred journey.

For American Indians, sacred places do not exist in isolation: they are connected to other sacred places, and these connections enhance the spiritual power of an area. The connections between sacred places are explained in the stories and in the songs.

It is not just "places" that are spiritually connected, but also the "people" who are associated with the places: the plants, the animals, the rocks. Again, the stories, songs, and ceremonies explain the nature and meaning of these connections (Ojibwa, 2013).

During the course of our research other Native Americans have shared the same thoughts with us.

Often, the Sacred Landscape covers a large area and is not obvious to those who are not familiar with Native American traditional beliefs. One place where the Sacred Landscape can be observed more clearly is in Chaco Canyon, New Mexico. Within the canyon there are several great houses, such as Pueblo Bonito. From these structures, Chaco Roads radiate outward to additional structures called outliers which replicate those in Chaco Canyon. (Figures 2 & 140 - 142) Some of the outliers are located more than a hundred miles from Chaco Canyon. Then, within the Sacred Landscape, there are Ceremonial Landscapes which consist of stone features, such as cairns and petroglyphs, which are associated with Chaco Canyon and replicated along the roads and within distant communities. Habitationscapes are communities located throughout the Sacred Landscape consisting of family units and outliers which resemble the structures found in Chaco Canyon. By connecting these sites and replicating various characteristics, the people who constructed them are defining their Sacred Landscape and expressing cultural uniformity.

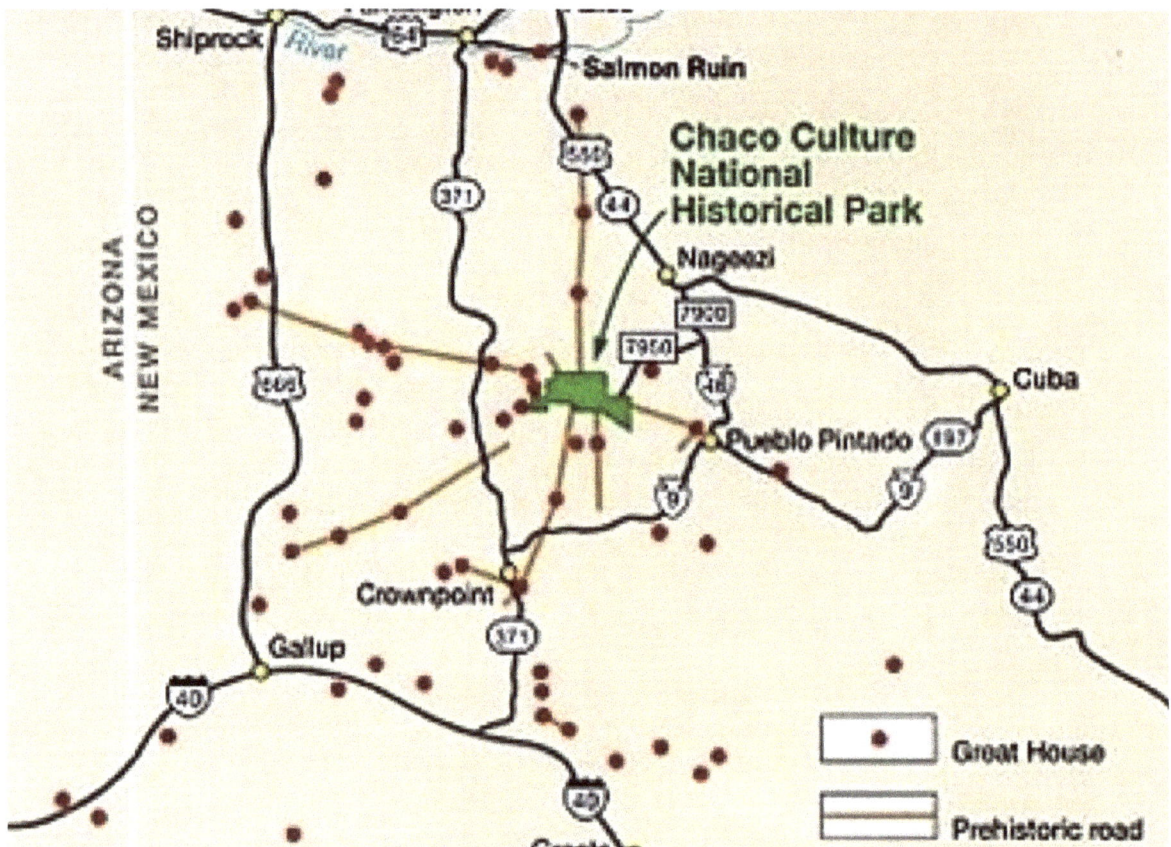

Figure 2: Chaco communities and roads, NPS Map, 2000

Although Ruth Van Dyke's description of the sacred geography and landscape was written in regard to Chaco Canyon, New Mexico, it reflects the basic beliefs of Native Americans throughout the Western Hemisphere:

> The Tewas, Keres, Zunis and Hopi place importance on spatial divisions and directions, dividing their physical, social, and spiritual worlds into horizontal and vertical dimensions of cosmologies expressed through landscape and agriculture. Multiple levels of social and spiritual meaning are inscribed on the landscape by topographic features and shrines, and the pueblo itself represents this organization

in microcosm. Horizontal divisions correspond to cardinal directions, and vertical divisions include upper and lower world. Nested layers or symmetrical quarters are connected at a center place - the pueblo. The center place is the place of convergence, where six directions (four cardinal directions plus zenith and nadir) join and where symmetrically opposing forces are balanced (Van Dyke 2004: 79).

The contemporary pueblo world cannot be considered a direct reflection of the Chacoan past. Nevertheless, some vital elements of Pueblo ideology, including notions of balance and center place, are clearly represented on the Chaco landscape. The Chacoans constructed buildings, roads, and shrines that express their ideas about the organization of the world. They also used elements of the natural topography to dramatic effect. The results were a landscape that was built to be experienced, to express ideas about sacred directions and dualistic balance. Oppositional dualisms such as those between the celestial and the subterranean, the visible and the invisible, and the north and south are represented in Chacoan great houses, great kivas, road alignments, earthworks, and shrines. The canyon itself was the center place, the fulcrum that balanced opposing forces, the intersection of the sacred directions, the axis mundi around which both space and time revolved (Van Dyke 2004).

In spite of being separated by thousands of miles, the Puebloan concept of the Sacred Landscape and the Andean Tradition are very similar. Anthony Aveni refers to the Andean Tradition in relation to Cusco, the Inca capital, as follows, "The principles of organization of Cusco has demonstrated, highland concepts of both time and space are inextricably bound to religious, social, and political organizing principles in the structural plan of the city. These principles can be understood only in their totality; they lose their meaning once we attempt to break them down into separate spheres of concern." He also comments "Moreover, the system is radial in its basic layout, a form that seems very special and important in Andean society (Aveni 1990)." The ceque system which, according to Aveni, "seems to have been a mnemonic device built into Cusco's natural and man-made topography that served to unify ideas about religion, social organization, hydrology, calendar, and astronomy." The ceques are 41 imaginary radial lines of sight that extend from Qoricancha which are documented by a line of huacas. Aveni states, "These huacas, which number 328 in all, according to the interpretation of Zuidema, are said to be temples (natural or man-made), arrangements of stones, bends in rivers, fields, springs or other natural wells called puquios, hills, even impermanent objects such as trees. In most cases, the water theme and its association with the agricultural calendar are given extreme emphasis." Cusco is divided into two halves, called Hanan and Hurin. Then they are divided into two sectors called suyus. Interestingly, Aveni comments, "The principle rationale for dividing the city has to do with the watershed environment rather than with any considerations of pure geometry. The boundaries between suyus demarcate the flow of groundwater in the Cusco Valley."

He also states that the suyus served as a way to delineate water rights to the various kin-related groups called ayllus that lived there. "These people receive, by right of birth, the underground water directly from their ancestors who are believed to reside within the earth." The suyus are distinguished by the four major roads leading out of Cusco which extend to remote regions of the empire (Aveni 1990, pp. 50-51). The beliefs expressed by the Inca were shared by cultures throughout this region during different historical phases.

These traditions share a complex intimate relationship with nature which was developed over thousands of years by observing, documenting and experimenting with their natural surroundings, and then implementing and adapting a lifestyle to accommodate these environments, thus enabling them to survive. Each site was multifunctional in scope to meet diverse parameters within their beliefs. To fully understand ancestral Native American structures and other features, each site needs to be examined holistically.

Ceremonial Landscapes

Figure 3: The Ceremonial Landscape, Spruceton Site, NY

Within the Sacred Landscape, there are Ceremonial Landscapes within a tribal sphere of influence which demonstrate cultural uniformity. (Figure 3) For example, several eastern tribes within the United States classify sites containing stone features, such as cairns and meandering walls, as Ceremonial Landscapes. The United South and Eastern Tribes (USET), consisting of twenty-six tribes, in Resolution #2007:037 describe these sites as follows: (Wikipedia 2014, Personal discussions with Narragansett Historical Preservation Office 2014)

> Elements often found at these sites include dry stone walls, rock piles (sometimes referred to as cairns), stone chambers, unusually-shaped boulders, split boulders with stones inserted in the split, and boulders propped up off the ground with smaller rocks.

> Within the ancestral territories of the USET Tribes there exist sacred Ceremonial Landscapes and their stone structures which are of particular cultural value to certain member Tribes.

> For thousands of years before the immigration of Europeans, the medicine people of the USET Tribal ancestors used these Sacred Landscapes to sustain the people's reliance on Mother Earth and the spirit energies of balance and harmony.

> Whether these stone structures are massive or small structures, stacked, stone rows, or effigies, these prayers in stone are often mistaken by archaeologists and State Historic Preservation Officers (SHPOs) as the efforts of farmers clearing stones for agricultural or wall building purposes (Wikipedia 2014).

The resolution goes on to request that the federal government work to understand and preserve the Ceremonial Landscapes.

Nearly three thousand miles away on the Pacific coast, the Klamath Tribe described the importance of stone features within their beliefs and history during a Committee on Interior and Insular Affairs meeting in 1992:

> Of equal weight is the spiritual importance of the River to the Klamath people. Spiritually, the River expresses the value of life. Its location and terrain have made it a focus for vision and crisis quests. Innumerable stone cairns throughout the canyon attest to its long and continued spiritual use. These cairns are pages in the Klamath people's history, a very real connection to the lives and spirits of those who walked the earth in the near and distant past. Studies of this area for the purpose of assessing the impact of further development have often looked at the `archaeological' value of various sites in the river canyon. Yet for the ancestral Native American peoples these archaeological sites are much more than scientific curiosities. These `archaeological' sites are all places where our ancestors lived and died, worshipped the Creator and buried or cremated their dead. These sites were not merely points of economic convenience: they were the places chosen by the Creator for our ancestors to worship, respect and serve the ends of creation, of life itself (Committee on Interior and Insular Affairs 1992, pp. 243, Gage 2015).

These tribal testimonials are supported by numerous historical documents. Several historical references to Native American Ceremonial Landscapes are found in early land patents and deeds. These documents clearly indicate Native American stone features existed prior to colonial occupation in the northeast. In 1878 in the History of Columbia County, New York, Captain Franklin Ellis discussed Robert Livingston's land deeds issued between 1684 and 1685. On August 10, 1685, Livingston purchased a vast tract of land referred to as Taghkanic from the Mohican Indians. In that deed, one of the boundaries is referred to as follows; "Wawanaquasick, stone-heaps on the north line, where the Indians have laid several heaps of stones together by an ancient custom among them." (Ellis 1878, Gaga 2015).

In colonial documents, people who were traveling with Native Americans commented on their relationship to the Ceremonial Landscape. For example, one reference refers to a stone pile in central New York State:

It was also on this road that the famous `stone-heap' was situated. There is a tradition that, long prior to the Revolutionary War, a white man was murdered at this spot, and the edict was issued that every Indian, in passing this spot, should throw a stone upon it. Who issued the command and when it was issued, are questions whose answers are lost in the dim distance of time. The fact remains that every Indian who passed the spot did cast a stone upon it. One authority says: `Somewhere between Schoharie Creek and Caughnawaga commenced an Indian road or foot-path which lead to Schoharie. Near this road *** has been seen, from time immemorial, a large pile of stones, which has given the name `Stone-heap Patent' to the tract on which it occurs, as may be seen from ancient deeds.' Rev. Gideon-Hawley, in the narrative of his tour through the Mohawk country, by Schoharie Creek, in 1753, makes the following allusion to the stone-heap: `We came to a resting-place and breathed out horses, and slaked our thirst at the stream, when we perceived our Indian looking for a stone, which, having found, he cast to a heap which for ages has been accumulating by passengers like him who was our guide. We inquired why he observed that rite. He answered that his father practiced it and enjoined it on him. But he did not like to talk on the subject. *** The custom or rite is an acknowledgement of an invisible being. We may style him the unknown god this worship. This heap is his alter. The stone that is collected is the oblation of the traveler, which, if offered with a good mind, may be as acceptable as a consecrated animal. But perhaps these heaps of stone may be erected to a local deity, which most probably is the case.' On this, Ruttenber remarks: `The custom referred to had nothing of worship in it. *** The stone-heaps were always by the side of the trail or regularly traveled path, and usually at or near a stream of water. The Indians paused to refresh themselves, and by throwing a stone or stick to a certain place, indicated to travelers that a friend had passed.' (F. W. Beers 1878, Gage 2015).

Ethnographic and archaeological evidence supports these statements. In Archaeological Expedition to Arizona in 1895, Jesse Walter Fewkes describes stone features he observed at Awatobi and reported they were still being used as shrines at the time of his expedition. One is described as "a circle of small stones in which were two large water-worn stones and a fragment of petrified wood, another was a small stone pile on the extreme western point of the mesa" and the last is a large boulder with a semicircular low wall extending from it (Fewkes 1895, pp. 619-621). Various forms of offerings, including prayer sticks, were associated with these shrines / stone features. While some appeared as though they had not been used in "modern times" others were still being used. He reported the semicircular low wall shrine "is still used by the *Mishoninovi priests* in their sacred observances" (Fewkes 1895, pp. 619-621). The four stone feature images accompanying his discussion are very similar to those we have investigated throughout the southwestern and northeastern United States.

In a discussion of Tewa cosmology in the Rio Grande del Rancho Valley, Severin Fowles, Department of Anthropology, Barnard College, along with extracts from Dr. Alfonso Ortiz, a Pueblo Indian and anthropologist, discusses the association of stone features with Tewa cosmology, shrines and spirits:

Ortiz's description of the location and morphology of these shrines (stone features) is especially interesting in light of the many similar features in the Rio Grande del Rancho Valley, discussed below:

Central to Ortiz's work was the Tewa conceptualization of the cosmos as a series of nested spheres or tetrads, each organized according to the four cardinal directions. These tetrads represent, in part, the various categories of living and deceased peoples in the religious hierarchy, the latter of whom reside in certain sacred locations surrounding the village center.

First in the directional circuit is Powa, "Sun, water, wind," represented by a pile of large stones at the northern edge of the village. At the western edge of the village is Awe Kwiyoh or Spider Woman, represented by a single stone; to the south is Nu Enu or Ash Youtg, also represented by a single stone. Approximately one mile east of the village is a low hill with a pile of stones on top; this is Ti tan He i or "Large Marked Shield," the shrine of the east. There are numerous other shrines dotting the landscape around each Tewa village..." (Ortiz 1969:20).

The outermost tetrad in the Tewa shrine system is represented by four sacred mountains located between fifteen and eighty miles from the village center. Each of these mountains has, at its peak, an "earth navel," home to the Towe spirits "who stand watch over the Tewa world" (Ortiz 1969:19). On the ground, the earth navel shrine appears as bermed rock circles with an opening out of which extends a path in the direction of the home village. Some, if not all, of these paths are outlined by rows of stones (Jeancon 1923:71-2, Parsons 1974:241). In Tewa understanding, earth and navel shrines were designed with a twofold function: to facilitate communication with the spirit world and to gather and redirect the blessings of the cosmos back toward the home village (Ortiz 1969:141, Fowles 2009:439-442).

Ortiz clearly indicates stone features were associated with the Tewa's concepts of the cosmos, physical and underworld:

In some cases First Nations recognize ancient stone features in their area as part of their cultural heritage, however they no longer know why they were put there. In 2012 following a blind survey in the Hopi Nation, Max Taylor, Water Resources Technician, Hopi Tribe Water Resources Program, who conducted the blind survey with me, commented in his report "Johnson was able to locate a spring and cairns he knew nothing about (Note: These cairns are very old and the purposes of the 2 markers are lost to the present day land users which are the Hopi)". He also mentions "Johnson located an archaeological site on the way to one of the cairns which the Hopi did not know about." (Taylor 2013). In addition to the Hopi, other Native American nations have also commented that they have lost some of their ancient oral history and the ancient function of some features. Frequently Native American Nations hold conferences to address these issues. For example, in 2017 I participated in a conference hosted by the Tsuut'ina Nation at their reservation near Calgary, Alberta, Canada, which was titled "Dene Migration Symposium, Mending the Holes in our Stories.

In spite of contemporary tribal testimonials, historical references and archaeological data from Ceremonial Landscapes, many non-native archaeologists and government agencies have neglected Native American nation's requests to protect these sites, since they attribute their construction to Europeans after 1492. During our research, my colleagues and I have been denied permits to investigate Ceremonial Landscapes on federal and state land for that reason. The reason given most frequently by the archaeologist in charge has been, they were constructed by settlers clearing land or sheepherders; or they are just stone piles. Other researchers have consistently encountered a similar response, for example, during the 1980s James Mavor, who documented several Ceremonial Landscapes in New England, urged the Massachusetts Historical and Indian Affairs Commission to protect several sites. The Indian Commissioner was interviewed by the *Providence Journal* and was quoted as saying, "Some farmer just started building a stone wall and never finished." (Mavor 1989,p.67, Whittall 1984). The Native American Nations, as well as the non-native researchers, investigating these sites strongly disagree. Anyone who has seriously investigated two or more Ceremonial Landscapes ultimately realizes striking similarities between them.

To fully understand these sites, archaeologists need to go beyond interpreting excavations and structures based solely on the artifacts they find. They need to develop a more in-depth understanding of Native American beliefs.

The various stone features are discussed in greater detail below.

Habitationscapes

During this research I was unable to find a word which best describes this concept, however when I read Severin Fowles' paper titled "The Enshrined Pueblo: Villagescapes And Cosmos In The Northern Rio Grande", the term Habitationscapes seemed most appropriate. In his article Fowles describes Villagescapes as follows:

> My central claim is that villages and the landscape that surrounded them were mutually constitutive and need to be viewed holistically as components of integrated Villagescapes that linked the dwellings of living to the dwellings of ancestral spirits, and the social order of the village to the spatial order of the cosmos (Fowles 2009).

Although I agree with Fowles' interpretation of this concept, I am concerned with the use of village to describe all ancestral Native American communities. The term village infers a small community, however one must consider the population of some ancient Native American communities surpassed contemporary cities in other regions of the world, such as Europe. "Cahokia was a city that, at its peak from 1050-1200 A.D., was larger than many European cities, including London. The city covered nearly six square miles and 10,000 to 20,000 people lived here." (Cahokia Official State Website 2014). With all due respect for Fowles' use of village, I replaced village with habitation which does not infer a limitation to the size of a community and accommodates all of the sites within the regions I am investigating.

Habitionscapes consist of one's immediate surroundings, the community, which is planned holistically to include components of the underworld, physical world and cosmos both within the community and radiating outward into the Sacred Landscape and Ceremonial Landscapes.

As mentioned above, one place where the Sacred Landscape can be observed more clearly is in Chaco Canyon. Great house outlier sites are frequently associated with habitation sites. The outlier reflects back to the focal point of the cultural heritage while the Ceremonial Landscape radiates outward connecting the community to others and defining the Sacred Landscape. This is demonstrated by the Chaco Roads and stone features associated with them which will be discussed more thoroughly below.

Both contemporary Native American beliefs and their ancestral heritage sites throughout the Western Hemisphere demonstrate a cultural uniformity regarding their concept of the Sacred Landscape, Ceremonial Landscape and Habitationscapes. To fully understand their origin and importance to Native

Americans, one must evaluate all three holistically and incorporate their ethnic beliefs.

Lost Knowledge

If concentrated flows within the groundwater played such an important role in the lives of ancestral Native Americans, why aren't there more references to the association between structures and stone features with areas of higher permeability within the groundwater among the current tribes? During private discussions with some Native American tribes, references to mapping areas of higher permeability have been discussed and examples shown to me; however, I agreed to keep this information confidential. As Fowles points out, as well as members of our research team, Native Americans are reluctant to share their deepest spiritual beliefs with the outside world (Fowles 2009).

One area where the loss of knowledge is apparent is associated with the Navajo. Our data indicates the location of Navajo hogans changed after the Long Walk which was:

> The 1864 deportation of the Navajo people by the government of the United States of America to Fort Sumner (in an area called the Bosque Redondo or Hwéeldi by the Navajo) in the Pecos River Valley, Navajos were forced to walk up to thirteen miles a day at gunpoint from their reservation in what is now Arizona to eastern New Mexico. Some 53 different forced marches occurred between August 1864 and the end of 1866. Some anthropologists claim that the "collective trauma of the Long Walk...is critical to contemporary Navajos' sense of identity as a people". On June 18, 1868, the once-scattered bands of people who call themselves *Diné*, set off together on the return journey, the "Long Walk" home (Wikipedia 2014).

During our investigation of archaeological sites in the Navajo Nation, hogans dating prior to 1864 were located on areas of higher permeability and closely associated with nearby stone features, however, most of the hogans dating to post 1869 were not associated with concentrated flows.

Since 1492, the conquest, pandemic diseases, warfare, displacement and forced assimilation took their toll on Native American Nations throughout the Western Hemisphere. These events often destroyed multiple generations within a short period of time and could have prevented oral history from being passed from one generation to another. As mentioned above, Max Taylor, Water Resources Technician, Hopi Tribe Water Resources Program, who conducted the blind survey with me, commented in his report "Johnson was able to locate a spring and cairns he knew nothing about (Note: These cairns are very old and the purposes of the 2 markers are lost to the present day land users which are the Hopi)".

Chapter 3

Research Data And Observations

Before addressing this issue one must consider the following. Native Americans, in general, are reluctant to share their deepest spiritual beliefs with those who are of non-Native American descent. During the course of this research Johnson and his colleagues, such as Kenneth Frye, Forrest Ketchin and Richard Friedman, have worked closely with several tribes, and on occasions, Native American tribal and spiritual leaders have shared their innermost beliefs regarding water in all forms with them. This has helped them develop a better understanding of the correlation between ancestral Native American surface features and areas of higher permeability within the groundwater. Typically these comments are shared with the stipulation that they are confidential and cannot be shared with the general public. Therefore, with respect to their wishes and spiritual beliefs, we cannot discuss all the information Native Americans have shared with us.

Native American Association With Water

Often when someone is introduced to this research, their first assumption is Native Americans were interested in groundwater because they were looking for potable water, for example, locating springs or near surface groundwater for wells. They also assume this was more important in drier regions and find it difficult to believe it also applies to wetter regions. However, this perception is misleading. To fully understand the Native American perception of water one must consider the following.

To Native Americans water is an integral component of all three worlds and is associated with life cycles, since water is life. Therefore, it would be logical for Native Americans in all regions to investigate groundwater resources as a spiritual component of the underworld. Even if they could not physically touch deep groundwater sources, they were still important within their concept of the underworld and origin concepts associated with Mother Earth.

The origin of this bond between Native Americans and water can be traced through their ethnography, as well as archeological evidence such as petroglyphs. Referring to petroglyphs, the Native American Encyclopedia comments, "The meaning of the water symbols were very important, as water in every form, is one of the most vital elements for the sustenance of life. The meaning of the water symbol was to signify life, fertility and purity." (Native American Encyclopedia 2014). In the southwest, tribes culturally affiliated with Chaco Canyon demonstrate through oral history and sacred ceremonies that groundwater is sacred to them. Springs and blow holes are considered sacred. The Hopi snake dance associates snakes as guardians of springs, and as their brothers, a means of passing prayers for rain and water through springs to the underworld where their ancestors live. Numerous springs and lakes are considered places of emergence from the underworld into the physical world by Native Americans. For example, Lake San Luis in the San Luis

Valley of Colorado is considered the place of emergence for the Tewa while Lake Titicaca in the Andes Mountains is the place of emergence for the Inca (National Park Service 2014, Wikipedia 2015). In Peru, both the Nasca and Inca cultures revered water in all forms. The Inca believed they received groundwater directly from their ancestors who resided in the underworld. All of the known Inca shrines (huacas) are associated with some type of water source (Aveni 1990) (Niles 1992) Modern Andean shamans still practice these beliefs. In spite of the fact that water was abundant in ancient times, as well as the present, Native Americans of the northeast consider springs, seeps and other associations with groundwater as sacred. Northeastern cairn sites are also considered sacred since they are located where groundwater surfaces through springs at the headwaters of river systems (Johnson 2009, Mavor & Byron 1989). (Figure 4)

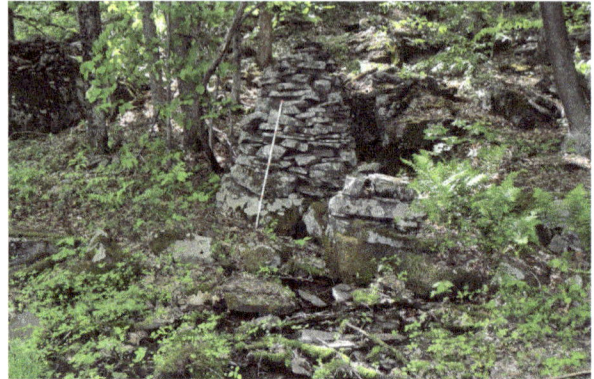

Figure 4: Tall cairn with spring below, Spruceton Site, NY

In 2017 I investigated the Blythe geoglyphs with Alfredo Acosta Figuero and several of his colleagues from the Native American Sacred Sites Protection Circle, Blythe, California. Prior to the investigation and before Figueroa was aware of my methodology, he told me the geoglyphs are associated with the aquifers within the lower Colorado Valley. Like the coastal geoglyphs of Peru and Chile, all of the Blythe geoglyphs and figures I investigated were associated with concentrated flows / aquifers. (Figures 5, 6, 70, 72, 154, 155, 157 & 175)

Figure 5: Trapezoid & triangle along concentrated flow, Nasca Lines, Peru

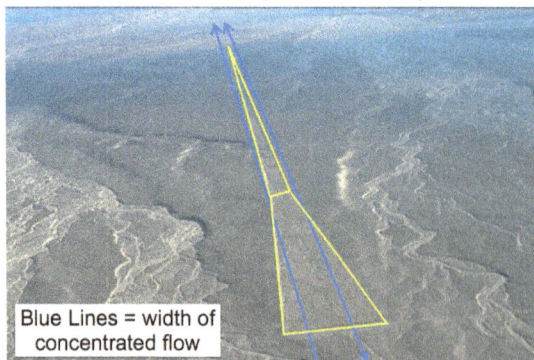

Blue Lines = width of concentrated flow

Figure 6: Trapezoid, circle, rectangle & line along concentrated flow, Blythe geoglyphs, CA

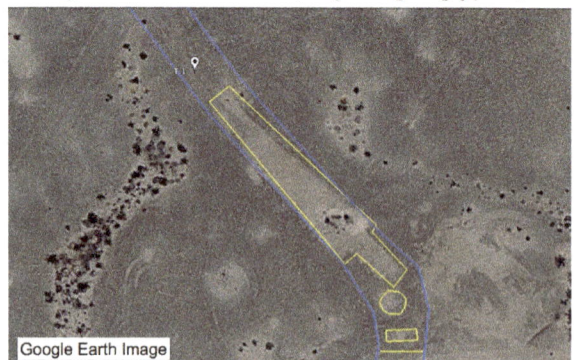

Google Earth Image

In his letter to Smithsonian Institution supporting submission of my Blythe site reports to my archival file he comments,

"The Blythe Giant Intaglios and other geoglyphs are all associated with the underground water. In the Nahuatl language, it is called A-Tla-Chinolli (water-earth-cosmos, the communicators). Mr. Johnson's testing of the sites emphasized the water connection with the geoglyphs. As one of the Chemehuevi Tribal Sacred Sites Monitors, I have spent most of my life researching these sacred sites and their connection to the oral history of the local tribes along he Lower Colorado River Valleys and the Mexica codices throughout their migration routes south to Mexico (Figueroa 2017, Johnson's Smithsonian Institution archival file).

In Peru and Chile, I observed several stones, boulders and bedrock panels which contained diagrams for ancient structures and agricultural fields. (Figure 7) Being aware of these features I looked for this type of petroglyph during my investigation of sites in North America. I prefer to map the areas of higher permeability first and then follow them to the site's features. Therefore my map of the concentrated flows is completed first. Then, features are added to the site map. In several cases, after

Figure 7: Map of irrigation system, Palpa Valley, Peru

completing the areas of higher permeability survey, we located a petroglyph which replicated my map of the concentrated flows at that site. This has happen enough times to be more than coincidental and indicates at some sites ancestral Native Americans were documenting the flow pattern of the areas of higher permeability in petroglyphs, and my data matches their's. For example, during our investigation of Palatki, near Sedona, Arizona, after I completed my map of the areas of higher permeability my colleagues and I began examining the petroglyphs and pictographs. In the Bear Alcove, we found a small petroglyph which replicated a section of my map of the concentrated flows at that location as shown in Figure 8. Where the petroglyph is located the main area of higher permeability branches and another flow

Figure 8: Petroglyph matching Johnson's map of flows, Bear Alcove, Palatki, AZ

Figure 9: Petroglyph matching Johnson's concentrated flow map, CO

crosses it. At the Smith Reservoir site in the San Luis Valley, Colorado, I had just completed mapping an area where several areas of higher permeability branch from the main flow. Due to the importance of this area and based on the flows, I asked Kenneth Frye, who is a petroglyph and pictograph specialist, to survey the area for any petroglyphs that resembled my map. Within a few minutes he located a petroglyph that replicated my map. (Figure 9)

Even if you do not believe I am mapping areas of higher permeability within the groundwater, our data strongly indicates I am mapping the same subsurface features the ancestral Native Americans were mapping.

Characteristics Of The Sacred Landscape

My colleagues and I have investigated several Sacred Landscapes throughout North America and Peru and Chile, South America. As mentioned above, even though they are associated with different cultures, historical phases and environments, each Sacred Landscape shared a degree of cultural uniformity with one another. The following discusses these similarities.

Sphere Of Influence

Today, our concept of the known world is very different from what it would have been five hundred or more years ago. Through technology we visualize earth as a planet consisting of oceans and continents divided into countries, as well as its position within the solar system. In the past, the known world consisted of the region you lived in and its immediate surroundings. Therefore, the world represented a smaller area. Within each region a cultural center developed which was the focal point of the regions government and spiritual beliefs which were disseminated to outlier communities. With this in mind, consider the following in regard to ancestral Native American cultures and their association with the Sacred Landscape.

Our research indicates by locating Ceremonial Landscapes and Habitationscapes on areas of higher permeability within a Sacred Landscape, ancestral Native Americans were able to establish a harmonious vertical alignment between the three worlds. Whether or not those who reside within the present world could touch the areas of higher permeability within the groundwater was not as important as establishing a vertical alignment with the concentrated flows which represent the pathways of those who live in the underworld. The regional centers I have investigated are located on a concentration of areas of higher permeability which are associated with unusual geological and hydrological features. Then this was replicated, as closely as possible, within the Ceremonial Landscapes and habitationscapes throughout the region where everything they constructed was located on a network of interconnecting areas of higher permeability. Thus, when someone in the present world is standing in a habitation structure or by a stone feature, such as a tall cairn, they are connected to everyone else within the site who is by one of these features, as well as, the underworld and cosmos, by the network of areas of higher permeability within the groundwater. For example, the site in

Figure 10 consists of stone features and a Paleo through contact habitation site. Each of the features are connected by areas of higher permeability within an area which is only .2 mi / .32 km square in size.

Figure 10: Paleo through contact habitation site, stone features & concentrated flows, CO

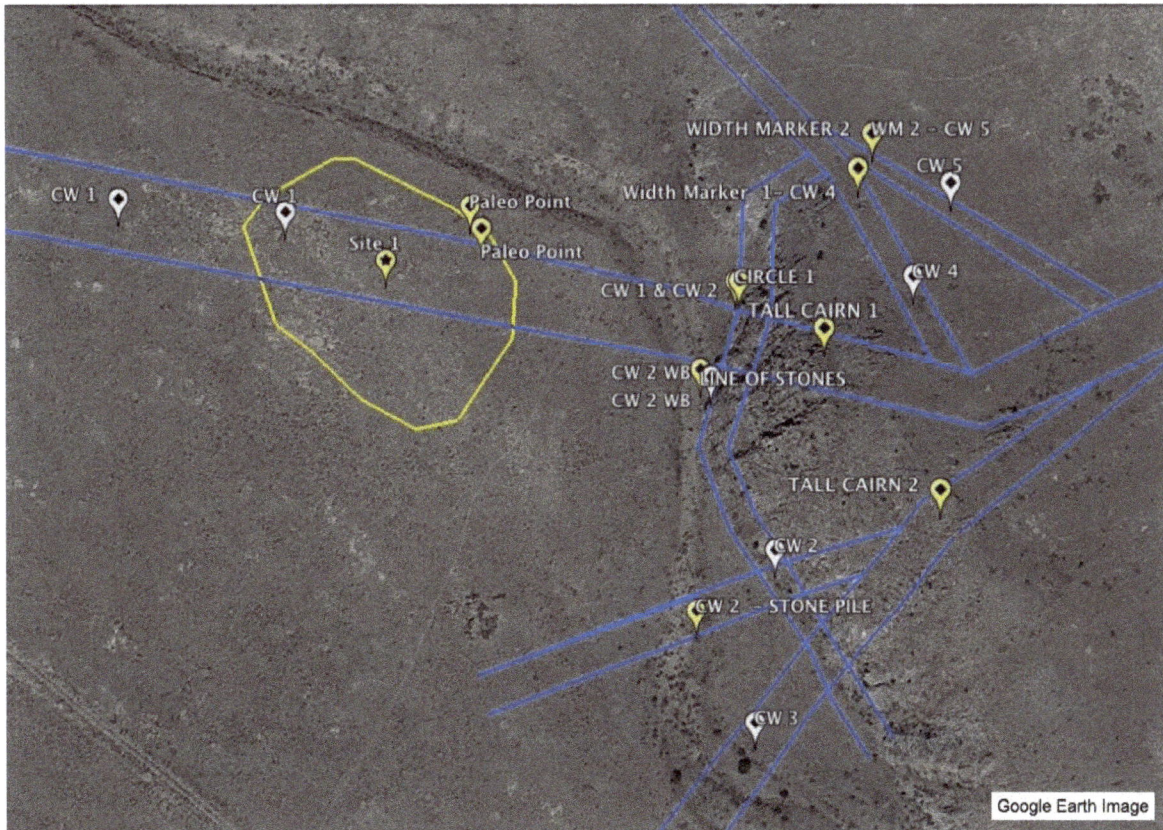

During the last twenty years I have studied four cultural centers: Cahuachi, Nasca culture in Peru; Cusco, Inca culture in Peru, Chaco Canyon, Chaco culture / Anasazi in northern New Mexico; and Cahokia, Mississippian culture. All four cultural centers share very similar characteristics and are located at the center of the culture's sphere of influence, which suggests it was also the center of their Sacred Landscape.

Cultural Centers

Archaeological evidence suggests only a small number of people resided at Cahuachi and Chaco Canyon year round, and people from the surrounding region made pilgrimages to these sites. Cusco became the capital of the Inca empire with a large population and pilgrimages brought in thousands of people for special occasions, such as the winter solstice (Judge 2012; Silverman, 1993). As mentioned above, "Cahokia was a city that, at its peak from 1050-1200 A.D., was larger than many European cities, including London (Cahokia Official State Website 2014).

Political and spiritual leaders resided at Cahuachi, Chaco Canyon, Cusco and Cahokia and the most spectacular structures within each region were located at these sites. For example, the only pyramids in the Rio Grande de Nasca drainage are found at Cahuachi. The largest Chaco structures are the great houses located within Chaco Canyon. All four sites had astronomical alignments associated with them. While roads radiated out from Chaco Canyon and Cusco, at Cahuachi it was geoglyphs (Nasca Lines) and at Cahokia it was trade routs. Along these routes the cultural identity of the region radiated out from the center.

All four cultural centers consisted of features which aligned the underworld, physical world and cosmos in the vertical and horizontal directions which corresponded to their perception of the Sacred Landscape and Mother Earth. These concepts generated by the regional centers radiated outward and were replicated in Ceremonial Landscapes and Habitationscapes.

Special Geological And / Or Hydrological Locations

Each of these regional centers are located where there is a special geological and / or hydrological feature(s). All four are centrally located within their region / sphere of influence, and each center was the focal point from which cultural and spiritual concepts radiated outward throughout what became their Sacred Landscape. For example, Cahuachi is located in the geographical center of the Rio Grande de Nasca drainage and Chaco Canyon is located at the geographical center of the San Juan Basin. Cahokia is centrally located along the Mississippi River while Cusco is located in the Andes Mountains near the source of the Amazon River between the Atacama Desert and the Amazon Rainforest.

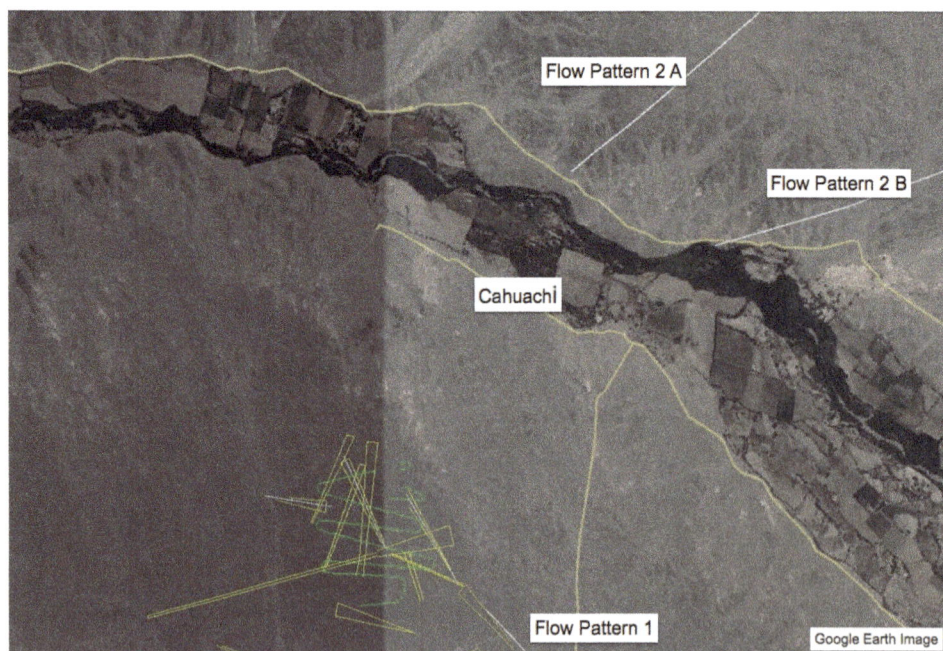

Figure 11: Cahuachi, areas of higher permeability, flow patterns & large geoglyph field, Peru

East of Cahuachi the Nasca River is dry for several miles. Further upstream, faults cut across the river and drain water from it. Northeast of Cahuachi and the Nasca River, geoglyph patterns (Nasca Lines) and areas of higher permeability cross the coastal desert from the Andean foothills to where they intersect the river at Cahuachi. At that location, springs along the valley's north slope contribute water to the river and surface water reappears. One of the largest geoglyph concentrations is located immediately south of Cahuachi where areas of higher permeability from the Andes to the northeast and Cerro Blanco to the east contribute groundwater to this area. Both Cerro Blanco and the Andes are sacred mountains (Johnson 2009). (Figure 11)

Saqsaywaman is a large complex situated above Cusco which has one of the most unique geological features in the Western Hemisphere, if not the world. In 1978 the Geological Society of America Bulletin published an article titled "The Extraordinary Striated Outcrop at Saqsaywaman, Peru" by Tomas Feininger. In the article he explains how the outcrop was formed: "The andesite reached the Earth's surface along an eruptive fissure. The first materials ejected were hot but solid blocks which built an elongated, steep-sided mound. Later, viscous lava was extruded though the crest of the mound and flowed down its flanks. The stretching of the lava during flowage caused its surface to become striated, analogous to the striations on the surface of pulled taffy." In geological terms this outcrop is also referred to as a mullion structure, which is defined as "consisting of a series of parallel columns composed of folded bedrock. The morphology of the outcrop is so remarkable that even the most casual observer is at once awed." (Feininger 1978). (Figure 12) My colleagues at the Geoscience Department of the University of Massachusetts and I examined this feature and came to the same conclusion. Consider the following. The mullion looks like the back of snakes coming out of the ground and going back down. The great zigzag wall of Saqsaywaman looks like a puma's head (Urton 1985). To the

Figure 12: The Mullion, Cusco, Peru

Inca, snakes represented the underworld and the puma the physical world. Thus, it appears as though the puma's ears are pointed towards the snakes for guidance. Cusco and Saqsaywaman were the political and spiritual focal points of the empire. For example, during the winter solstice the Inca ruler, along with the mummies of past rulers which were carried to the site, went and sat on the mullion to ask the spirits and their ancestors for guidance (Johnson 2009, Chap. 7) (Wikipedia 2014).

Within the strata beneath Chaco Canyon there are important regional sandstone aquifers which include the Point Lookout Sandstone, Gallup Sandstone,

Dakota Sandstone and Westwater Canyon Member of the Morrison Formation (Martin 2005). "Recharge occurs in and adjacent to outcrop areas at the western and southern margins of the San Juan Basin. Most groundwater in the Gallup sandstone flows northeasterly toward the basin center, then moves northwestward and discharges into the San Juan River in the vicinity of the four corners." (Stone 2006). (Figure 13) The great houses in Chaco Canyon are located where the

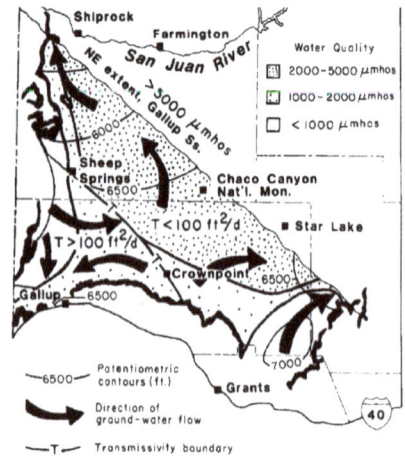

Figure 13: Stone's ground water flow chart for Chaco Canyon

Gallup aquifer's flow turns from northeast to the northwest at the center of the San Juan Basin. Cahokia is centrally located along the Mississippi River and its watershed. It is also strategically located at the confluence of the Mississippi, Missouri and Illinois Rivers. This enabled Cahokia to develop as a commercial and cultural center within the midwest.

At these sites, the people who chose the location for their cultural center selected a place which exhibited special geological and hydrological features within their Sacred Landscape.

Sacred Mountains

Sacred mountains are an important component of religions all over the world, as well as, Native American spiritual beliefs. Throughout the Western Hemisphere, ancestral and current Native American cultures have revered specific mountains within their sphere of influence, and those occupying large areas had a sacred mountain in each region of their nation, for example the Tewa mentioned above. Sacred mountains have a variety of functions within their culture. They functioned as portals between the three worlds and emergence sites into the present world from the underworld for some Native American cultures.Pilgrimages to the mountain brought them to a sanctuary where they were closer to the Great Spirit and from which they could pray and see their homeland / nation. For example, the Nochpeem Tribe was one of the member tribes of the Wappinger Confederacy along the Hudson River in New York State. Nimham Mountain was sacred to them and their last spiritual leader, Daniel Nimham, frequently visited the mountain. As shown in Figure 14, anyone who has stood on top of Nimham Mountain has to agree that Nimham could see all the land of the Wappinger Indians from that

Figure 14 - Looking westward towards the Hudson River & Catskill Mountains

location,. (Maxson, 2009. All of the stone features I documented on the sacred mountains I researched map the course of concentrated flows. Some sacred mountains contain unusual geological features, such as exceptionally large glacier erratics, for example, Split Rock which is discussed below.

In Alberta, Canada, the Tsuut'ina First Nation's sacred mountain functions the same way. In 2019 I accompanied members of the Tsuut'ina First Nation, which included their chief, council members, elders and historic preservation staff, to the top of their sacred mountain to survey the Native American stone features located there. Today, the mountain is owned by the province and leased to an oil company for drilling, thus providing the Tsuut'ina limited access to this site. When we arrived on the summit, they took this rare opportunity to conduct prayers, offerings and a feast in accordance with their traditional cultural and spiritual beliefs. They admired the panoramic view of their homeland which has been reduced to the Tsuut'ina reservation. Then, as we conducted the survey, Jim Big Plume, who assisted with the archeological surveys of the mountain in the 1990s, pointed out the location of stone features that no longer exist. The stone features we documented that day are the fragmented remains of their ancestors' testimonial to their sacred mountain and the Great Spirit. Without protection, the remaining stone features will be destroyed within their generation. The stone features on this sacred mountain, as well as others, need to be protected as part of their cultural and spiritual heritage for future generations.

Characteristics Of Ceremonial Landscapes

One of the problems I encounter as I move from one region to another is the diversity of names for some of the stone features. Often, when I ask other researchers if a particular feature is located within their region, they say no. Then, when I am conducting the site surveys in that region, I find the feature I asked about which they said did not exist. Then, we realize we are talking about the same feature, only we are using a different name or term for it. For example, in the northeastern states, semicircular cairn shaped features (Figure 133) are referred to as crescent cairns, in the San Luis Valley of Colorado they are referred to as inverted game blinds and those associated with the Chaco culture are called herraduras. (Figure 176) However, when I examined them, they all served the same function and had the same shape. This was also true for great cairns, mounds and earthworks which serve the same function. This strongly suggests some form of standardized classification is needed for these features. Hopefully, the classification and name applied to various features within this discussion will help overcome this problem.

When you first observe features within a ceremonial landscape, they appear to have been placed randomly without any purpose. However, our data indicates their location served a specific purpose.

For example, Figure 15 shows a site consisting of several stone features and a multi-component habitation site dating to Paleoindians. Each feature appears

41

randomly placed with no apparent correlation to one another. However, when you add the areas of higher permeability, all the features are located on one or more concentrated flows, and they are all connected to one another by the intersecting flows. (Figure 16) Thus, anyone standing by one of the features is connected to all the features within the site, and to anyone else who is standing by a feature or on a concentrated flow.

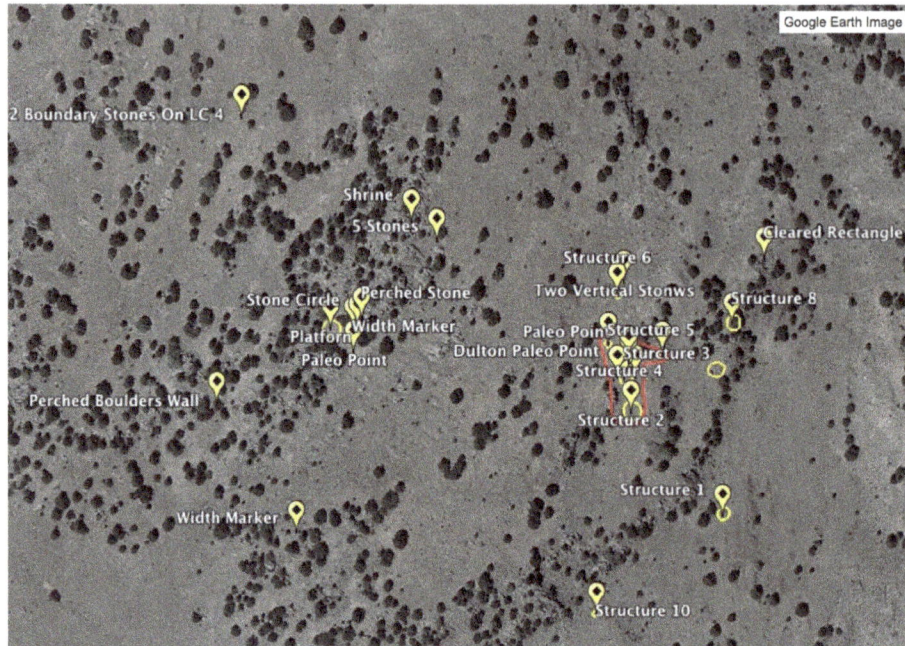

Figure 15: Paleo through contact habitation site & stone features

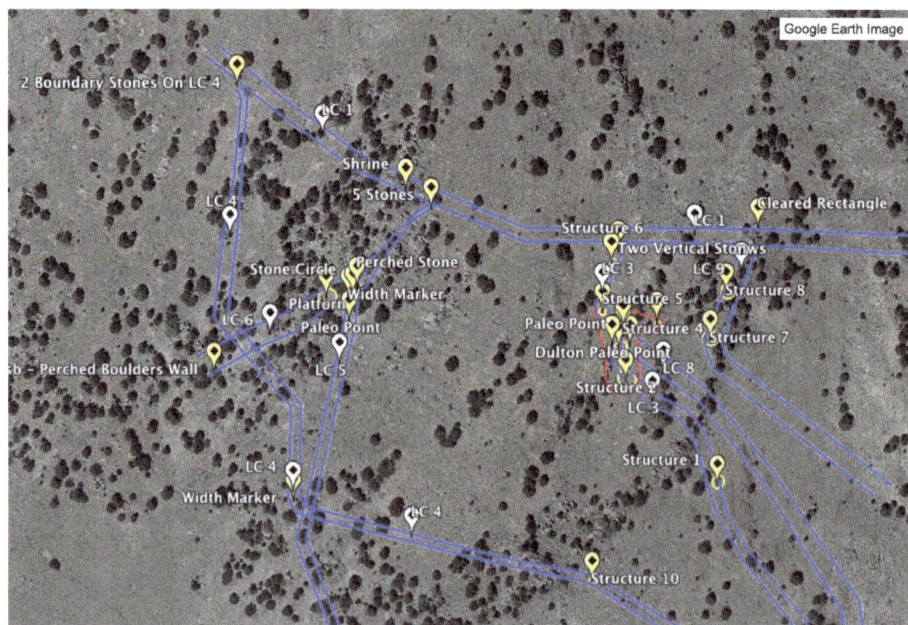

Figure 16: Paleo through contact habitation site & stone features with concentrated flows

Geological And Hydrological Observations

Before discussing various ancestral Native American surface features associated with Ceremonial Landscapes and Habitationscapes, it is beneficial to consider some of the geological and hydrological features which influenced the placement of these sites and the features contained within them. The following are some examples:

Concentration Of Areas Of Higher Permeability

Ceremonial Landscapes are typically located where several areas of higher permeability intersect one another. Often a small number of areas of higher permeability conduct groundwater into and out of the area. However, within the area there are several bedrock fractures, faults, contacts, dikes or alluvial channels which disperse the flows creating a concentration of areas of higher permeability. For example, north of Chaco Canyon nineteen areas of higher permeability were located trending towards the canyon. Within the canyon seventy-five areas of higher permeability were documented. (Figure 17) In Chaco Canyon all the structures and stone features we surveyed were located along areas of higher permeability. At the Lewis Hollow Site in New York State, fifty-one areas of higher permeability were located within the site, while only five intersected it, and all of the stone features were located along areas of higher permeability and several on springs. (Figure 18) While areas of higher permeability which connect sites are mapped with stone features, those which do not connect sites are not mapped.

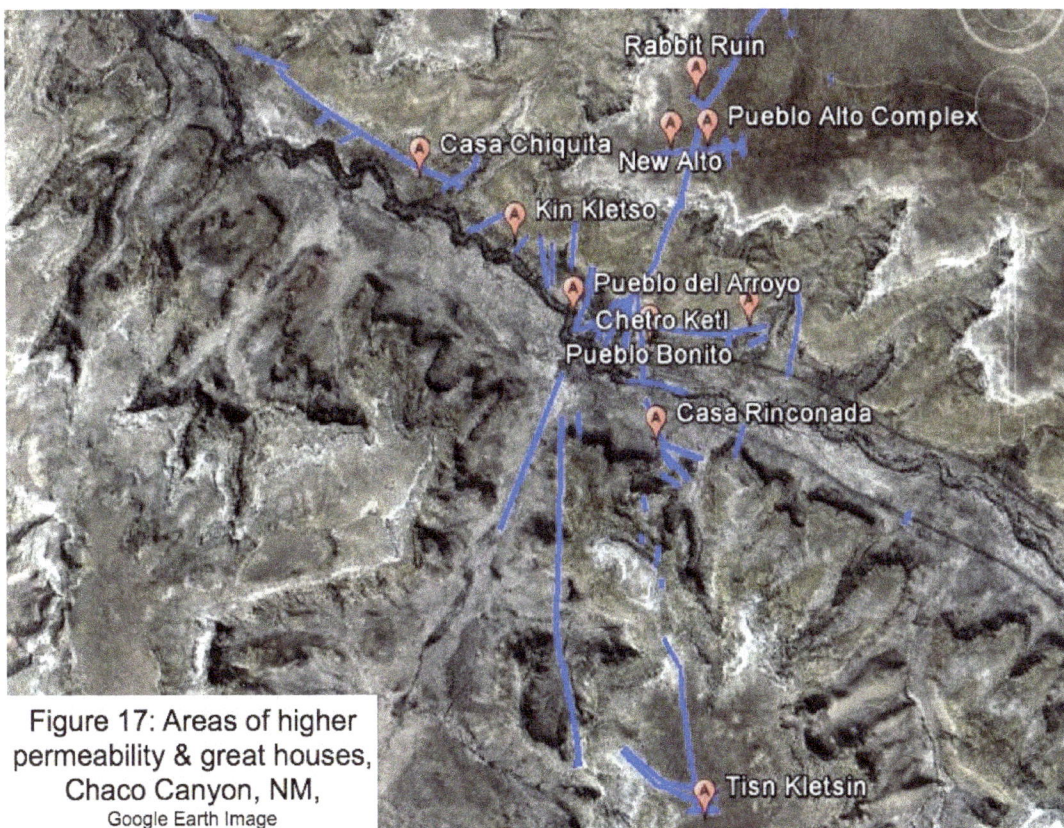

Figure 17: Areas of higher permeability & great houses, Chaco Canyon, NM, Google Earth Image

43

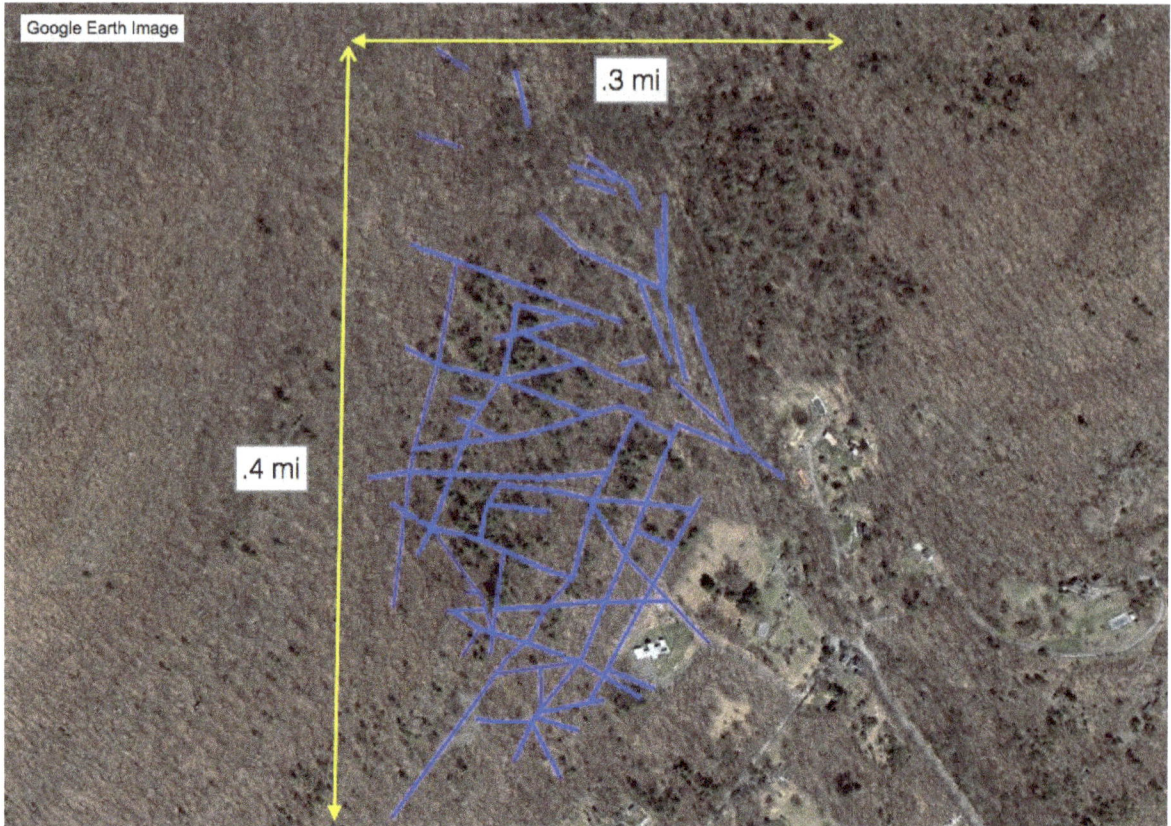

Figure 18: Areas of higher permeability, Lewis Hollow Site, NY

Meandering Patterns

Since the flow of an area of higher permeability is dependent on geological features which meander, they also meander along their course and can extend for miles. Therefore, structures and features located on areas of higher permeability also meander across the landscape. (Figure 19)

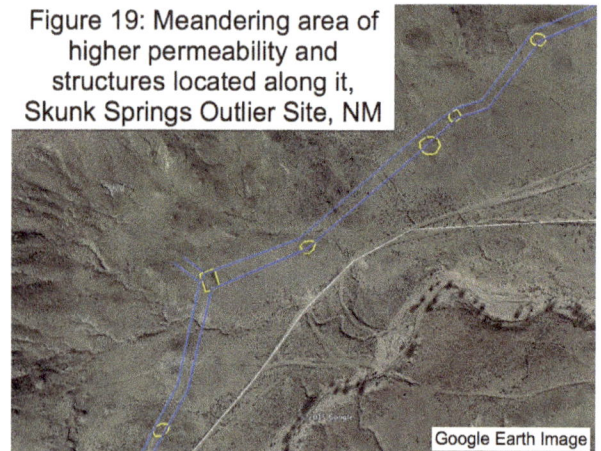

Figure 19: Meandering area of higher permeability and structures located along it, Skunk Springs Outlier Site, NM

River Or Stream's Sudden Changes In Rate Of Flow

When the surface and/or subsurface water flowing down a river or stream intersects a fault which crosses it and extends deeper into the ground, some or all of the flow can drain into the fault and follow a different course. During the Rio Grande de Nasca River survey in Peru we documented several locations where this occurs, and important archaeological sites were associated with each one. For example, at Estaqueria, a fault crosses the Nasca River where there is an important ancient cemetery located on the south side of the valley and an ancient community on the north side. Several geoglyphs cross the desert and intersect this site. When the river floods, the volume of water above the fault is much greater than below the fault, and, at times, the flood is completely absorbed by the fault (Johnson 2009, Ch 3, Pt 2, p. 34). Although we haven't found examples of this during our research in North America, it cannot be dismissed as a possibility.

Sudden Change In Direction

At some sites, while following an area of higher permeability the trend of the concentrated flow can change abruptly. This can occur at the intersection of faults and fractures. If a fault or feature conducting an area of higher permeability intersects another fault or feature and does not cross it, the concentrated flow can flow into the other feature and follow its trend. The change in the flow's course can be at ninety degrees or a very oblique angle. The alignment of any structures or stone features on the surface will map this abrupt change in direction. For example, while documenting the concentrated flows at one of the great house outliers, one of the flows turned at nearly 90°, and is documented by the three structures located along it as shown in Figure 20.

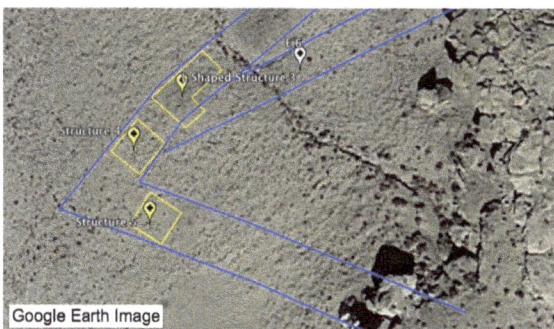

Figure 20: A flow changes course abruptly & the offset of the structures indicate the change in direction

Concentrated Flow's Width Changes

Where two or more areas of higher permeability merge, the width of the flows before the intersection can be narrower than the flow beyond the intersection. If the flows are being mapped by cairns on each of the width boundaries, there will be a noticeable change in the distance between them before and after they merge.

Dikes

A dike is a sheet of rock that forms in a fracture in pre-existing bedrock. Magmatic / igneous dikes form when magma intrudes into a crack and then crystallizes. In some cases, when a dike crosses an area and groundwater intersects it, the flow will change course and flow along the trend of the dike. In other situations, the dike can function like a dam. As the groundwater collects along one side of the dike, it can reach the surface creating a spring. In some cases, these springs can be substantial. The USGS study of Montezuma Well concluded, "The presence of an impermeable vertical basalt dike forces the deep water to travel to the surface. The average rate of flow for Montezuma Well is 1,500,000 US gallons (5,700,000 L; 1,200,000 imp gal) of water emerge each day from an underground spring." (National Park Service, 2012). The location of structures and stone features will be concentrated on the side of the dike which intersects the groundwater and along the trend of the dike.

Watersheds

Often, Ceremonial Landscapes are associated with watersheds which lead to rivers. In this case, as you follow the tributaries away from the river, you will locate Ceremonial Landscapes along them where groundwater from the surrounding hills/ mountains reaches the surface forming streams, which eventually merge with the river.

Mountain Slope Groundwater Flow

In the northeast, Ceremonial Landscapes begin along the upper slopes of a mountain and extend downslope. At higher elevations springs are not present. However, when the stone features are followed downslope, they lead you to springs near the base of the mountain where the areas of higher permeability reach the surface. At these locations, the springs are marked by cairns placed on them. In Figure 4 a tall cairn is located on a spring. Unfortunately, at many sites the ancient cairns have been replaced by spring houses.

Springs

Sites are often located on or by springs which serve at least two purposes. One is to obtain potable water, and other is springs were considered a means of communicating with the underworld. (Figure 21)

Figure 21: Area with four cairns and springs, NY

These examples represent only a few of the numerous geological and hydrological features and their characteristics which can influence the location of structures and stone features at archaeological sites.

These Sites Are Everywhere

Frequently researchers say certain groups of features, such as petroglyphs and pictographs, are everywhere in a given area or region. However, one does not have to look very far to realize this is an exaggeration, since surrounding the site there are additional suitable bedrock and boulder surfaces without these features. Therefore, there must be a reason why a particular location was chosen, and others dismissed. Our data consistently indicates stone features and petroglyphs / pictographs are located along concentrated flows. Since concentrated flows are not located everywhere beneath the surface, neither are the surface features which are mapping them. When you look at the accompanying site maps, as well as those of other researchers, this becomes apparent.

Topography

The topography of the area does not appear to interfere with the location of stone features in spite of the slope, bedrock or wet and dry areas. For example, if a concentrated flow passes beneath a mountain, the stone features cross over it in spite of cliffs. Thus, in very steep areas petroglyphs and pictographs replace cairns. (Figure 22)

Figure 22: Pictographs on cliff, San Luis Valley, CO

Interpreting The Stone Features

When interpreting stone features it is important to remember that each one is associated with cultural and spiritual beliefs as well as areas of higher permeability within the groundwater. For example, a turtle cairn can map the course of a concentrated flow, represent the turtle clan and be a component in a creation story. (Figures 23, 3, 98, 118, 137 & 138). This discussion well focus on their association with concentrated flows within the groundwater. Several types of stone features, such as crescent cairns / herraduras have the same function throughout North America, as well as Peru and Chile, South America. This strongly suggests a degree of cultural uniformity.

Figure 23: Turtle Cairn, Spruceton Valley, NY

Since vegetation makes it difficult to observe stone features in photographs and satellite images, Figure 24 demonstrates the relationship between stone features and concentrated flows, thus providing a clearer explanation. Images for each of these stone features are provided in Part 2. In the image blue lines represent areas of higher permeability and yellow the stone features. The dots represent cairns or stone piles which form parallel or single

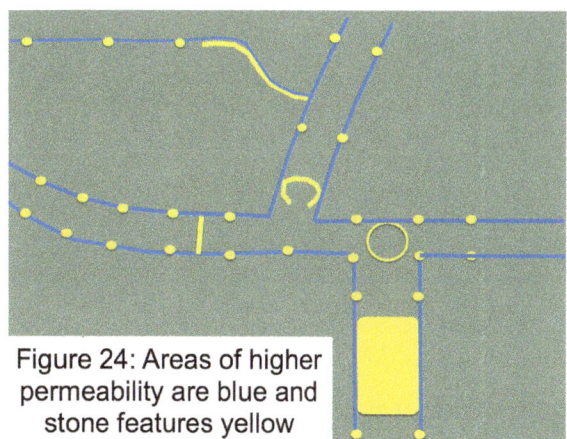
Figure 24: Areas of higher permeability are blue and stone features yellow

linear patterns that map the concentrated flow's trend, while the distance between them is its width. A single linear pattern maps the trend of a narrow concentrated flow. The crescent shaped feature, also known as a herradura in the southwest, is equal to the width of the flow it is located on and has been associated with Native American trails in the northeast and Chaco roads in the southwest. The circle indicates an intersection of two concentrated flows and is equal to the width of one of them. Where appropriate, they were also used as teepee sites. The straight yellow line represents a width marker which is equal to the flow's width. The yellow curving line represents a snake / serpentine effigy wall which is common to Ceremonial Landscapes throughout the regions we have investigated. The wall follows the trend of the concentrated flow. Frequently, the snake's head is located where two concentrated flows intersect. The large rectangular shape represents a great cairn / mound / earthwork. Consistently, their width is equal to the concentrated flow they are located on, and their length is along the flow's trend. These large cairns can have various shapes, however their function remains the same. They are located where an area of higher permeability turns sharply, and where two or more intersect. Although this pattern is from a site in New York State, the same interpretation applies to sites in other regions.

The description and function of several Ceremonial Landscape stone features are discussed in Part 2. When you know the meaning of several features you can follow a concentrated flow without dowsing it.

Similarities And Differences Between Sites

Specific styles of stone features are replicated from site to site and region to region regardless of different cultural and historical periods. For example, cairns, circles, crescent shaped stone piles, snake walls and great cairns / earthworks are consistently grouped together within a Ceremonial Landscape. Although the two tall cairns shown in Figures 25 and 26 are separated by 2,000 mi / 3,218 km, their construction and shape are remarkably similar. Another striking similarity is the location of similar stones within each cairn. This is also true for the Blythe geoglyphs in southern California and the Nasca Lines of Peru. (Figures 5, 6, 156 & 157)

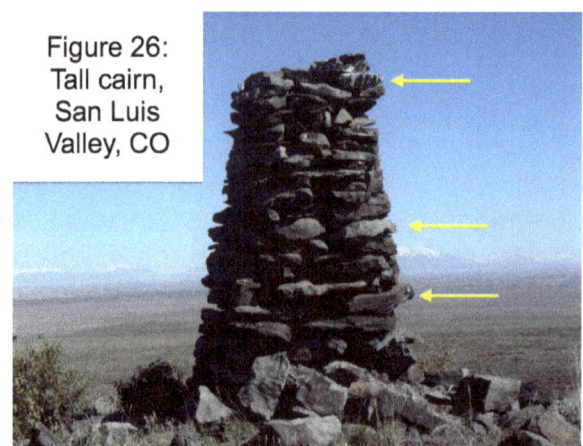

Figure 25: Tall cairn, Spruceton, NY

Figure 26: Tall cairn, San Luis Valley, CO

Each of the stone features we have documented are discussed in Part 2. Therefore, once you know the association between a particularly shaped stone feature or petroglyph with a specific characteristic of an area of higher permeability in one region, you can apply it to other regions. Thus, the surface features serve as a written language which can lead you across the landscape as if you are reading a modern map.

In the southwest, stone features, as well as petroglyphs and pictographs, are commonly found within a Ceremonial Landscape, however in the northeast, this is not as common. It is possible more petroglyphs and pictographs existed in the northeast during ancient times, however weathering and modern construction destroyed many of them. Another problem in the northeast is they may be covered by soils and the dense vegetation.

Petroglyphs And Pictographs

During the course of this research, numerous Native Americans have expressed their concern with the term "rock art". Often non-natives associate Native American petroglyphs and pictographs with what the western world considers art, such as a portrait or landscape. However, Native Americans consistently refer to petroglyphs and pictographs as their ancient written language, and I agree with this concept. Therefore, the term "rock art" will not be used in this discussion.

When mapping an area of higher permeability, the changing topography poses a challenge. On relatively flat ground surfaces, stone features, such as cairns, can be used. However when the area of higher permeability passes under a steep mountain slope, stone features are impractical. Therefore, petroglyphs and pictographs were used on both vertical and horizontal surfaces. Many of the stone features' geometric shapes are replicated in the petroglyphs and pictographs. For example, the circular shape of a cairn's base is represented by

Figure 27: Sun / Shield petroglyphs are located along the width of an area of higher permeability, Agua Fria, AZ

a circle in a petroglyph or pictograph panel as shown in Figure 27. When two are next to one another, the distance between them represents the width of the areas of higher permeability. A single circle indicates a narrow concentrated flow. At the same time a particular shape, for example a circle, can have cultural adaptations. The feature in Figures 27, 28 & 29 are all circles and have the same meaning. However each has been culturally modified by a different tribe or during a different historical phase by adding rays, concentric circles or lines crossing one another. Like the stone features, by knowing the meaning of various petroglyph and pictograph symbols, it is possible to follow an area of higher permeability without using dowsing. Refer to Part 2 for a more comprehensive list and description of these features.

Figure 28: Sunburst, Smith Reservoir, CO

Figure 29: Shield pictograph, Palatki, AZ

Like stone features, when you map petroglyphs and pictographs they can appear isolated and unassociated. However, when you include the areas of higher permeability, they are connected. For example, Figure 30 shows a traditional petroglyph site survey map, and Figure 31 the same map with the areas of higher permeability added.

Figure 30: A traditional map of petroglyphs, San Luis Valley, CO

Figure 31: Petroglyphs & areas of higher permeability added, San Luis Valley, CO

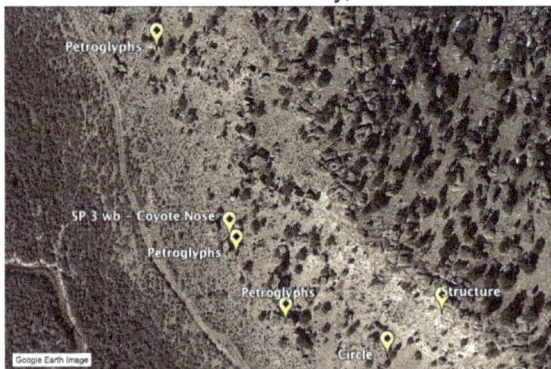

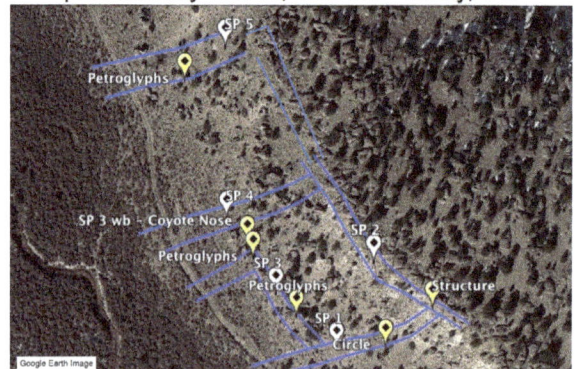

Culturally Modified Trees

A culturally modified tree is the term used to describe the modification of a tree by Native Americans. They are another important component within the Sacred Landscape, Ceremonial Landscapes and Habitationscapes concepts. Unfortunately, non-native archaeologists often dismiss Native American peeled and shaped trees as natural growth. While some peeled trees have been placed on historical preservation lists, most remain without protection and are vulnerable to modern land use. The following summarizes the data my colleagues and I have gathered from investigations of culturally modified trees throughout North America.

Within Sand Dunes National Park there is a grove of ponderosa pines which has been culturally modified by the Ute and other regional tribes. The trees have had a section of bark peeled off on one or more sides. (Figure 32) Some of the trees predate the European migration into this region. Several of the trees are registered with Smithsonian Institution as living artifacts.

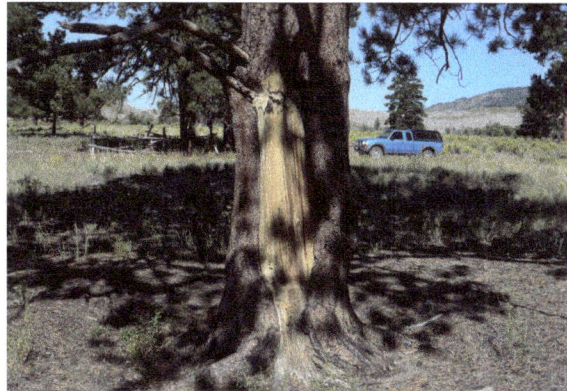
Figure 32: Peeled tree, Sand Dunes NP, CO

According to the Great Sand Dunes National Park's website, "the Grove contains approximately 200 ponderosa pine trees, of which 72 show evidence of having been culturally peeled. They are classified as "living artifacts" protected by the National Register of Historic Places (Mayers, Patrick, National Park Service)." The scared trees within the park are considered sacred to the Ute and other regional tribes. Alden Narango, Southern Ute tribal historian, describes the Grove as follows:

"This was one of the places that the Utes used to gather...the Capota band were the ones that used to camp in this area. Neighboring families would come here and camp with them, this was maybe early in the spring or late in the fall. The Utes used to use the bark from the ponderosa pine for medicinal purposes, and also for food sources... they would cut the bottom, pulling it apart. That's the way they harvested. The younger kids would help, to a certain age, but basically it was all the women that did the harvesting of the trees, and they're the ones that picked the trees out..."Alden Narango, Southern Ute tribal historian (Sand Dunes National Park, 2014).

Within the grove's current population of living peeled trees, there are some dead ones. Since many of the peeled trees are nearly 500 years old, it is possible some of the original trees died and decayed or could have been cut down and removed. Therefore, the current population could be smaller than the original number.

Florissant Fossil Beds National Monument, National Park Service, lists four categories of culturally modified trees which are medicine, prayer, burial and message. Dr. James Jefferson, Ute elder, has been an advocate for the documentation and preservation of culturally modified trees / prayer trees, and my colleagues and I have been collaborating with him. Jefferson recognized several basic categories of culturally modified trees, and some are discussed below (Dr. Jefferson personal conversations, Anderson 2015, National Park Service). Within each of these categories there are subcategories, and some of them are also discussed below.

The following descriptions were taken from John Anderson's book and the Florissant Fossil Beds National Monument website (Anderson 2015).

1. Arborglyphs / Message Trees:

Messages or Ute signs were often carved into the bark of a tree and depict events, such as a tribal fight or hunt. In some cases, they are trailmarkers. For example, Figure 33, the bark contains an image of a person walking towards the left, thus indicating the direction of the trail.

Figure 33: Culturally modified tree with man walking, San Juan Forest, CO

Figure 34: Burial tree, San Luis Valley, CO

2. Council Trees:

As the name implies, these trees indicated the place where meetings were held, often between tribes.

3. Burial Trees:

The Ute burial tree can be either a ponderosa tree with two distinctive nearly 90° bends which point to where the Ute tribal leader is buried, or a cedar tree planted to mark the general location of possibly their honored leader's burial site. (Figure 34)

4. Peeled Bark / Medicine Trees:

A Ute medicine person would make a small cut on a tree at a spot that matched the site of a person's ailment. A sharp stick would then be inserted into the tree and leveraged upward to peel the bark away. The inner layer of the bark would then be used in a healing ceremony. (Figure 32)

5. Peeled Bark Trees:

They also map the trend of areas of higher permeability. For example, if two peeled trees are located on the same concentrated flow, at least one of the bark peels on each tree will face the other tree, thus indicating the trend of the flow. (Figure 32)

Figure 35: Prophecy tree, New York

Figure 36: Trailmarker tree, New York

6. **Prophecy Trees**:

Two trees are grafted / fused together. They are believed to foretell future events. The tree in Figure 35 points to a nearby spring and is next to the trailmarker tree in Figure 36.

7. **Trailmarker Trees**:

Often they have one 30° bend to the trunk before extending upward. The bend points towards some geological or navigational reference such as a trail, stream, mountain pass or stone feature, to mention few. (Figures 36) In some cases signs of cultural modification may still be present on a tree. For example, when a rope is wrapped around a tree and

Figure 37: Bark with ring around it caused by rope binding it, San Juan Forest, CO

then staked to the ground to hold the sapling or branch in place for a long period of time, it can leave a permeant scar. Figure 37 shows a rope scar on a culturally modified tree.

Our data demonstrates that while culturally modified trees are affiliated with tribal, cultural and spiritual concepts, among others, they are also associated with mapping areas of higher permeability within the groundwater. Various types of culturally modified trees and stone features also serve the same function.

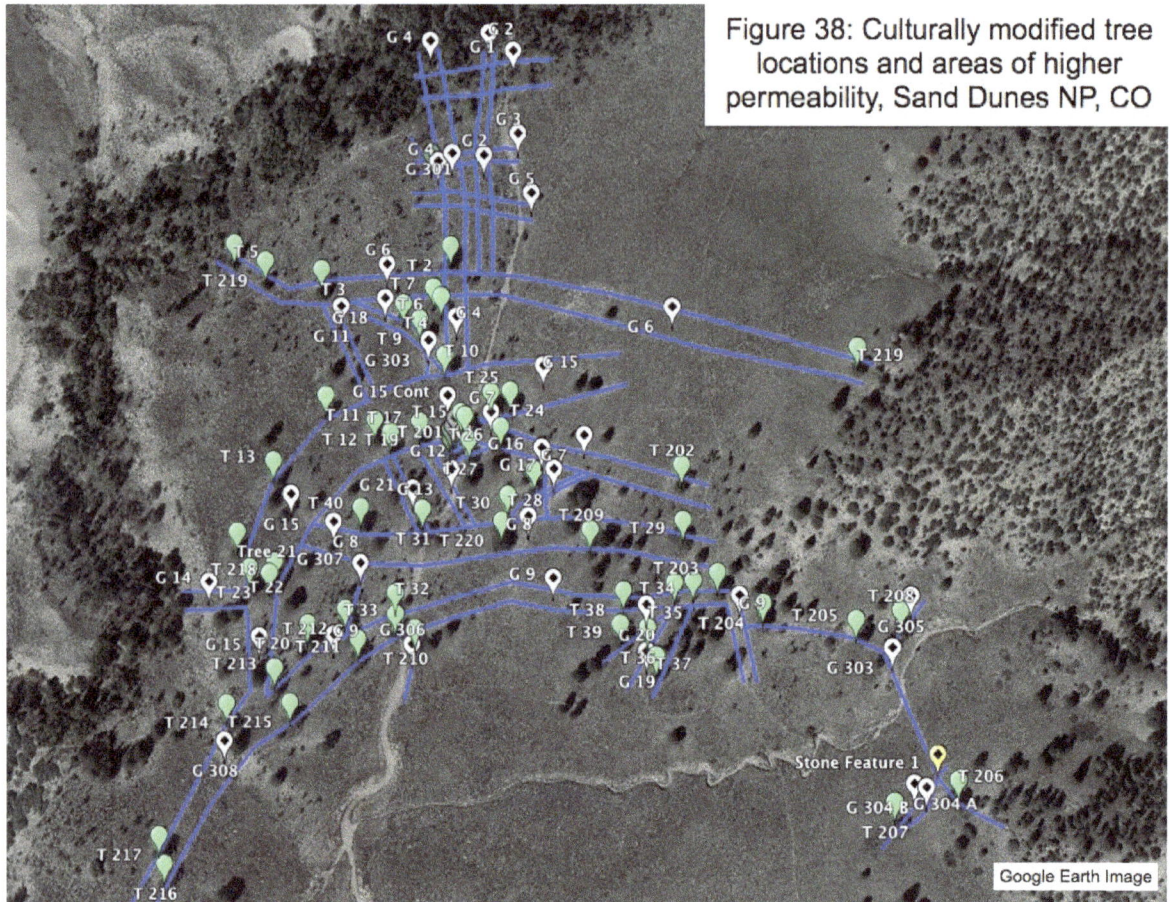

Figure 38: Culturally modified tree locations and areas of higher permeability, Sand Dunes NP, CO

Culturally Modified Trees And Areas Of Higher Permeability

These observations are characteristic of the culturally modified tree sites Johnson and his colleagues have researched.

1. Not all areas of higher permeability are mapped extensively by structures, stone features, trees and petroglyphs. However, Ceremonial Stone and Tree Landscape sites are located where several areas of higher permeability intersect one another. Of the seventy-two culturally modified trees within Sand Dunes National Park, we investigated forty-one of them which is a little more than two thirds of the grove. They were associated with twenty-nine areas of higher permeability. This suggests there are additional concentrated flows within the grove. (Figure 38) All of the culturally modified trees are located along one or more concentrated flows. This is characteristic of ancestral Native American sites regardless of size or function. For example, within the Chaco Canyon where the Chaco great houses are located, seventy-five areas of higher permeability were documented. (Figure 17) At the Lewis Hollow Site in New York State fifty-one areas of higher permeability were located. (Figure 18) This is also true for small habitation sites as shown in Figure 10.

2. When you walk through a group of culturally modified trees or map their location, their placement appears to be random. However, when you include the location of the areas of higher permeability a distinct pattern emerges. All of the trees are located along concentrated flows and thus connected to one another. (Figure 39) As mentioned above, this pattern also applies to ancestral Native American stone features, habitation and ceremonial sites as shown in Figures 15, 16, 17 & 18.

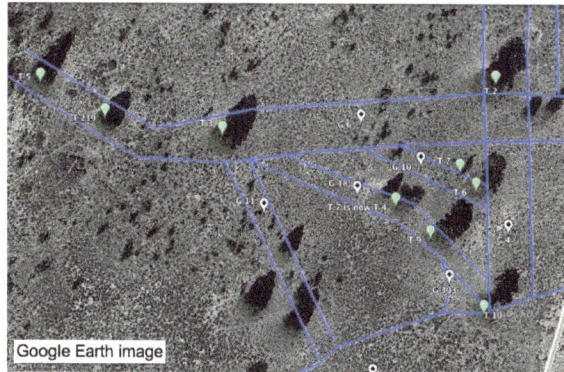

Figure 39: Culturally modified trees & concentrated flows, Sand Dunes NP, CO

3. Since the trees are located along concentrated flows and are peeled indicating cultural modification, this strongly suggests the ancestral Native Americans who peeled the trees were also aware of the areas of higher permeability. (Figures 32 - 44)

4. While some of the trees are centered on areas of higher permeability, others are located along the width boundary of concentrated flows, and where two flows intersect. This suggests specific trees may have been selected when they were very young due to their association with an area(s) of higher permeability and culturally modified or possibly planted. (Figures 38 & 39)

Figure 40: Three trees located along a concentrated flow

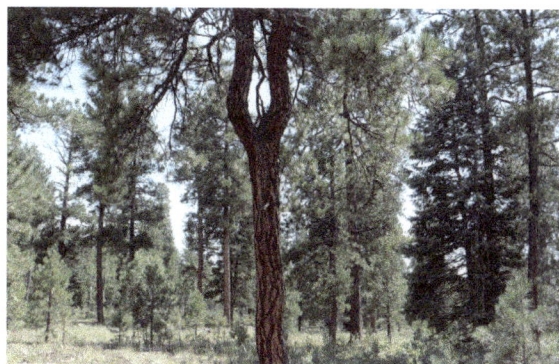

Figure 41: Tall culturally modified forked tree, San Juan NF, CO

5. With peeled trees, nearly all the peels are located along the trend of an area of higher permeability. At several locations you can determine the trend of a concentrated flow by looking for a series of peels forming a dotted line from tree to tree. This is also true for stone features, such as cairns, along concentrated flows. (Figure 40)

6. The culturally modified trees also serve as a map while traveling through an area. For example, while walking along a trail you observe the direction the peel is pointing and continue in that direction. As you encounter other peeled trees, you continue to follow the direction the peels are pointing. Then you might encounter a tree in line with your direction, however in the bark it has the image of a person walking in another direction at ninety degrees to your direction. (Figure 33) This tells you the trail turns to the right or left and you follow that direction. As you continue, you may see a tall forked modified tree which confirms the direction you need to follow along the trail. (Figure 41) Although all the culturally modified trees are located on a concentrated flow, in dry areas the flows may not be connected.

7. Some shaped trees have an L shaped or curved branch(es) extending from the trunk which have the same trend as the concentrated flow it is located on. Others have a similar shaped branch on each side of the trunk and appears as a forked tree. This suggests they were culturally modified when they were very young to form a particular shape. In Figure 42, a tree has a branch extending outward on each side of the trunk. The tree in Figure 43, which is located in Alaska, shows a single branch aligned with the trend of a concentrated flow.

Figure 42: Forked tree along concentrated flow, CO

Figure 43: The L shaped branch on old growth tree along concentrated flow, Alaska

8. Some of the trees have been grafted together to form a particular shape. (Figure 35) The direction of the graft is along the trend of the concentrated flow it is located on. With other trees, two trees have been twisted together, thus their trunks merge forming a spiral.

9. When you compare the correlation between stone features and culturally modified trees with areas of higher permeability, both of these features map the course of concentrated flows and can consist of a variety of styles. For example, a group of stone and tree features are located along the same area of higher permeability as shown in Figure 44.

Figure 44: Culturally modified tree & stone features on a concentrated flow

Throughout the regions we have investigated, culturally modified trees strongly suggest a high level of cultural uniformity among different Native American cultures, historical periods and diverse environments.

Culturally Modified Glacier Erratics

Another important feature within Ceremonial Landscapes are culturally modified glacier erratics. A glacier erratic is a rock that differs from the type of bedrock native to the area it is located in. In areas affected by glaciation, small stones to very large boulders were carried by glaciers, often over long distances. Then, when the glacier retreated, the stone / boulder was left behind. In some cases glacier drops formed very interesting configurations. Some propped boulders are an example. (Figure 45) They occur when large stones and boulders were left on top of a pile of rubble as the glacier retreated. As the smaller pieces of rubble eroded away the largest boulder can remain supported by a small group of rocks or on a single

Figure 45: Propped glacier erratic along a concentrated flow, Salem, NY

rock in various positions. Although there is a naturally occurring explanation for unusual configurations, some show evidence of cultural modification.

Fortunately, I have had the opportunity to examine glaciated landscapes throughout North America and the Andes Mountains in Peru and Chile. During this research, numerous small to large glacier erratics were investigated, both on and off Native American archaeological sites. In areas that were not associated with Native American archaeological sites, some were on concentrated flows while others were not. This suggests their association with areas of higher permeability is coincidental. However, within Ceremonial Landscapes, glacier erratics that appear to be or are culturally modified were located on areas of higher permeability, which also had stone features associated with them. When stone and tree features were compared, some of them were associated with a particular concentrated flow characteristic. Within these sites it is also possible that some erratics were moved to accommodate an alignment with an area of higher permeability. Unfortunately, many archaeologists and geologists still dismiss culturally modified glacier erratics as naturally occurring. The following discusses some of the more predominate types of culturally modified glacier erratics.

Alignment

When two or more erratics are aligned along a the trend of a concentrated flow, they might point to another site or feature. In the Shawangunk Mountains of New York, two erratics of equal size lean against one another and are centered on a concentrated flow. (Figure 46) When you sight along the flow's trend and between the two boulders, the direction is to High Point, New Jersey, which is the state's highest mountain and the location of a Ceremonial Stone Landscape.

Figure 46: Two large boulders on concentrated flow

Astronomical Alignment

Some large erratics were modified to align with astronomical events. The large erratic in Figure 47 has the appearance of a turtle and is located on a concentrated flow within a large Ceremonial Landscape. The area under it has been cleared of debris. During solstice and equinox sunrise and sunset, the sun casts a beam of light on one side or the other of the turtles's head, thus indicating a particular time of year.

Figure 47: Turtle Rock, NY

Figure 48: Great Turtle Rock, NY

Balanced / Rocking Boulder - In some cases, one boulder is balanced on the narrow point of the supporting boulder and can be rocked back and forth to make a loud sound. (Figure 162)

Effigy Boulder

Turtle - Some large erratics have been modified to appear as a turtle. (Figures 47 & 48) In Figure 48 small boulders extend out from the main boulder to form the neck and head of a turtle, while on each side others form its front legs. Turtles are an important component of creation beliefs and clans with many Native American cultures.

Profiles - Some erratics have been shaped to form human or animal profiles. In Figure 49 the top of the erratic appears to have been culturally modified to resemble a buffalo's profile. It is located on a concentrated flow, and when I followed the flow, it lead me to a nearby buffalo jump which I did not know about. This erratic is sacred to the Tsuut'ina Nation in Alberta, Canada.

Figure 49: Vertical view of buffalo looking towards the sky, Alberta, Canada

Largest Glacier Erratic - Within different regions affected by glaciation, the largest glacier erratic is sacred to the local Native American Nations, for example, Big Rock / Okotoks Erratic in Alberta, Canada, Cochegan Rock in Connecticut and Split Rock in New York. I have included this discussion in the section on Intersecting Areas Of Higher Permeability With Ponding. (Figures 82 & 90)

Leaning Propped Boulder - This consists of a boulder leaning up against another boulder. Within Ceremonial Landscapes they are located along a concentrated flow. (Figure 50)

Figure 50: Propped leaning boulder, Turtle Rock Site, NY

Figure 51: Placed boulder, NY

Placed Boulder - It is placed on the ground or bedrock and centrally located on an area of higher permeability. (Figure 51)

Propped On Single Boulder - This is when one boulder sets on top of another boulder. Typically, the length of the top boulder is aligned with the trend of the concentrated flow. (Figure 52)

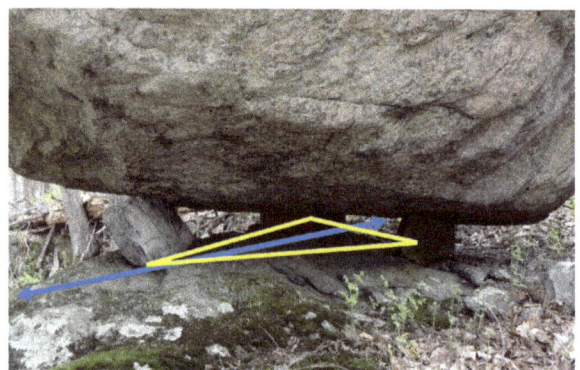

Figure 52: Boulder propped on another boulder, NY

Figure 53: Triangle indicates trend of flow, Tripod Rock, Hudson Valley, NY

Propped On Several Rocks - A large erratic is propped on several stones and is centrally located on an area of higher permeability. Like the one in Figure 53, however there are more stones under the propped boulder.

Tripod Boulder / Propped On Three Rocks - All of the propped boulders supported by three rocks that I have investigated on Ceremonial Landscapes are located along a concentrated flow. The supporting stones / boulders form a triangle, and its longest side is aligned with the trend of the flow. (Figure 53) This characteristic has been observed throughout the glaciated regions I have researched and appears to be more than coincidental. One possibility is during modification, as humans removed the debris, the three rocks which formed a triangle and coincided with a concentrated flow's trend were left in place. Another possibility is the three supporting rocks were placed in their current position during modification. Since some of the boulders are quite large, we often hear the comment humans could not have lifted them. However, archaeological evidence throughout the Western Hemisphere, such as the Inca walls in Saksaywaman, Cusco, Peru, and throughout the world indicate ancient people were capable of moving and lifting exceptionally large megalithic boulders.

Vertical Boulder - In this case, an elongated boulder is propped vertically. The one in Figure 54 is located where an area of higher permeability changes course at ninety degrees.

We have also found propped boulders on several sites in the southwest which were not affected by glaciation. In Figure 55, the propped boulder is located where two areas of higher permeability intersect near Pueblo La Pato in Agua Fria National Monument, Arizona which was not glaciated. These rocks have the same characteristics as the surrounding bedrock, however their positioning is very similar to those of culturally modified glacier erratics. This suggests propped boulders were used by ancestral Native Americans to map the course of areas of higher permeability in both glaciated and non-glaciated regions. I have also investigated perched boulders which were not on areas of higher permeability or associated with other Ceremonial Landscape stone features. This suggests, in some cases, ancestral Native Americans constructed propped boulders at some sites and utilized glacial erratics at others.

Figure 54: Glacial erratic where course of concentrated flow turns, Turtle Rock Site, NY

Figure 55: Propped boulder where two concentrated flows intersect, AZ

Expanding Generally Accepted Interpretations

When I first introduce my methodology to Native American Nations or government agencies, I offer to conduct a demonstration at one or more of their sites. I tell them they do not have to provide any information about the site and suggest they choose sites which they cannot explain since they have unusual features and / or are located where you would not expect them to be. Some of the sites have included Chaco great house outliers, drive lines and teepee rings, to mention a few. Inevitably, the features are located along areas of higher permeability and often, during or immediately following the survey, those accompanying me begin to rethink the generally accepted interpretation of the site's features. Here are some examples.

Drive Lines And Buffalo Jumps

On their website, the U.S. Department Of The Interior, Bureau Of Land Management, Wyoming defines a drive line "as long lines of stone piles that marked a path used to channel the bison in the proper direction during a hunt. The drive lines caused the animals to move toward a jump-off or corral location." (Bureau Of Land Management 2016). Generally speaking this is true, however, all of the well preserved drive lines my colleagues and I have investigated consist of several "long lines of stone piles" which intersect one another at oblique angles. At some of the sites, the stone cairns and walls are tall enough to drive a herd to a kill site. However, at other sites, some of the parallel lines are a few feet wide, while others are thirty or more feet wide consisting of a variety of stone features, which can include low stone piles, cairns, short low walls, as well as, circles and ovals with cleared centers, to mention a few. Frequently, they do not lead to a kill site.

In the northeastern states, most Ceremonial Landscapes have paralleling lines of stone piles and cairns which are very similar to those associated with drive lines in the western states; however, only a few have been associated with a suitable kill site. Nevertheless, they consistently lead to springs which often have a cairn located on them. (Figure 4) As mentioned above, our data indicates most of the stone features are mapping the course of areas of higher permeability, and there is a high level of cultural uniformity between ancestral Native American Ceremonial Landscapes. Therefore, the function of the various stone features should also be similar from region to region.

Within these sites most of the stone features are too low or too far apart to deter a stampeding herd from going one way or the other. Placing people by specific stone features along a drive line could help direct the herd, however it could put the participants in the path of the stampede. Also, if all the branching "drive lines" at a site were staffed with people, it would develop into a maze and be uncontrollable. The Lewis and Clark Journals describe the procedure used by some of the Native Americans they encountered as follows:

> "most active and fleet young men is selected and (being) disguised in a
> robe of buffaloe skin, having also the skin of the buffaloes head with

the ears and horns fastened on his head in form of a cap, thus caparisoned he places himself at a convenient distance between a herd of buffaloe and a precipice proper for the purpose, which happens in many places on this river for miles together." Then, a group of Indians surrounds the buffalo on three sides and begins to drive the herd. As they begin to run, the person in the buffalo robe stands to get the buffalo herd's attention and runs toward the cliff as the herd follows. Then just before the herd starts to fall over the cliff, the lead person takes shelter at a predetermined location (Moulton 2001).

At several animal kill jump sites, pre-planned drive lines are apparent due to the remaining stone features such as high walls and cairns. For example, there are several high long walls in Agua Fria National Monument which are associated with animal jump sites. However, this does not explain the function of other stone feature groups which do not lead to a kill site. This suggests some of them had another function.

For example, at the Madison Buffalo Jump (Figures 56 & 57) I followed MB 11 eastward for .25 mi / .4 km. Only two concentrated flows, MB 12 and 13, intersected it, and all three flows had teepee rings associated with them. Teepee rings (TR) 11 through 14 were centrally located on a flow. The diameter of TR 11 through 13 were equal to the width of the concentrated flow they are located on, while TR 14 was slightly wider. This is consistent with the other buffalo jumps and drive lines I have investigated in the northern plains. If these stone features were mapping the buffalo drive, it would seem impractical to use them for habitation.

Figure 56: The Madison Buffalo Jump is the only jump site along .50 mi / .80 km of escarpment

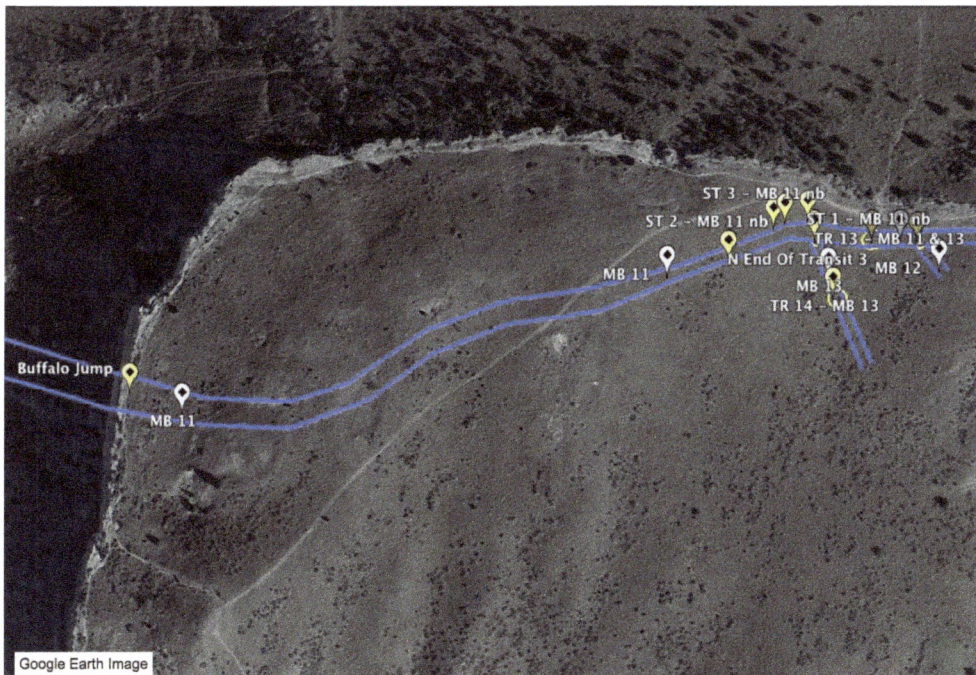

As of this article, antelope, big horned sheep, elk and buffalo drive lines which lead to cliffs have been investigated by my colleagues and I from Arizona to Alberta. Most of the sites were located along a broad mesa which has a long steep escarpment along one or more sides which was sufficient for a kill site; however, animals were driven over the edge at only one or a few locations along it. For example, in Figure 56 the Madison Buffalo Jump is the only jump site along

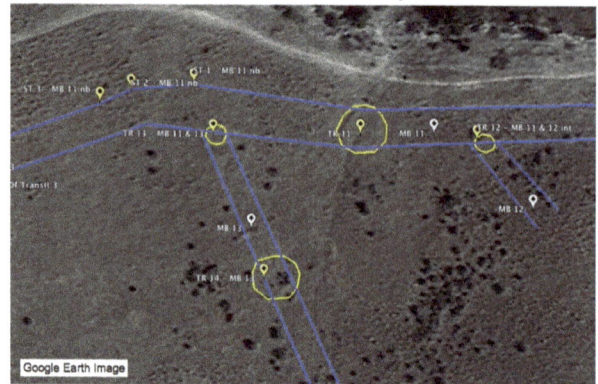

Figure 57: Teepee rings / stone circles, Madison Buffalo Jump, MT

.5 mi / .8 km of the escarpment, however this entire distance is suitable for a jump site. This strongly suggests the persons who chose these sites had associated them with something which was not characteristic of the rest of the escarpment.

Our drive line data strongly suggests the stone features are mapping something else, and we believe it is areas of higher permeability within the groundwater, some of which coincide with drive lines which lead to kill sites. For example, prior to choosing the location of the buffalo jump certain criteria appear to have been considered. First, locating an area frequented by buffalo or other animal herds during their migration; secondly, finding a cliff or other natural features suitable for a kill site and thirdly, mapping the areas of higher permeability with stone features and determining where one or more intersect an appropriate kill site. Once completed, only those areas which coincided with these requirements were chosen as kill sites.

At the Vore Buffalo Jump in northeastern Wyoming, I located two areas of higher permeability, VB 1 and VB 2, which intersected the site and are associated with a buffalo jump, dive line cairns and geological features which indicate the presence of an area of higher permeability. (Figure 58) Dr. Greg Pierce, Wyoming State Archaeologist, comments, "The Vore Buffalo jump was used at least twenty times between approximately 1550 and 1800 A.D." "The tribes who most likely used the sinkhole were the Lakota Sioux, Cheyenne, Arapaho, Crow, Kiowa, Plains Apache and Shoshone." (Pierce 2014, Vore buffalo Jump 2016).

Sinkhole 1 and the buffalo jump are centrally located on VB 1 which crosses the site from northwest to south. VB 2 intersected VB 1 at sinkhole 1 and trends westward and then northwestward to where it intersects sinkhole 2. The average width of VB 1 was 55 ft / 16.76 m and VB 2 58 ft / 17.67 m. Due to Route I-90, I was unable to follow VB 1 southward. However, Jacqueline Wyatt told me the buffalo were driven towards the site from the south along a shallow depression, and the remnants of a drive line consisting of cairns was documented along it before the road was constructed.

Within the vicinity of the buffalo jump, there are three sinkholes, and two of them have a sinkhole within them, thus totaling 5 sinkholes when counted separately. I have labeled them Sinkhole 1 through 5. (Figure 59)

Figure 58: Sinkholes & concentrated flows, Vore Buffalo Jump, WY

The site's geological report comments:

Although the dissolving of limestone within the Minnelusa Formation is a feasible hypothesis for the creation of the sinkhole found at the Vore Buffalo Jump (this is how the Mammoth Site sinkhole, which is also located within the Spearfish Formation, originated), other evidence seems to suggest that dissolution in the Minnelusa may not be the direct cause which led to the formation of the Vore site sinkhole (sinkhole 1). Instead, evidence suggests that the sinkholes of this region are formed by a collapse into open passageways near the bottom of the Spearfish Foundation and the top of the Minnekahta limestone. This hypothesis is backed up by evidence found in a neighboring larger sinkhole (sinkhole 2 and 3), found just across the frontage road from the Vore Buffalo Jump. In 1985, the north end of the sinkhole collapsed to form a smaller 60-foot deep sinkhole. At the time of its formation, local ranchers heard water running beneath in a cavern that extended horizontally beyond the

65

limits of their flashlights. Because the stream and cavern the ranchers discovered were relatively close to the surface, this incident supports the idea that both this sinkhole and the Vore site sinkhole were formed in the higher up Spearfish and Minnekahta Formations and the layer of gypsum which is sandwiched between them, rather than in the much deeper Minnelusa Formation. The presence of a cavern underneath the larger sinkhole also suggests that the Vore site sinkhole and its neighbor may in fact be linked together by means of a subterranean cavern system which formed within the gypsum layer (Schnorenberg & Gade 2015, Vore Buffalo Jump 2016).

Figure 59: Sinkholes associated with Vore Buffalo Jump, WY

This hypothesis is supported by Ted Vore's observations when he was working the ranch. There is a large sinkhole north of the road approximately .5 mi / .81 km west of the buffalo jump sinkhole 1 and sinkholes 2 and 3. (Figures 58 & 59) In 1957 Ted and his brother where riding by sinkhole 4 and noticed sinkhole 5 had appeared within it. They lowered themselves to the bottom and found a hole which went deeper, and they heard water running. Ted crawled into the hole, while his brother held his ankles, and reported he could see a large cavern with water running through it (Personal conversation with Ted Vore in February, 2017).

Although I have not investigated sinkholes 4 and 5, when you compare my map of VB 1 and 2 with the geological report, they support one another. Although I did not investigate the cairns, they seem to be associated with the trend of VB 1. This suggests the Native Americans who constructed the cairns were mapping VB 1, as well as establishing the location of a drive line.

At the Wahkpa Chu'gn Buffalo Jump in Havre, Montana, I located six areas of higher permeability which intersected the site from the south. (Figure 60) Excavations conducted on three of the concentrated flows revealed a large number of buffalo remains and artifacts which date to the following:

> The earliest of these groups is known as the Besant. Besant peoples used the site extensively a number of times between 2000 and 1500 years ago. After its use by Besant peoples the site was abandoned for a 200 to 300 year period. The site was then used briefly by the Avonlea people between about 1200 and 1300 years ago. This was followed almost immediately by the Saddle Butte peoples who continued to use the site until about 600 years ago when the site was finally abandoned (Wahkpa Chu'gn Buffalo Jump 2016).

Figure 60: Concentrated flows at Wahkpa Chu'gn Buffalo Jump, MT

Since the areas of higher permeability are relatively close together, it is possible there are remains on all of them.

Similar characteristics have been observed at all the animal kill sites we have investigated.

Teepee Rings & Stone Circles

Another controversial stone feature is the teepee ring. (Figures 61 - 70, 99 & 146) When various researchers described this feature to me, and I looked up the definition, the descriptions seem to be ambiguous. For example, Wikipedia provides the following descriptions which I also heard from various researchers:

Figure 61: Stone circle on concentrated flow and no artifacts, MT

They are generally found in the Great Plains of the United States and Canada, but are also found in the foothills and mountains, near good areas for hunting, supplies of water and fuel, and main routes of travel. The rings are often 6 to 25 feet (1.8 to 7.6 m) in diameter and often occur in groupings. The rings of stone held down the edges of animal skin hides of the cone-shaped tipis, to keep them snug against the ground. The general pattern of a tipi (also "tepee") ring is an east-facing entrance, where there are no stones, and a heavily anchored side with extra stones for protection against prevailing winds, often on the northwestern side of the ring. Hearths found in the center of tipi rings suggest a winter encampment. In the summer, food was cooked in open-air hearths. There are generally few artifacts found at these sites (Wikipedia 2016, Cassells 1997, Malouf 1961).

Stone circles, of which tipi rings are an example, may be simply assembled rocks placed in single or multiple courses. More elaborate circles have been constructed in walls of stone or with horizontal logs and stone, possibly for a fort or corral.[2] Other stone circles – some more than 39 feet (12 m) across – may be the remains of special ceremonial dance structures. A few cobble arrangements form the outlines of human figures, most of them obviously male. Perhaps the most intriguing cobble constructions, however, are the ones known as medicine wheels. Tipi rings are nearly all of the types of stone circles, except those that are medicine wheels or of very small diameter (Wikipedia 2016, Malouf 1961).

From a study of 137 sites on the 2,000 square mile Blackfeet Indian Reservation, tipis were often arranged in a pattern, such as a single or double row, semi-circle, circle, triangle, V-shape or a haphazard shape.[5] Artifacts found were limited to tools or fragments of tools made of stone or bone, such as broken projectile points, hammerstones, grooved mauls and pieces of flint or imported obsidian. When horses were introduced after about A.D. 1730, camp materials were pulled by horses rather than dogs and the tipis became larger, from holding 6-8 people to up to 50 people (Wikipedia 2016, Kehoe 1958).

Our data indicates stone circles are located along one or more areas of higher permeability. When you compare the teepee ring descriptions mentioned above, certain discrepancies emerge. While one comments few artifacts are found at these sites, another indicates they accompany these sites. One states they can be associated with other stone features, and the other describes a variety of patterns they are arranged in, however, one excludes certain circular patterns. Additional discrepancies emerged during several of the teepee ring field surveys. I was told many teepee rings do not have an entrance, and we observed several of them at each site. We observed others large enough to house six to eight people on slopes as steep as forty-five degrees or more, while some were located in narrow drainages. At several sites, teepee rings were located along drive lines, which does not seem practical. Frequently, a group of teepee rings were adjacent to one another making it difficult to maneuver from one to another if they were all used for habitation at the same time. Conversely, if some were used for habitation while others within the group were not, the unused stone circles would be obstacles while moving about. It would have been more practical to remove the unused stone circles. Consistently, I have read site reports which determined a site is a teepee / habitation site, however, when I surveyed the site, some of the teepee rings documented in the report are only 2 ft / .609 m in diameter. In some cases they were identified as hearths, however, there was no evidence of charcoal, fire cracked stones or any other form of artifacts. This strongly suggests they had another function.

Another observation researchers agree with is some teepee rings are located considerable distances from water. It is possible these sites were utilized during the winter when snow augmented their potable water supply, however, it is not practical in regions which do not receive snow. These observations suggest stone circles / teepee rings may have another function which was not considered by previous researchers. Our data indicates they were mapping concentrated flows within the groundwater, whether or not they were used for habitation.

As mentioned throughout this text, Native American features consistently have more than one meaning or function, and this is true for stone circles. While collaborating with various northern plains First Nations, I was told that stone circles were also used as prayer and vision quest sites. A small prayer circle is used by an individual and could only be used once while groups use two large adjacent stone circles for prayer and ceremonies. Therefore, if a particular location was used for prayers over hundreds or thousands of years, there could be a considerable number of prayer circles with various diameters at that site. Since these sites are sacred, cultural material and debris were not deposited at these locations. Thus, although the stone circles remain, there would not be evidence of habitation at these sites. This helps explain why some sites consisting of hundreds of stone circles remain without any to very little evidence of habitation.

Where stone circles are associated with household artifacts, the evidence indicates they were associated with teepees, and sites can consist of hundreds of them. However, when there is very little or no evidence of household artifacts, it suggests the stone circles were used for other purposes. Interestingly, both teepee rings and stone circles are consistently located on one or more areas of higher permeability. Figure 69 shows a section of a teepee ring habitation site which contains numerous artifacts throughout it.

Within a large cluster of stone circles, some may not be located on an area of higher permeability. A possible explanation for this is long term use and congestion. I first encountered this in Peru where there were large ancient communities. The first habitation structures were located along the area(s) of higher permeability which crossed the site; however, as the community expanded, the area along the concentrated flows filled up. (Johnson 2009) Therefore, later structures were located as close as possible to the concentrated flows. This same pattern could easily apply to large clusters of stone prayer circles if they are only used once.

Figure 62: A large group of stone circles & concentrated flows connecting them, MT

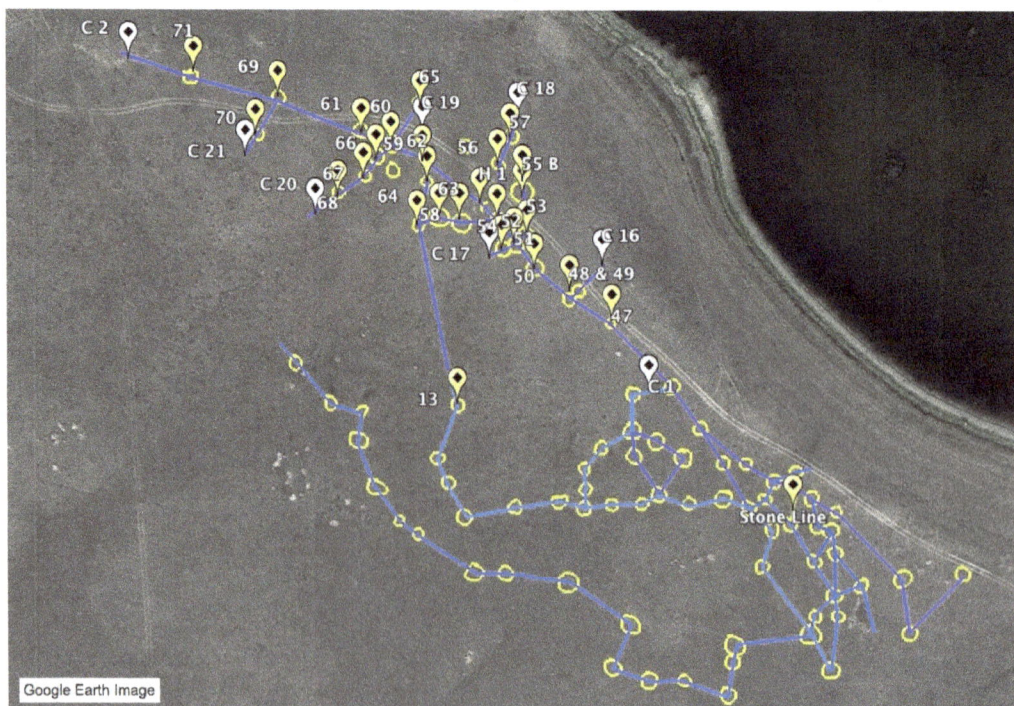

70

My colleagues and I have had the opportunity to examine large clusters of stone circles from Wyoming to Alberta, and the results are interesting. While some sites contained evidence of habitation, others did not, for example:

At one of the sites in northern Montana, we ground surveyed and mapped the areas of higher permeability which were associated with one hundred twenty-eight stone circles and tested for concentrated flows at several others. (Figure 62) This site is charismatic of other stone circle sites that did not have artifacts associated with them. This indicates the stone circles were not used for habitation however they served another function.

1. All of the stone circles were located on one or more areas of higher permeability.

2. The lines of stone circles followed the concentrated flow's meandering trends.

3. The width of the concentrated flows varied and the stone circles' diameters were equal to the width of the flows they were located on.

4. Some of the stone circles have stone features within them such as circles, lines and triangles as well as others. These inner features indicated intersections of concentrated flows, where it curves and the trend of the flow. In Figure 63 there is a triangle within a stone circle which indicates the trend of the concentrated flow it is located on. In Alberta, Canada, some of the small circles had medicine plants growing within them as shown in Figure 64.

Figure 63: Stone circle with a triangle within it, 14 ft / 4.26 m diameter, MT

Figure 64: Small stone circle with medicine plants within it, 4 ft / 1.2 m diameter, Alberta, Canada

5. In addition to stone circles, half circles, low cairns, triangles, figures and stone lines were also associated with the concentrated flows. (Figures 65) This pattern was also documented in Peru. (Figure 68)

Figure 65: Two varieties of stone circles indicate where two concentrated flows intersect

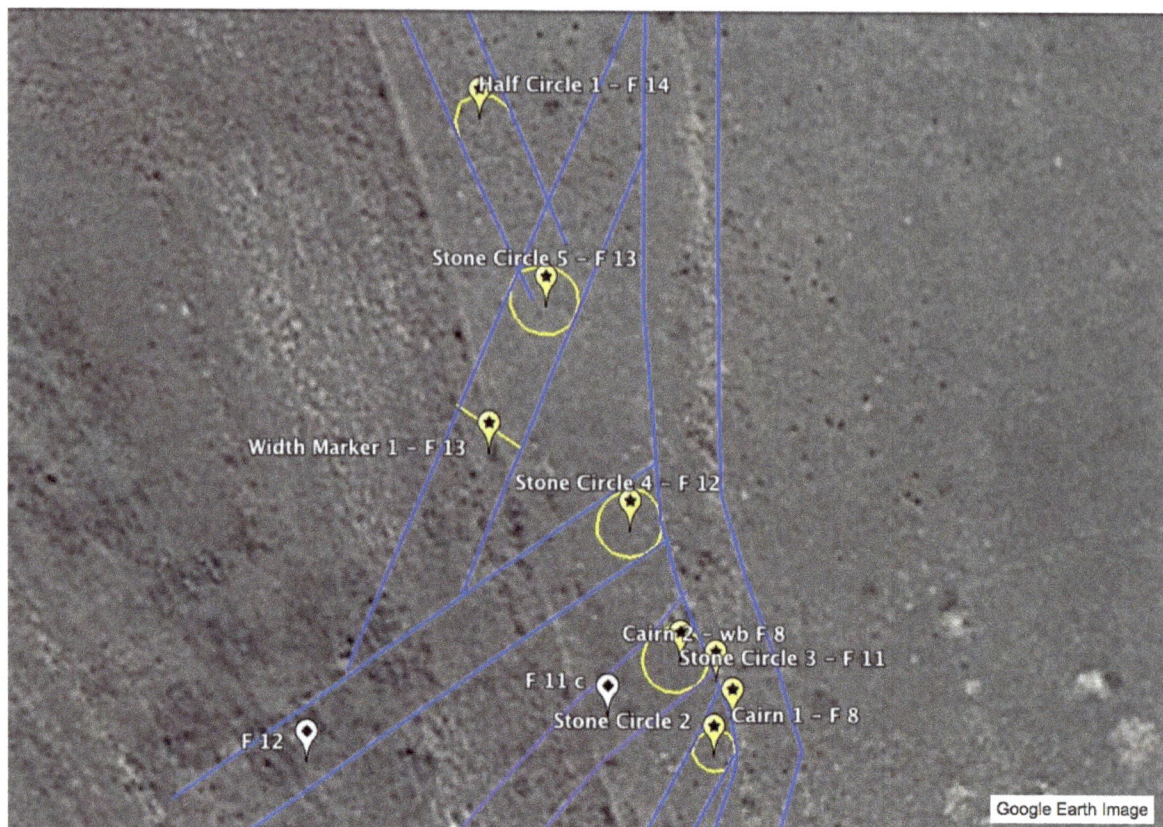

6. At the site shown in Figure 62 we did not find any artifacts associated with habitation.

7. In some cases, two or three stone circles or a stone circle and half circle were placed adjacent to one another where two concentrated flows intersected one another. (Figures 65 & 68) We also documented this in Peru as shown in Figure 68.

When the southwest and northern plains data was compared, some stone circle variations were observed. During the southwestern investigation, circular shaped habitation structures, such as pithouses and hogans, were located along areas of higher permeability. Their diameter was equal to the width of the concentrated flow and often associated with other stone features on the same flow. (Figure 66) At other sites, circular stone features which did not contain artifacts shared the same association

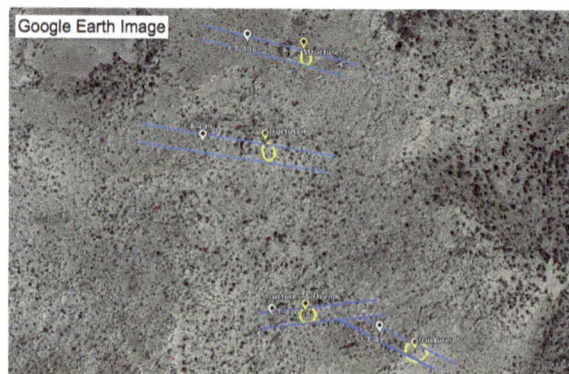

Figure 66: Navajo hogans & concentrated flows, NM

with areas of higher permeability. Fewer stone circles of either type were documented in the southwest than in the northern plains, even though the concentration of areas of higher permeability at each site was similar. In the northern plains, there was a variation in the location of stone circles where two areas of higher permeability intersect. For example, where two concentrated flows intersect, the circle was the width of one of the flows, while half of it was on each flow. (Figures 65)

During our investigation of the coastal geoglyphs of Peru and Chile, stone circles were similar in appearance to teepee rings; however, the archaeological data indicated they were not used for habitation. (Figures 67 & 68) In each case, they were located along an area of higher permeability, where two or more intersect or a concentrated flow changed direction. The diameter was always equal to the diameter of the flow they were centrally located on (Johnson 2009, Ch. 2, Pp. 30 & 40).

Figure 67: Stone circle with cleared center, Conanoxa, Chile

Figure 68: Half circle next to a circle where two concentrated flows intersect, Nasca Lines, Peru

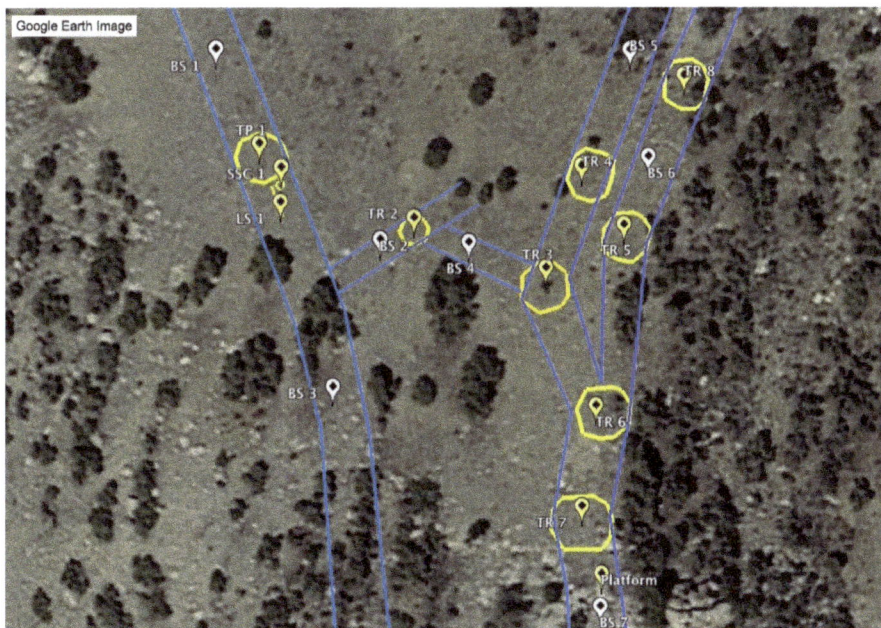

Figure 69: Teepee rings located along areas of higher permeability, WY

At this point in time, the location of stone circles within the northern plains suggests the following.

1. <u>Mapping the course of an area of higher permeability</u> - When you are following a line of circles with equal diameters, it indicates the trend and width of the area of higher permeability. (Figure 69)

2. <u>Areas of higher permeability Intersecting</u> - Thus far, two patterns indicate where two areas of higher permeability intersect.

   A. Where two concentrated flows intersect, a stone circle may be located half on one of them and half on the other, however its diameter will be equal to one of the flows if their widths are different. If the concentrated flow's widths are the same, the diameter of the stone circle will equal their widths. Near the circle, on one or both of the flows, there may be other features, such as width markers and / or half circles whose length or diameter is equal to the width of the concentrated flow they are located on. However, if one of them is not directly in line with the circle and it is offset by half of the circle's width it indicates two concentrated flows with different widths are intersecting. For example, in Figure 65, stone circle 5, half circle 1 and width marker 1 indicate this.

   B. When you have a line of circles with equal widths mapping an area of higher permeability, and there is a smaller or larger circle out of and adjacent to the alignment, it indicates another concentrated flow is intersecting the one you are following. (Figure 69)

Figure 70: Two areas of higher permeability cross one another & two different sets of stone circles indicate width and trend

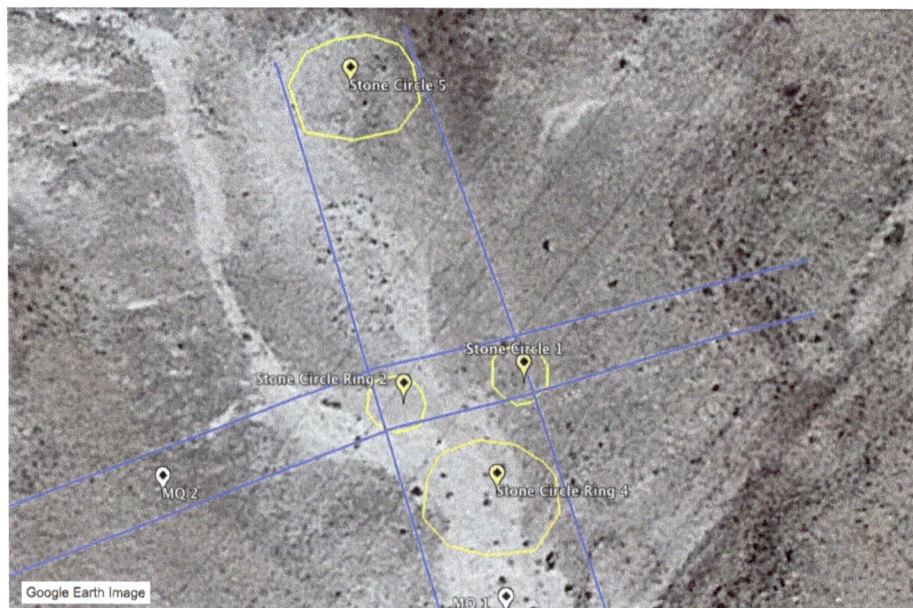

74

3. <u>Two areas of higher permeability are crossing one another</u> - When you have four circles located in a square or rectangular pattern, it indicates two areas of higher permeability are crossing one another.

A. If all four circles have the same diameter, it indicates both concentrated flows are the same width.

B. If the concentrated flows are not the same width, the four circles are divided up into two sets, with each set having different diameters. (Figure 70)

Thus, in the northern plains stone circles were multi-functional. Some stone circles functioned as teepee rings, prayer and vision quest circles while mapping the area of higher permeability they are located on. Others only mapped the area of higher permeability they were located on. This aligned these features with the three worlds.

Intersecting Areas Of Higher Permeability With Subsurface Ponding

It is important to mention the circumstances which led me to the sites discussed in this section. Prior to my investigation, native and non-native reachers directed my attention to these sites since they have unusual features associated with them which they could not explain. By applying my methodology to these sites, they hoped they could obtain a more in-depth understanding of them.

In Peru and Chile, our data indicated where a group of areas of higher permeability either intersect or cross one another creating ponding within the bedrock, ancestral Native Americans mapped these locations with surface features. Then, as we expanded our research into the United States and Canada, very similar patterns emerged. The following discusses the various locations where this has been documented from Peru northward to Alaska, and the Native American features which are associated with them. Each of these sites share similar characteristics indicating cultural uniformity among them and, in some instances, oral history can be associated with them, which strongly supports why they were considered sacred sites in the past, as well as the present.

Line Centers In Peru

Within the coastal geoglyphs of Peru and Chile, where two or more concentrated flows intersect or cross one another creating ponding, the concentrated flows are mapped with geoglyphs dating to 2,100 B.P. to 1,500 B.P.. (Figure 71) Along the Andean foothills line centers are frequently located where a ridge line begins to disappear below the alluvium deposited along the base of the hills, and where a ridge protrudes above the alluvium. Often the topography at these locations is higher than the surrounding area which provides a panoramic view of the landscape. Some of the line centers are connected to one other by lines which function like the page numbers of a book. By following the lines they take you from one line center to the other. From the top of a line center you can observe various geoglyphs in that area, and if you know their meaning, you can determine the number of areas of higher permeability intersecting that location and follow them outward. The top of a line center usually contains one or two small stone circles, either with or without a cleared center. Frequently there are shallow circular depressions indicating the location of

Figure 71: Line center with several geoglyphs & concentrated flows intersecting it, Peru

burials and offerings. Often they have been looted thus exposing the fragmented remains of burials and offerings (Johnson 2009, Ch 2). The burials and offerings suggest these locations were considered sacred.

Figure 72: Socos line center and ponding area, Peru

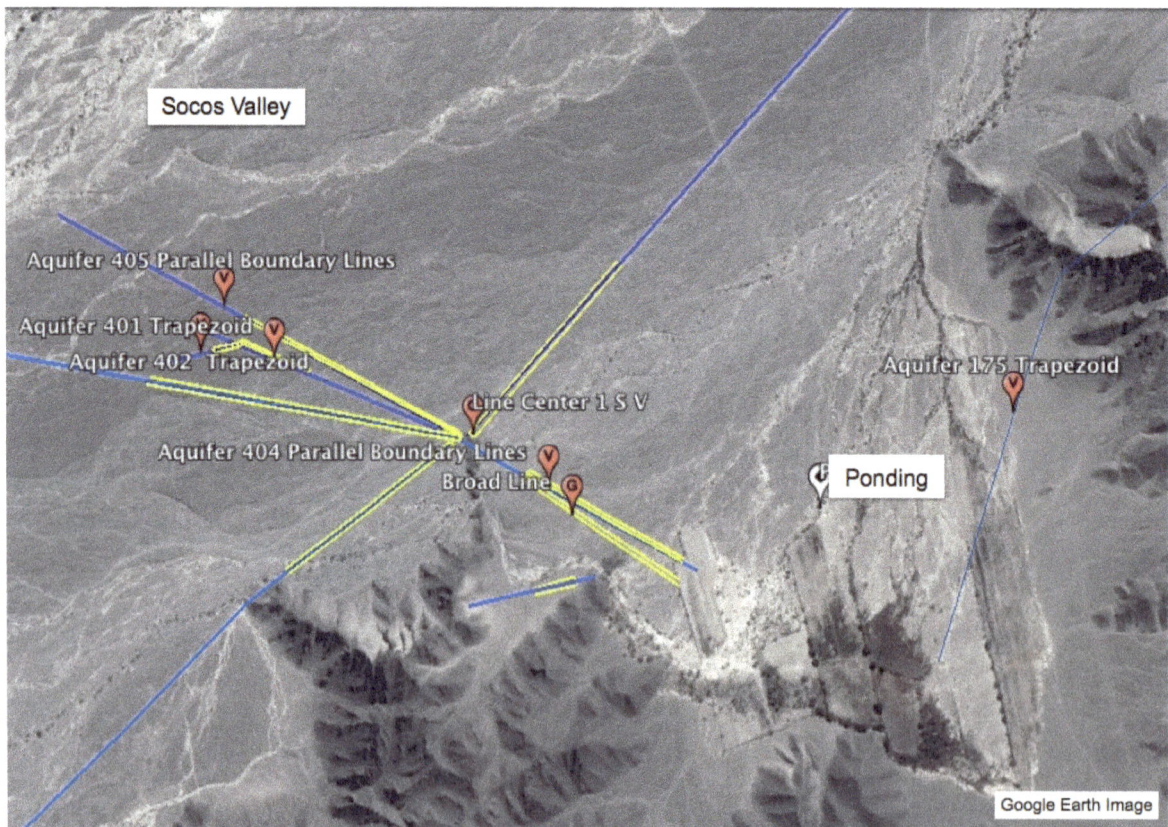

Intersecting concentrated flows can be caused by various factors. One example is located in the Socos Valley near Nasa, Peru. At this location an area of higher permeability within the groundwater flowing down the valley intersects the valley wall were there is a shallow side valley. When this happens, groundwater in the alluvium can be trapped or damed up creating ponding. Then some of the groundwater may seep out through faults, fractures, bedding contacts or along dikes, to mention a few possibilities, within the bedrock to the other side of the ridge thus creating a ray like pattern of flows. In Figure 72 line center 1 is located where the ridge line extending northward sinks below the alluvium. At this location groundwater flowing along the east side of the valley is channeled into the side valley along the east side of the ridge. The ponding is evident by the presence of agriculture in the side valley. Where line center 1 is located, six areas of higher permeability intersect it and are mapped by seven geoglyphs. Some of the areas of higher permeability are bringing groundwater to or from the east side of the valley and the subterranean flow along the center of the valley.

Figure 73: Circle with concentrated flows & ponding, Ripley Intaglio Site, CA

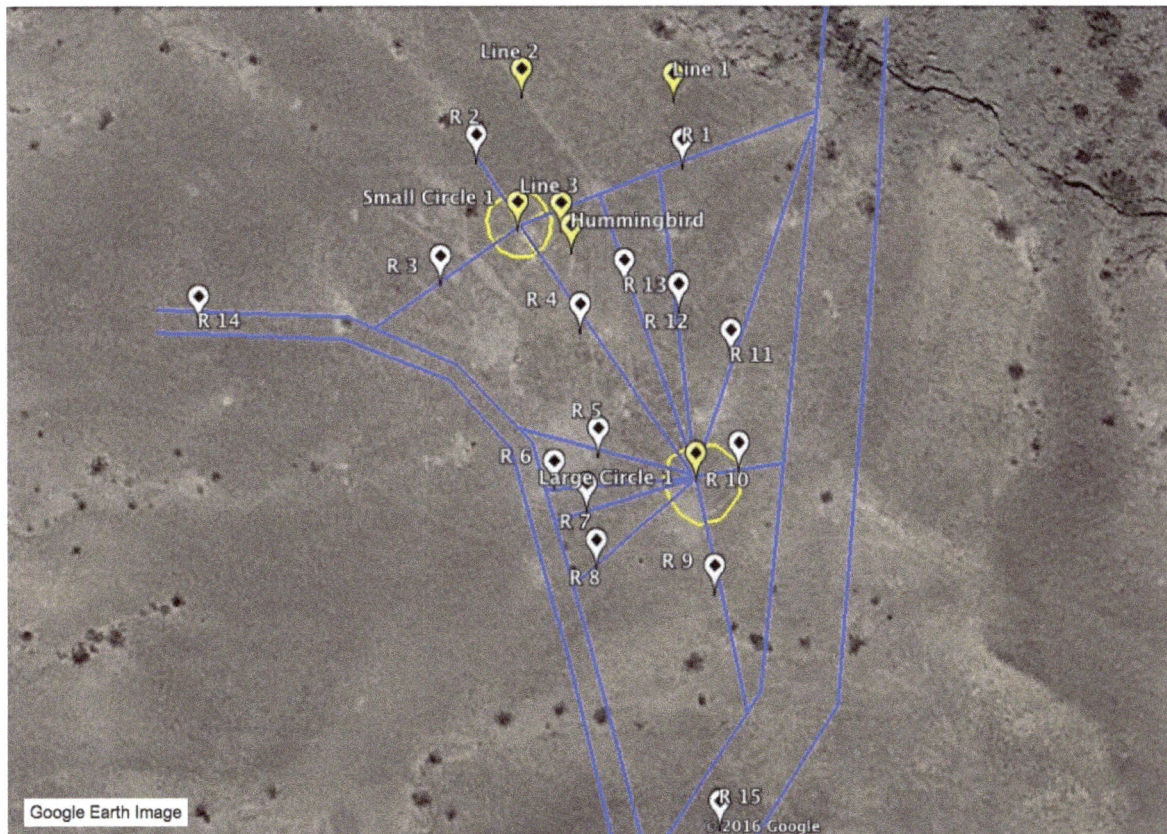

Line Centers And The Blythe Geoglyphs

In southern California and Arizona, there are geoglyphs which are very similar to those found in Peru and Chile. At some sites, such as the Ripley Intaglio Site, there are stone circles with lines, human figures and other varieties of geoglyphs intersecting them. (Figure 73) When I dowsed around large circle 1, I located ten areas of higher permeability intersecting the center of the circle where there is ponding. All the other nearby concentrated flows were also mapped with geoglyphs. This may be caused by a small dome within the bedrock which has created fractures that are receiving groundwater from R 14 and R 15. As mentioned above by Figueroa, "The Blythe Giant Intaglios and other geoglyphs are all associated with the underground water. In the Nahuatl language, it is called A-Tla-Chinolli (water-earth-cosmos, the communicators)....I have spent most of my life researching these sacred sites." (Figueroa 2017, Johnson's Smithsonian Institution archival file).

Buttes With Intersecting Concentrated Flows

During the investigation of Chaco Canyon's great houses and outliers, a few outlier sites contained a small butte with a structure located on top and either a ramp or a way to climb to the top. (Figure 74) Each of these buttes have several areas of higher permeability intersecting an area of ponding beneath them. (Figure 75) Thus far, I am aware of six of these sites located in northern New Mexico; however, I believe there are others.

Figure 74: Butte with ramp and structure on top, Escalone Chaco outlier, NM

Figure 75: Butte and areas of higher permeability radiating out from it, Escalone Chaco outlier site, NM

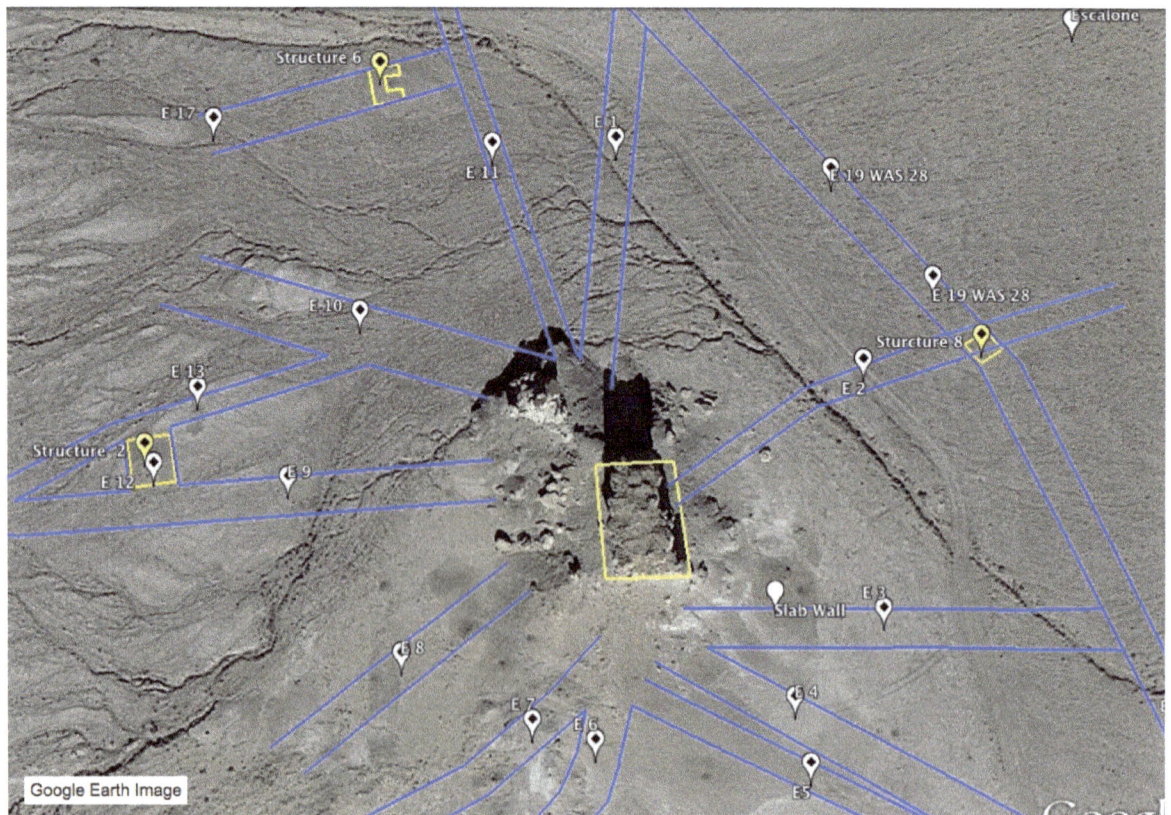

This also appears to apply to Fajada Butte, which is located in Chaco Canyon. I have not received a permit to dowse around the base of Fajada Butte; however, I did receive permission to document the areas of higher permeability crossing the roads on the north and west sides of the butte. Even through the data was taken between .7 mi / 1.12 km to 1 mi / 1.6 km from the butte, thus far, I have located six areas of higher permeability which trend towards Fajada Butte. (Figures 76 & 77)

Figure 76: Fajada Butte

Within the canyon Fajada Butte is an important component. It is sacred to several Native American Nations, and when approaching the canyon, it stands out like a beacon. There are several Native American features on the butte, including the sun dagger astronomical petroglyph, structures and a ramp. Fajada Butte is centrally located within the San Juan Basin. When you compare the ray pattern of areas of higher permeability at Fajada Butte with those found by Pueblo Bonito, they are very similar to the trend of bedrock fractures in that area.

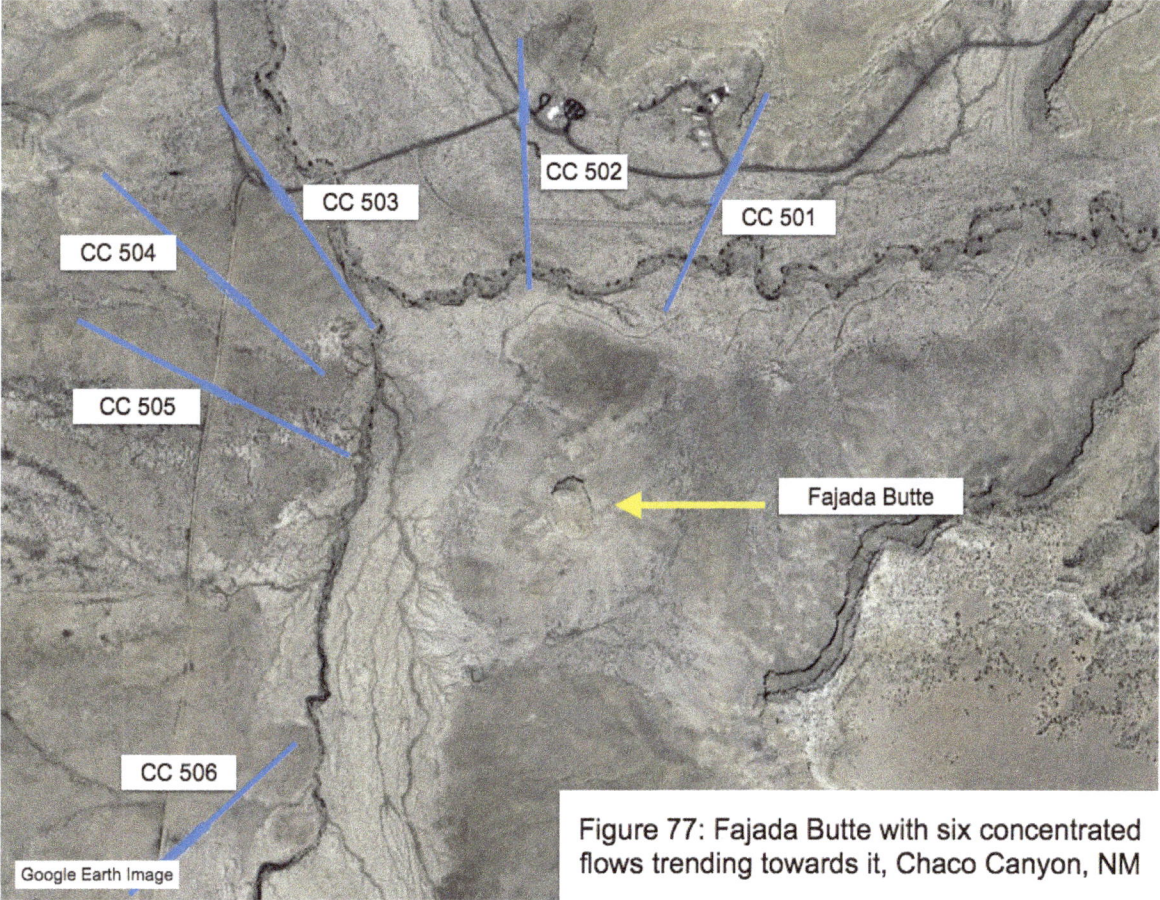

CC 502

CC 503

CC 501

CC 504

CC 505

Fajada Butte

CC 506

Google Earth Image

Figure 77: Fajada Butte with six concentrated flows trending towards it, Chaco Canyon, NM

79

The three buttes I circled at outlier sites had between five to fourteen concentrated flows intersecting them. Some crossed from one side to the other, while others intersected each other. When mapped, ponding was concentrated below the buttes, and areas of higher permeability radiated outward from it like rays. All of the site's structures and stone features are located along the areas of higher permeability radiating from the butte or others crossing between them. Thus, all of the site's features are connected to one another by one or more areas of higher permeability, and all of the astronomical observation points are located along these flows.

Figure 78: Plaza located at center of habitationscape containing pithouses & roomblocks, NM

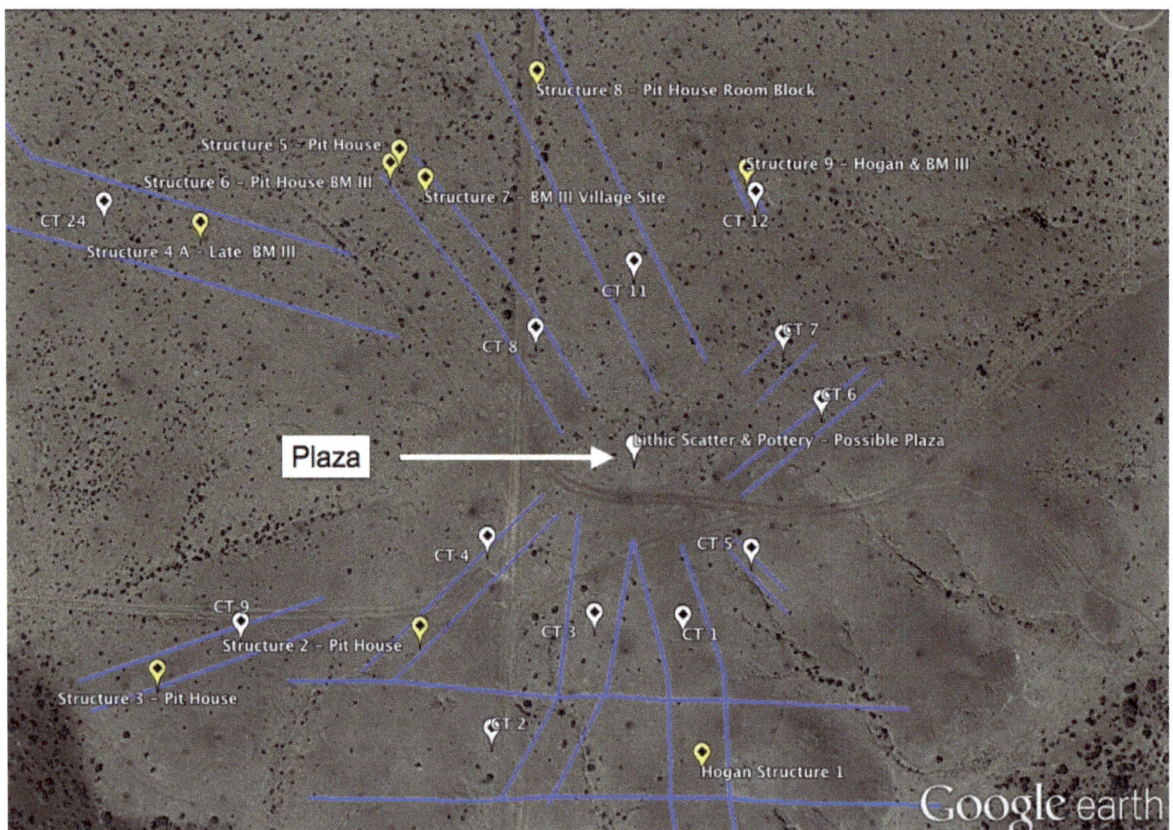

Some sites which do not have a small butte associated with them have ponding with several areas of higher permeability intersecting at the center of the site. For example, some of the Chaco outliers have several areas of higher permeability intersecting them, while some Basketmaker and Chaco roomblock sites have a central plaza where several areas of higher permeability intersect. (Figure 78) This is also true for several Sinagua sites. All the sites' structures and stone features are located along the flows. (Figure 79)

Figure 79: Sinagua roomblock, AZ

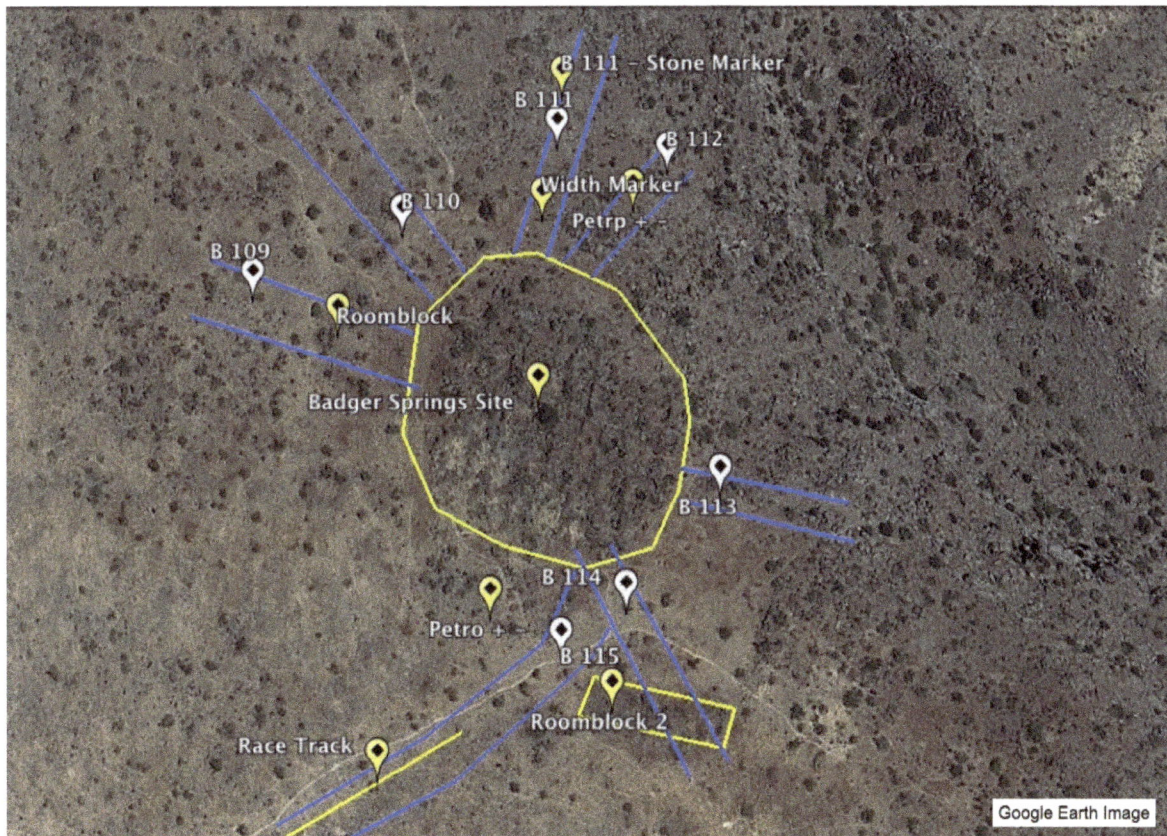

After you map the areas of higher permeability intersecting one of these buttes, your first inclination is the pattern resembles rays or the spokes of a wheel. During these phases Native Americans did not know about wheels. However, when you consider the southwestern Native American legend of Spider Woman, you realize this pattern also resembles a spider web, which is referred to in several of their legends and is discussed below.

Medicine Wheels

In the northern plains, ancestral Native Americans constructed what are presently referred to as medicine wheels, which are described as follows by John Brumley, who has researched them extensively. (Figure 80)

Figure 80: Medicine wheel, WY

All medicine wheels consist of a combination of at least two of the following three primary components:

a. A prominent, centrally located stone cairn of varying size

b. Usually one, but sometimes concentric stone rings of generally circular shape

c. Multiple (two or more) stone lines radiating outward from a central origin point, central cairn, or margins of a stone ring (Brumley 1986).

He has divided them into eight subgroups as show in Figure 81. Brumley also commented "these features are rare and poorly understood."

Figure 81: Brumley's eight medicine wheel subgroups

Courtesy of Brumley 2017

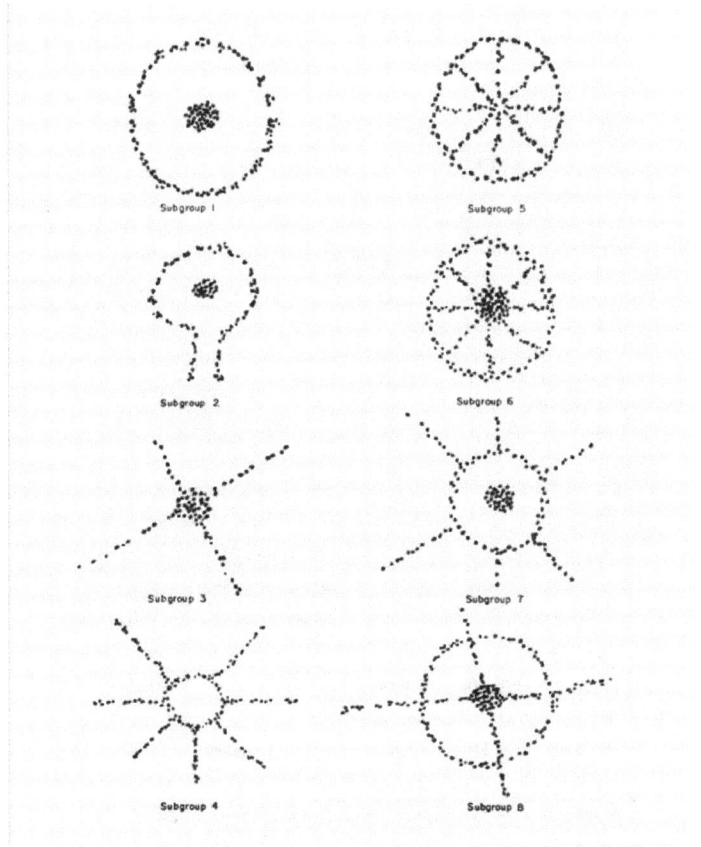

Figure 2 : Defined Medicine Wheel Subgroups. (from Brumley nd)

I was introduced to medicine wheels by a colleague who suggested I look up the Big Horn Medicine Wheel National Monument in Wyoming on the internet. As soon as I saw the photograph of the medicine wheel I reflected back to the line centers and buttes with areas of higher permeability intersecting them and wondered if they were similar. Although I have not investigated the Big Horn Medicine Wheel, I had the opportunity to investigate others in Wyoming, Montana and Alberta which represented three of the eight medicine wheel subgroups described by Brumley. I began by circling the outer circle to determine if any areas of higher permeability intersected it. Interestingly, a concentrated flow intersected each spoke / ray, and the rods indicated the area between them was dry. The medicine wheels I surveyed had between eight and fourteen spokes. Like the line centers and buttes, some crossed from one side to the other while others intersected each other, and where they intersected there was ponding. Each had a central stone pile / cairn with a stone circle around it. Where the spokes intersected the outer ring, the width of the spoke was equal to the width of the area of higher permeability. When the areas of higher permeability were followed outward from the medicine wheel they lead to other stone features which included circles, stone piles and cairns, to mention a few. Amazingly, these features closely resembled the line centers and buttes with areas of higher permeability intersecting them, and when you consider the southwestern Native American legend of Spider Woman, you realize this pattern also resembles a spider web, which is referred to in several of their legends and discussed below.

In addition to these observations, other researchers have shown some of the medicine wheels have "alignment with the cardinal directions is common, some are also aligned with astronomical phenomena involving the sun, moon, some stars, and some planets in relation to the Earth's horizon at that location (Brumley 1986, Wikipedia 2016).

Dr. Philip LaPorta, a stratigraphy raw material and prehistoric quarry specialist, suggests the following explanation for the areas of higher permeability associated with these features:

> Domes and basins: circular or oval zones of uplift or depression, respectively, causing sedimentary layers to be convexly or concavely bent. Sedimentary layers in many places show a warping into broad dome-like or basin-like structures, which may range from 100 to 200 miles in diameter, but in which sedimentary layers are inclined only about 1 to 2 degrees from the horizontal.

> As domes are topographically expressive, they are subject to weathering and erosion from the elements. As the central part of the dome is eroded, older rock layers are exposed. As each layer is cut through, it is eroded back from the center, creating cuestas that face in toward the central part of the dome. Basins, on the other hand do not suffer from erosion to the same extent as domes. As such, their centers tend to preserve rock due to the protective embrace of the central depression. In contrast to domes, basins tend to preserve younger rocks in their centers, with older rocks flanking the younger rocks as one moves away from the basin center. Cuestas in basins have their steep faces outwards, and as erosion progresses, the cuestas retreat toward the center of the basin.

> Domes are known to preserve oil, gas and water in their sedimentary strata. Such fluids tend to accumulate in domed sandstone layers overlying or sandwiched between impervious shales.

> The compressive stresses which generate domes or basins are also responsible for creating finer scale structures known as joints in the outcrop. Joints are parallel fracture sets along which there has been no movement. Statistical patterning of joint sets, or the plexus of

genetically related fractures, is often arranged radially or centripetally around the dome or basin, respectively. The crests of domes often contain the most severely eroded joint-bounded lithologies. This geometric arrangement of fractures can localize water flow into a radial convergent pattern in domes or a centripetal pattern in basins. From an aerial view, the drainage pattern or configuration on the landscape, would resemble that of the spokes of a wheel (Strahler 1965).

Wikipedia defines cuesta as follow:

A cuesta is a hill or ridge with a gentle slope on one side, and a steep slope on the other. In geology the term is more specifically applied to a ridge where a harder sedimentary rock overlies a softer layer, the whole being tilted somewhat from the horizontal. This results in a long and gentle backslope called a dip slope that conforms with the dip of resistant strata, called caprock. Where erosion has exposed the frontslope of this, a steep slope or escarpment occurs. The resulting terrain may be called scarpland (Wikipedia 2017).

By including a third dimension, the areas of higher permeability within the groundwater, with archaeological research, Native American oral history and mythology a more in depth understanding of their ancient past can be achieved.

Large Glacier Erratics And Concentrated Flows

As mentioned above, during the course of this research, numerous small to large glacier erratics were investigated, and some were on concentrated flows while others were not. However, within Ceremonial Landscapes, glacier erratics that appear to be or are culturally modified were located on concentrated flows. Interestingly, some of the largest glacier erratics also share similar characteristics and are considered sacred to the Native Americans who occupy the regions

Figure 82: Okotoks Glacier Erratic Site, Alberta, Canada

affected by glaciation. The "Big Rock" glacier erratic in Okotoks, Alberta, Canada is an example. (Figure 82)

This massive angular boulder, which is broken into two main pieces, measures about 41 by 18 meters (135 by 60 feet) and is 9 m (30 ft) high. It consists of thick-bedded, micaceous, feldspathic quartzite that is light grey, pink, to purplish. Besides having been extensively fractured by frost action, it is unweathered (WIKIPEDIA 2017, Stalker 1975, Cruden 2003).

Near the end of the Pleistocene Period, between 12,000 and 17,000 years ago, a massive landslide occurred within the upper reaches of the Athabasca River valley. As a result of this landslide, millions of tonnes of beige to pinkish quartzite and quartzitic conglomerate slid from the side of a mountain and onto the top of a valley glacier within the Athabasca River valley. On its top, the narrow valley glacier carried eastward this mass of Gog Group quartzite and quartzitic conglomerate. Because it lay on and within the top of this glacier, the highly fractured boulders were neither broken up into smaller blocks nor rounded by movement of the glaciers that transported it. After leaving the Rocky Mountains, the valley glacier collided with the westward moving ice streams of the Laurentide Ice Sheet and both it, other Rocky Mountain valley glaciers, and Laurentide ice streams coalesced as ice streams and were diverted southward and parallel to the eastern flanks of the Rocky Mountains. Together they flowed as far south as northern Montana as an ice sheet before they stagnated and melted. When the ice sheet melted, erratics of Gog quartzite and quartzitic conglomerate were dropped to form the line of rocks known as the Foothills Erratics Train. Big Rock is one of these glacial erratics of Gog quartzite and quartzitic conglomerate that originated as part of a landslide in the Athabasca River valley and carried on the top of a glacier, later ice stream, to its present site (WIKIPEDIA 2017, Jackson 1999 & 2008).

During September 2017 I was conducting research with the Tsuut'ina Nation at their reservation which extends westward from Calgary, Alberta, Canada, with Jim Big Plume, Specific Claims Research Director, Land and Treaty Research. His grandmother and several elders regarded some of the glacier erratics within the area as special places, however the historical significance was vague. He wondered if my methodology and data from other Native American archaeological sites could provide additional information regarding these features. During this investigation he accompanied me to the Okotoks glacier erratic site since it is considered a sacred site by five First Nations within the region, which include the Tsuu T'ina, Blackfoot, Blood, Pikaani and Stoney. These tribes associate the erratic's shape with a bat in flight. Big Plume pointed out several spiritual features within the boulders including a Sundance mediation area as well as images on the feature which included a horse and face among others.

Prior to seeing the feature I knew it was very large, however standing next to it, I was amazed at its size and commented our data indicated Native Americans considered unusual and unique geological features as sacred sites. Secondly, Native Americans were especially attracted to sites where several areas of higher permeability within the groundwater intersect creating ponding.

Figure 83: Concentrated flows intersecting ponding, Okotoks Glacier Erratic Site, Alberta, Canada

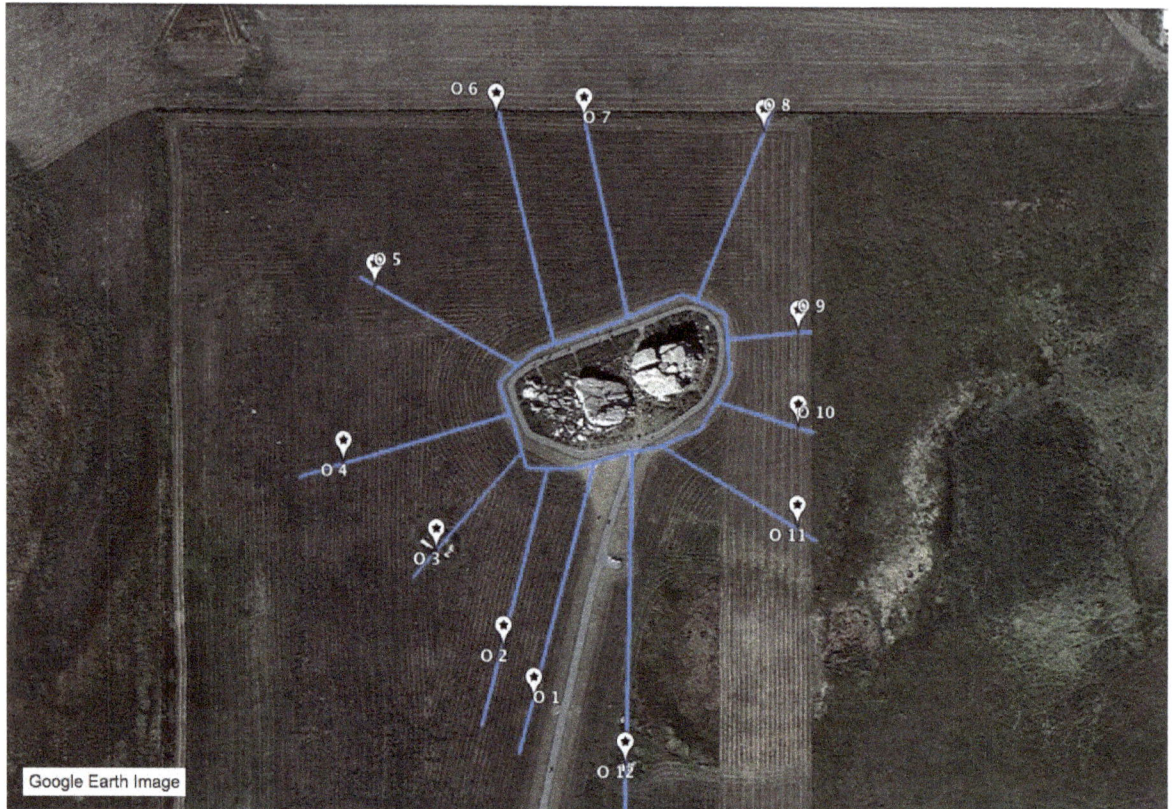

We began the survey by dowsing clockwise around the feature and located twelve concentrated flows intersecting it forming a pattern like those associated with the line centers, buttes and medicine wheels. (Figure 83) Like the other features, where the concentrated flows intersect there is ponding. It seems unlikely that the glacier coincidentally deposited the erratic on this groundwater pattern, however the weight of the glacier erratic could be exerting enough stress to create a depression and / or stress features which collect and / or conduct groundwater. Since this groundwater pattern is also associated with the features mentioned above, it would seem logical for the regional Native Americans to associate with it as they did with medicine wheels. Interestingly, Alberta has one of the highest concentrations of medicine wheels (Brumley 1986).

If this was the only large glacier erratic site I documented, I would consider it coincidental. However, a month before I surveyed the Okotoks glacier erratic, I was asked by one of the Native American First Nations in Alaska to examine a similar site which consists of very large glacier erratics.

The site is dominated by five large glacier erratics which form a circle. In addition to the large boulders there are a few smaller ones in between them. All of the large boulders appear to be naturally placed, however some of the small ones could have been moved by humans to their present location. (Figure 84)

Figure 84: Native American Glacier Erratic Site & areas of higher permeability, AK

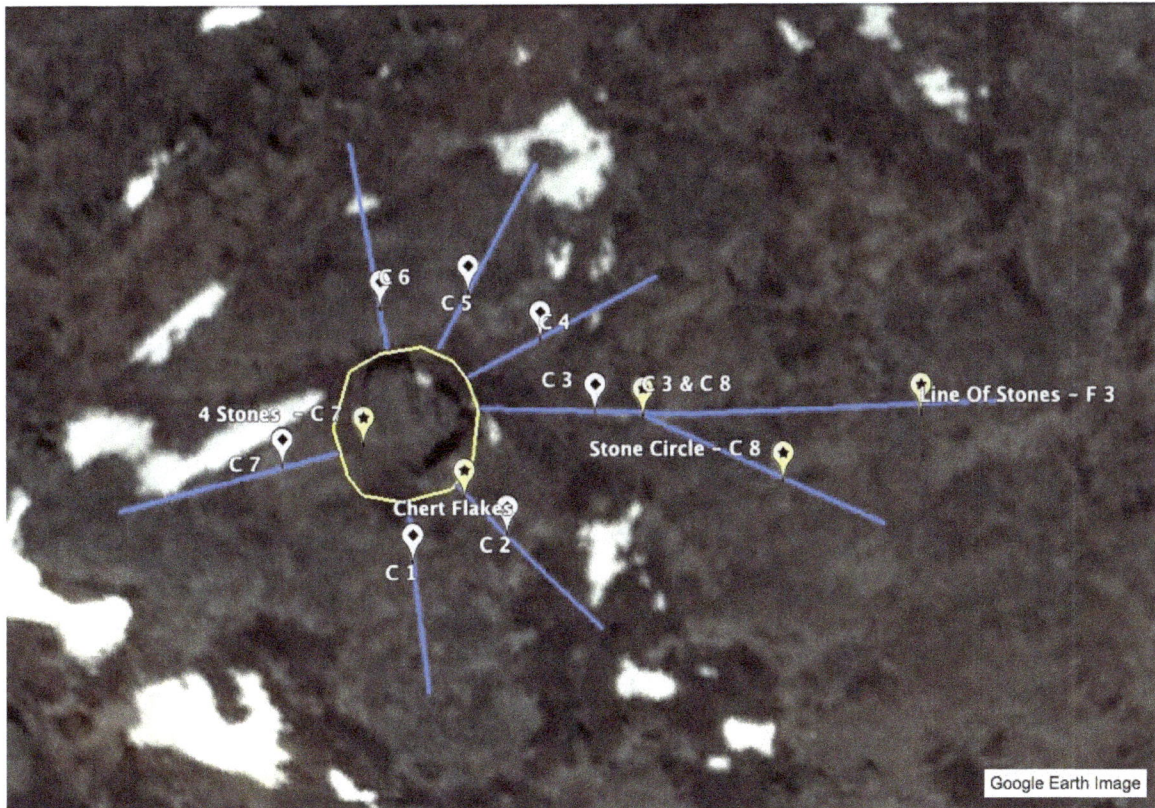

Figure 85: Stones in center of glacier erratic circle, Alaska

Figure 86: Large glacier erratic looks like face looking upward, Alaska

There is a circular stone pattern in the center of the site, and some of the stones are not characteristic of the surrounding bedrock in this area suggesting they were brought to the site. (Figure 85) Throughout the regions I have investigated, various types of stones were used as offerings at sacred sites. For example, red round river cobbles and quartz stones are shown in Figures 140 and 141. Some stone tools were found within the circle. When you look towards the stone circle, the largest stone appears to be a human face looking up towards the sky. (Figure 86)

One of the large boulders is pointed, and when you sit in the middle of the circle and look at it, it appears to have the same outline as one of the mountain's peaks. (Figure 87) It is possible this boulder was culturally modified to resemble the sacred mountain. Johnson and his colleagues have documented similar boulders in Peru and throughout the United States. (Figure 88) As I followed the concentrated flows outward, I located some stone features along them including stone piles and lines of stones. An area of ponding is located where the circle of glacier erratics is located, and seven areas of higher permeability intersect it.

Figure 87: Possible culturally modified glacier erratic, shape resembles mountain peak, AK

Figure 88: Stone cut to replicate distant mountain, Machu Picchu, Peru

Figure 89: SR 6 - 8 & Split Rock, NY

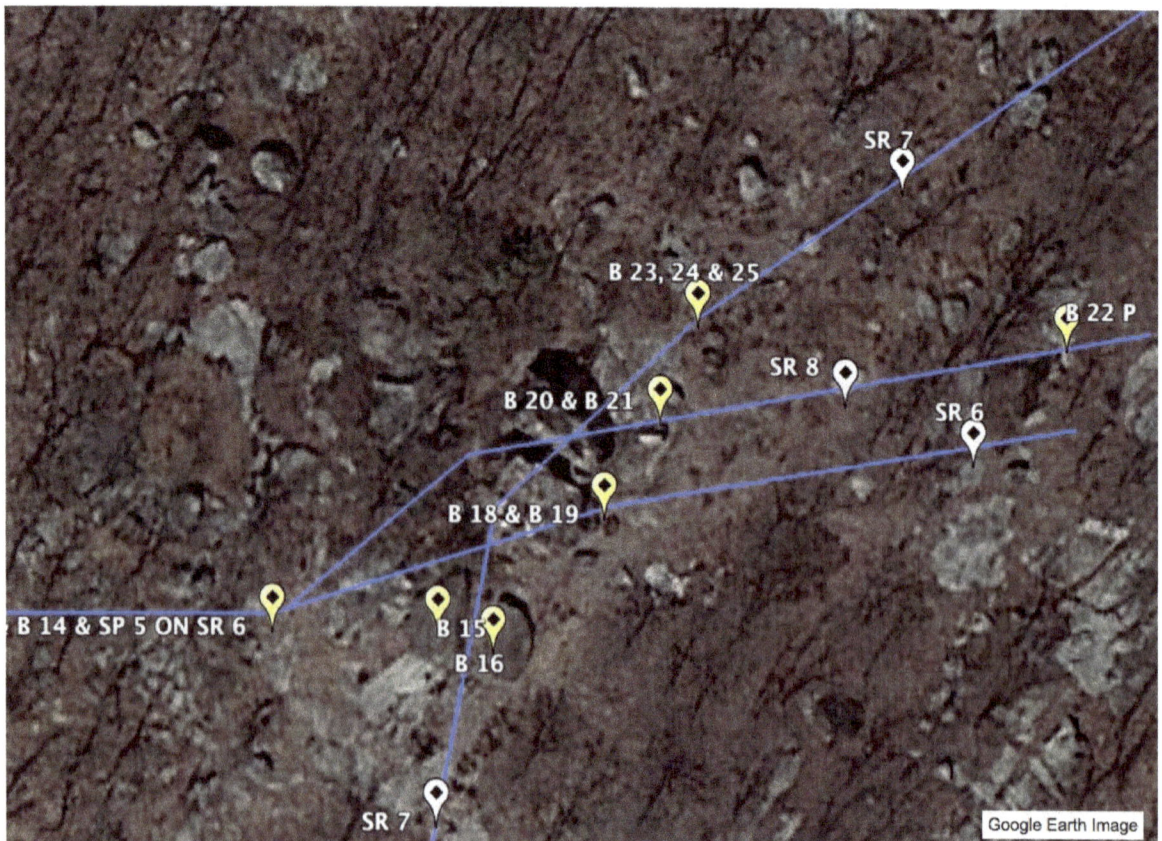

Another example exists along the New Jersey - New York boarder. Like Okotoks, Split Rock is a large glacier erratic which is split in the middle. (Figures 89 & 90) This site is sacred to the Ramapough Lunaape First Nation since it is a portal between dimensions and a place of emergence into this world. At this location three areas of higher permeability cross one another creating six rays and ponding beneath the feature. When the concentrated flows are followed outward from the site, several additional stone features, such as cairns, propped boulders and width markers, map their trends.

Figure 90: Split Rock, NY

Within New England, Cochegan Rock is the largest glacier erratic and sacred to the Mohegan Nation. (Holtz 2007, WIKIPEDIA 2018)

It seems unlikely that the glacier coincidentally deposited the erratics on this groundwater pattern, however the weight of the glacier erratics could be exerting enough stress to create a depression and / or stress features which collect and / or conduct groundwater.

Mounds, Earthworks And Great Cairns

During the course of this research, my colleagues and I have investigated mounds associated with the Adena, Hopewell and Mississippian cultures. It is important to keep in mind that my discussion is focused on the association between mounds and the areas of higher permeability they are located along. In addition to this correlation, they are also associated with numerous Native American cultural and spiritual beliefs.

All of the mounds we investigated are located on one or more areas of higher permeability. As mentioned above, Cahokia was a cultural center like Cahuachi, Cusco and Chaco Canyon. I located a group of areas of higher permeability that cross the site from north to south and east to west. Although I did not throughly investigate the western section of the site due to limited access, the trends of the areas of higher permeability indicate additional concentrated flows cross that area. (Figure 91) Where these concentrated flows intersect, there is an area of subsurface ponding immediately south of Monk's Mound and Collinsville Road, where the main plaza is located. This pattern is very similar to the sites discussed below under intersecting areas of higher permeability and ponding. Within the central area of Cahokia several mounds are located along the areas of higher permeability I documented. In most cases, the width of the mound equalled the width of one of the areas of higher permeability it was located on as shown in Figure 91. I realize I

89

investigated only a portion of the site's mounds, however, this strongly suggests the other mounds associated with Cahokia are located on concentrated flows. Also, as mentioned above, since this was the cultural center, it strongly suggests the outlier mounds are also located on concentrated flows.

Figure 91: Cahokia mounds & areas of higher permeability

Figure 92: Mounds along concentrated flow, Indian Mounds Regional Park, MN

Figure 93: Mounds along concentrated flow, Indian Mounds Regional Park, MN

Throughout the mound sites we surveyed, mounds ranged in size from a few yards in width or diameter and from a yard to several yards high. The largest

90

mounds indicate the width of the widest areas of higher permeability. At some sites mounds were linear in shape and extended along a narrow concentrated flow's course for several yards. The width of the mound and concentrated flow were equal and the mound's hight was about 3 ft / 0.9 m. A line of mounds, which may be in a straight line or meander, indicate the course of the concentrated flow. Where two areas of higher permeability intersected and one is wider then the other, the larger mound(s) is on the widest flow with a smaller mound next to it on the narrower flow. Figure 92 shows mounds 1 though 3 along concentrated flow M 1 and mound 4 along M 2. Figure 93 shows mound 4 offset from mound 2 when looking west. Effigy mounds are located along the course of a concentrated flow as shown in Figure 94. Within the Ceremonial Landscapes that have not been partially destroyed, mounds are also accompanied by stone features such as cairns, circles and low meandering walls.

Figure 94: Effigy Man mound, WI

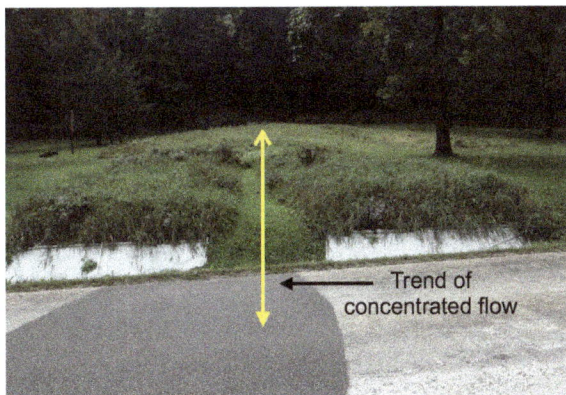

Trend of concentrated flow

Figure 95: Chaco roomblock, earthwork and concentrated flows, NM

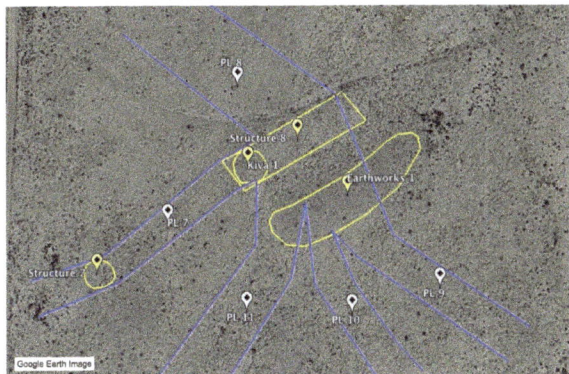

During the investigations of Basketmaker and Chaco culture sites, many but not all of the earthworks were located along areas of higher permeability; however, they often extended beyond the width of the concentrated flow as shown in Figure 95.

When I began to research northeastern Ceremonial Landscapes, it was obvious there was a discrepancy between small and very large stone features, which were collectively referred to as cairns. While some of the cairns ranged in size from a few yards in diameter and height, others exceeded 15 x 15 x 5 ft / 4.57 x 4.57 x 1.5 m in size. The largest I documented, thus far, was 75 x 30 x 12 ft / 22.8 m x 9.14 m x 3.65 m. (Figures 96 & 134) When I compared the correlation between small and large cairns with the areas of higher

Figure 96: Great cairn, 75 x 30 x 12 ft, Lewis Hollow Site, NY

permeability they were located on, it indicated they had different functions. The smaller cairns were along the width boundary of concentrated flows, especially those wider than 8 ft / 2.4 m or centered on narrow ones. The large cairns were the width of the widest concentrated flow and often extended along its course. Therefore, to distinguish between them, I labeled the larger cairns 'great cairns'. Then, when I began to investigate mounds, I realized their function was the same as great cairns within Ceremonial Landscapes. Consistently, great cairns are equal to the width of one of the concentrated flows they are located on and often extend along its course. They are also found where concentrated flows turn sharply. Great cairns are also accompanied by a variety of other stone features within the immediate area including smaller cairns, meandering walls and stone piles, to mention a few. Great cairns are usually the largest stone features within a Ceremonial Landscape site and are located along the main concentrated flow(s), which are often the widest within a site. Typically, the stones within them are slanted towards the structure's center to give it stability. Some have depressions on top of them which may have been intentional or suggest an inner chamber has collapsed. At some sites, a group of great cairns may represent a constellation. It can be a vertical representation of what is observed in the sky or a mirror image if a reflecting pool was used to document it. Like other Native American stone features, non-native archaeologists have neglected them.

Even though intersecting areas of higher permeability with ponding have been documented from Peru to Alaska, a distance of 6,600 mi / 10,800 km, and across the continent to the northeast, as well as associated with different cultures, historical periods and environments, the site's characteristics are remarkably similar. This demonstrates a high level of cultural uniformity among ancestral Native Americans throughout these regions.

Consistently, when you incorporate areas of higher permeability within the groundwater into your data base, various site components which appear to be isolated from one another on the surface become connected with one another. This, in turn, helps explain the function of the features.

Associating Oral History With Sites And Johnson's Methodology

Throughout this research a common theme has been observed. In spite of different historical periods and diverse environments, Native American nations have consistently mapped similar geological and hydrological features, and there are references to some of these sites in their oral history and mythology. By adding a third dimension, the areas of higher permeability within the groundwater, to archaeological research, Native American oral history and mythology can be linked to the past more completely, thus providing a more in depth understanding of their ancient past. For example, Spider Woman is an integral part of several Native American beliefs.

Spider Woman is one of the most important deities of traditional Navajo religion. Unlike the Hopi Spider Grandmother, the Navajo Spider Woman is not considered the creator of humans, but she is their constant helper and benefactor. Spider Woman was the advisor of the heroic twins Monster-Slayer and Born-for-Water, taught the people the arts of weaving and agriculture, and appears in many legends and folktales to "save the day," protect the innocent, and restore harmony to the world." (Native American Language 2016). According to Navajo legend Spider Woman lives on top of Spider Rock in Canyon de Chelly National Park which is one of the most sacred sites to the Navajo (First People 2016, Rudolph 1997, Wikipedia 2016).

She is creator of the world in some southwestern Native American religions and myths, such as that of the Pueblo, including Hopi peoples. Although accounts vary, according to mythology she was responsible for the stars in the sky; she took a web she had spun, laced it with dew, threw it into the sky and the dew became the stars (Native Languages of the Americas 2016, Wikipedia 2016).

The Ojibwe people (Chippewa) of southern Canada and northern US speak of Spider Woman, known as *Asibikaashi,* (Pratt 2010) as a helper of the people, and inspiring mothers (or other close female relatives) to weave dreamcatchers, styled after a spiderweb, for their infants that filters out bad dreams, allowing only good thoughts to enter (Lusty 2001, Wikipedia 2016).

When you compare the sites which contain ponding with areas of higher permeability intersecting them to a spider's web, there is a resemblance. It is possible the Spider Women concept inspired ancestral Native Americans to seek out these locations or the interpretation of these features lead to the Spider Women stories.

Often Native American chants and stories refer to sites whose location has been lost. In 2017 I was invited to present at the Tsuut'ina Nation conference titled the "Dene Migration Symposium, Mending the Holes in our Stories". Interestingly, a site survey conducted a few days later exemplified the conference's goal. After my presentation, some of the elders mentioned several years ago they had heard the story of a medicine wheel which existed somewhere in a large area along the east side of the reservation, however its exact location was lost.

Jim Big Plume obtained permission to attempt to locate the site using my methodology. At the time of the investigation the area where they thought the medicine wheel was located was within the construction zone of a major four lane highway, and none of the surface features shown in Figure 97 or stone features were present. When we arrived at the site, Chief Lee Crowchild turned on his cell phone's maps and ran his finger over a large area where they thought the medicine wheel was located. I informed the chief that I was going to cross the construction site from east to west to determine if there were any areas of higher permeability intersecting the site from a north south direction, and then I would survey along the west boundary of the construction site to determine if any flows were intersecting it from east to west. Within minutes I located a concentrated flow which intersected the site from north to south, and then a few feet further east, I located a second. When I determined the trend of the concentrated flows, I realized they intersected a short distance away, and while determining if they merged or crossed one another, I realized they both intersected where there was ponding. As I circled the ponding, I located a total of eight areas of higher permeability which intersected it. (Figure 97) As demonstrated above, this pattern of rays intersecting ponding is characteristic of the other Native American sacred sites discussed above. By combining their traditional oral story with my data base and methodology, some of the "Holes" in their history were filled in.

Figure 97: Tsuu T'ina medicine wheel, Alberta, Canada

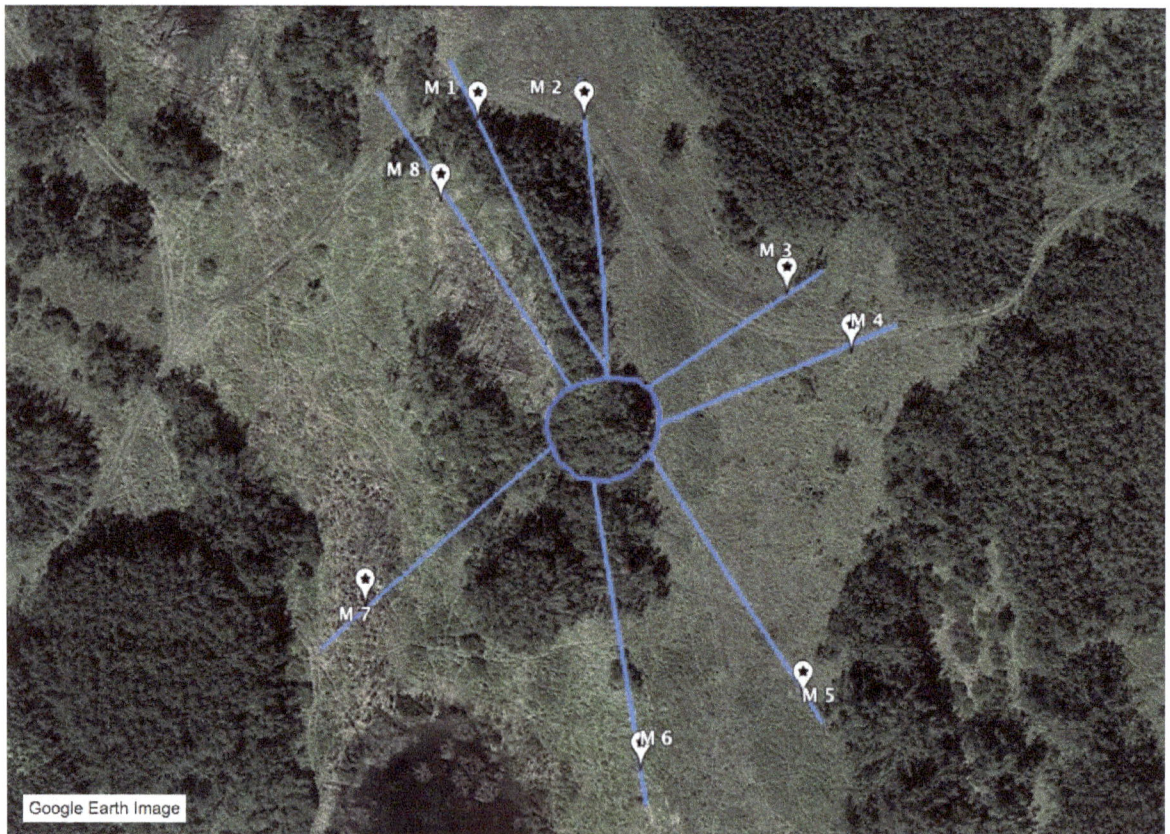

Another example of locating a site based on oral history is discussed in the conclusion below. I was able to locate a section of an outcrop which looks like the profile of a coyote's head at the site mentioned in a Navajo chant / story. (Figure 234)

Another comparison to consider is the similarities and differences between Ceremonial Landscapes within different linguistic groups such as the Algonquin and Athabaskan / Den'e. Our data indicates Ceremonial Landscapes are very similar throughout the different linguistic groups my colleagues and I have investigated. The main reason for variations within Ceremonial Landscapes is the influence of diverse environments and climates which require adaptation.

Dating Ceremonial Landscapes

It is important to note that several types of stone features commonly associated with Ceremonial Landscapes were also used during the historic period. Stone features, such as cairns, have been used to designate property lines and trails. Some ancient Native American cairns and other features could have been incorporated into historical features such as walls or barbed wire fence lines. Therefore, it is important to determine the age of these features. In addition to scientific methods, this can be done by examining historical documents such as deeds, as well as various characteristics of the stones.

Some archaeologists argue many of the stone features, such as cairns, were constructed by farmers, sheepherders and miners etc.. Within the northeastern region, nearly all of the Ceremonial Landscapes I have surveyed are located along the upper slopes of mountains where soils are very thin and barely cover the bedrock. While clearing fields, stones are typically placed where wetlands, depressions and other natural obstacles are located. Over the years I have both helped and observed Amish farmers in Pennsylvania clear field stones by hand. This work is labor intensive and time consuming. In each case, stones were randomly thrown or dumped onto a pile in an out of the way location. With the exception of wall construction, the piles were not stacked or evenly placed along a linear pattern paralleling one another. Often they were deposited in areas to help prevent slope erosion or fill a depression. Northeastern ceremonial landscape sites do not fit into an agricultural format. In the southwest, other archaeologists argue cairns and other stone features were constructed by sheepherders or other post-1492 settlers. In the southwest our data demonstrates, where Native American stone features are located along areas of higher permeability, they are consistently accompanied by pre-Columbian archaeological sites.

We are not advocating that all sites containing cairns and stone piles are ancient Native American Ceremonial Landscapes. However, many of the sites we have investigated contain features which are replicated from site to site and associated with ancestral Native American historical phases, in spite of cultural and geographical diversity. The features are concentrated within a given area and associated with the topography, geology and hydrology of that area.

Some critics argue, if the ancestral Native Americans constructed features like tall or turtle cairns hundreds or thousands of years ago, they would have collapsed by now. At Crestone, San Luis Valley, Colorado, there is a site which contains a wide variety of stone features including turtle cairns (Figure 98) which have a chamber inside. They were constructed with large round stones and boulders which would appear to be unstable. In 2014, our team asked Mark Jones, architect, to examine their structural stability. He reported:

Figure 98: Turtle cairn, CO

We observed four dome shaped crude stone structures, with small openings, and each with a straight line of rocks extending from it 6 to 8 ft long on the opposite side from the opening; all within a small area of +/- 200 ft from each other. Three of the structures had their openings oriented facing 259 degrees, with the accuracy of a simple hand held compass. One had its opening facing north.

The structures are built using a very primitive but very effective technique for making domed structures that is based on the concept of a "Compression Ring". What this simply means is that you place stone or other solid building components (could be stone, bricks, ice, etc) in a ring, as tightly together as you can. Then you place another similar ring of slightly smaller diameter concentrically on top of the first ring, and continue up ring by ring. What happens is that if the components have their surfaces tight to each other, the gravitational force resolves itself by pressing one component horizontally against its neighbor, with all components similarly pressing against their neighbors, so that the horizontal forces within the "ring" are greater than the vertical force of gravity trying to make the "ring" fall down. Then, in turn, each ring exerts vertical force on the ring beneath it, which actually adds to that ring's effective weight, increasing the pressure between its components—in effect making it stronger. This only works if the components (in this case stones) are all tightly placed.

This is the same basic technique that has been used in all component-built dome structures, whether it is a stone dome, an ice igloo, or the enormous, iconic brick Pantheon dome in Rome. Same principle. As far as I know this technique has been known and used for an indeterminate time since man figured out how to stack stones on top of one another. Clearly, the Romans didn't invent the arch, or the dome, even though they took them to new levels of perfection. So, my observation would be that there is nothing about this method of building that would prove it to be from any period in historical times-- indeed from a structural standpoint it could be as old as whenever people first set foot in this area.

The structures are all made of local stones, similar to the stones plentiful in the area, and there is no evidence of any tools having been used to dress, shape or otherwise "work" the stones before placing them. So there is nothing in the technique of building that places the structures at any particular point in time. There are two techniques used to make the doors: One, a "tilt arch" where two larger stones are tilted toward each other and held apart at the top by a "keystone". The arch is held up by the same principle as used for the horizontal rings, except that it is vertical. The other technique is a modified "lintel arch", where a flat stone is used to close the top of the arch. Both of these techniques are primitive and so, again, not associated with any particular technology associated with a particular time.

As to stability, my observation is that because of the inherent structural stability of this building method, and because of the durability of the (stone) material, these structures are stable (as long as not disturbed) and could have remained that way indefinitely, as in thousands of years.

Even though the stones are placed tightly together, so that the "compression ring" structural stability works, they are inherently uneven in shape and size, resulting in a lot of gaps between them, which is illustrated in some of the interior photos below with daylight coming in at numerous points. There is only one of the four structures that shows any evidence of any kind of mud or mortar possibly having been placed between the stones. What this says is that these structures appear not to have been weather-proof or weather-resistent, nor are they in any way rodent-proof or rodent-resistant.

Some evidence of staining on certain areas on the interior of the stones could have been from a variety of causes, among them rodent middens, or fires. However, the structures do not appear to have been capable of supporting significant size fires (as for an oven) since there is no evidence of any kind of flues. To support significant fire in an enclosed structure you need not only incoming combustion air, but also some kind of proportionally compatible sized flue. (This is the same problem that causes a lot of old fireplaces not to "draw" properly).

The structures have the curious feature of being quite small, maybe even too small for more than one or two people to get into, and the entry openings are extremely small, making access/egress difficult at best.

Because of the characteristics of the structures noted above, my observation is that the structures are poorly suited for human habitation (small size, lack of weather resistance, tight access), for any kind of storage of food or seed products (lack of weather resistance, easy rodent access), or for any more demanding materials storage use for the same reasons. They also appear to be of dubious functionality as ovens (lack of proportional flue area). I'm not going to speculate on what their actual use may have been, whether practical or symbolic, only to observe above what they appear not to be well suited for.

Certainly these are unusual structures of indeterminate origin, and they deserve further study (Mark M. Jones, AIA, Report, 2014).

In addition to these features others, such as cairns, have been observed using the same construction. We have asked architects in other regions to examine the structural stability of Native American stone features in their area, and they came to the same conclusion.

Techniques used to date sites and features vary from region to region. In the northeast, one of the problems is Ceremonial Landscapes rarely contain visible habitation components and diagnostic artifices on the surface.

Thus, archaeologists argue excavations are needed to determine if artifacts are present and date them. However many Native American Nations do not permit this, thus archaeologists are reluctant to conduct these investigations. In the past some Ceremonial Stone Landscape features have been excavated which provided diagnostic artifacts and scientific dating which concluded the features predated 1492.

Between 1952-54, Frank Glynn excavated two stone heaps at Pilot's Point on coast of Connecticut. Heap I, an oval shaped stone mound, measured 12 feet by 21 feet with a maximum elevation of 2 feet. Heap II, another oval shaped stone mound, measured 9 feet in diameter with maximum elevation over two feet. It was built against a large glacial boulder. A small shell heap abutted the heap. Both heaps had 19th and 20th century artifacts on their top surface. The presence of these artifacts had led to local speculation of their colonial or later origins. Heap I revealed upon subsequent excavation to contain 20 features (primarily hearths and fire pits) some superimposed on top of lower features. Artifacts recovered included "stemmed and barbed projectile points, a stemmed knife, a scraper and a chisel, suggestive of the Archaic-Woodland overlapping periods." In addition, rim shards, a mortar and pestle, and hoes and spades described as "Adena-like" were recovered. Glynn noted that "The immediate sealing-off of fires either by covering them with stone or rolling a large stone into them was evident." Heap II was a mix of burnt stone and shell and had strong evidence that the glacial boulder was used as a reflector oven for cooking clams. Artifacts recovered included "Quartz cores, flakes and chips ...broken choppers and scrapers ..." (Glynn 1973, Gage 2015).

In some cases carbon-14 dating has been used to date stone features. For example, in the 1980s a mound was excavated near Freetown, Massachusetts. The excavation recovered charcoal from two features which was c-14 dated to 875 +/- 160 years B.P. and 790 +/- 150 years B.P.. Nearby artifacts included red ochre or soft hematite, as well as stone tools including hammerstones, scrapers and anvils. Mavor concluded, the mound "was built by pre-historic Native Americans for ceremonial use, and was certainly not the result of English colonial field clearing." (Mavor 1989, p. 75).

In some cases the alignment of stone features can also help date a site. This is discussed below in the in the section on Astronomical Alignments and the Council Rock Site.

In the southwest, structures, diagnostic pottery and lithic scatter are commonly associated with stone features. Johnson and Frye have found Early Archaic projectile points on stone features dating to c.a. 6,000 B.P. in the San Luis Valley. (Figure 99) Johnson and Friedman have also found stone features such as herraduras incorporated within habitation sites which contain structures, pottery and lithic material associated with the Pueblo II, 900 to 1150 A.D. and Pueblo III, 1150 to 1350 A.D. Periods.

As Ceremonial Landscape research continues, our team believes additional evidence will confirm many, if not all, of these sites are hundreds or thousands of years old.

Figure 99: Stone circle with 6,000 B.P. obsidian projectile point, San Luis Valley, CO

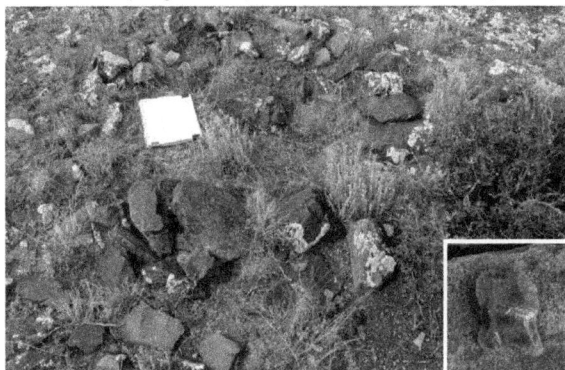

Figure 100: Surface flooding has damaged a broad line which maps a groundwater flow, Casma, Peru

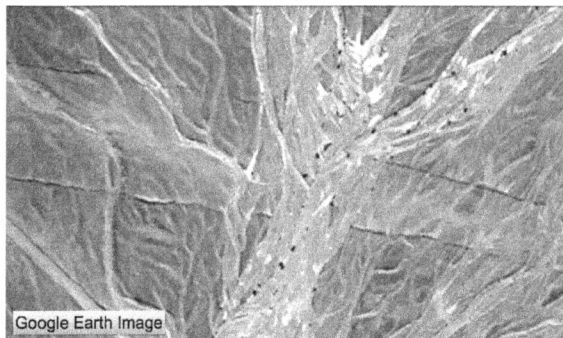

Destruction Of Ceremonial Landscapes

Until recently Ceremonial Landscapes have been neglected by non-native archaeologists, as well as local, state and federal government agencies. Therefore, they have been subject to destruction by various forces. It is also safe to assume natural forces have destroyed sites. Therefore, when a stone feature pattern suddenly ends look for landscape alterations. If damage has occurred, follow the trend of the areas of higher permeability across the damaged area to determine if the pattern continues on the other side. For example, in Figure 100, surface flooding has damaged the broad paralleling lines along each width boundary.

Characteristics Of Habitationscapes

As mentioned above, Habitationscapes can vary greatly in size from large complexes to a single structure. In spite of this, they share common characteristics.

Choosing A Site Location

Based on our data, ancestral Native Americans chose habitation and ceremonial sites based on a specific criteria. First, an area was chosen based on human sustainability. Then the vertical and horizontal alignments of the three worlds were put into place. Both the present world and the cosmos are visible, therefore they could see features in both, such as mountains and planets, and align them. However, areas of higher permeability within the underworld are not visible, and in some bedrock features, they can be scarce. Our data indicates ancestral Native Americans were locating areas of higher permeability, and if they were, in order to assure a structure or Habitationscape is in alignment with all three worlds, the concentrated flow would have to be located first. Then habitation and ceremonial structures, as well as stone features, petroglyphs and pictographs, would be placed along the areas of higher permeability. (Figures 101, 10, 16, 17, 19, 20, 78, 79 & 102) In order to achieve astronomical alignments, such as solstice events or rising or

Figure 101: Habitationscape / structures & concentrated flows, Pueblo La Pato, Agua Fria NM, AZ

setting celestial bodies, the site for the proposed observatory would be moved along the area of higher permeability until the desired astronomical alignments can be achieved. However, some sites like Chimney Rock suggest the site's location was influenced by an astronomical event, which is discussed below.

Locating Structures

All of the pre 1492 structures we surveyed within North America are consistently located along areas of higher permeability. Within large roomblocks, such as Pueblo Bonito, typically, the earliest rooms are located along areas of higher permeability, and after those locations are occupied, additional rooms are placed as close as possible to the concentrated flows even though they may not be on one. (Figure 106) Often where larger structures, such as Chaco great houses, outliers and large roomblocks, have two or more areas of higher permeability intersecting them, within the structure, various features, such as walls and kivas, are aligned with the concentrated flows. For example, at Kin Bineola Chaco outlier shown in Figure 102, the north wall and roomblock located along it are aligned with the trend of KBCF 2. KBCF 3 and KBCF 4 intersect KBCF 2 and KBCF 1 along the north wall at the center of the structure. Then KBCF 1 trends southward at an oblique angle and the central roomblock is orientated along it while the east and west roomblocks are aligned at right angles to the north wall. The great kiva is centered on KBCF 5, central kivas along KBCF 1 and the north kivas parallel KBCF 2. Frequently, a smaller structure's length is orientated along the trend of a concentrated flow, and its width is equal to the flow's width. (Figures 19, 20, 69, 75, 101, 106 & 108) However, at some sites there are variations. For example, in Figure 103, at the Caughnawaga Mohawk Site near Fonda, New York, inhabited from 1666 to 1693, the south row of longhouses are located along concentrated flow C 1 however their length extends beyond its width. The northern row is not on a concentrated flow. This may have been the results of the southern row of longhouses filling the available space along the concentrated flow within the compound, so the additional longhouses were placed as close as possible to the concentrated flow along

Figure 102: Concentrated flows aligned with walls and great kiva, Chaco great house outlier, Kin Bineola, NM

Figure 103: Longhouses along area of higher permeability, Caughnawaga Site, NY

the north side. At the time this site was occupied, the Dutch were trading with the Iroquois, and Jesuits established a mission by the village. These forces were influencing the Iroquois' culture. The only exceptions have been a few small temporary hunting camps and rock shelters which were not located along an area of higher permeability.

Astronomical Alignments And Habitationscapes

Since astronomical sites are found within Ceremonial Landscapes and Habitationscapes, I decided to include both of them in this section.

Consistently, astronomical alignments are incorporated within Ceremonial Landscapes. For example, at one of the sites within the San Luis Valley in Colorado, various styles of features and their placement are aligned with different constellations including the Hunter (Orion) and Snake (Scorpio). On a small hill there is a cairn with a small platform located along its northeast side and three boulders whose alignment resembles the Hunter's belt. Both look towards the Hunter in the winter months. Southeast of the cairn along the base of the slope, there are two snake walls with the heads facing each other and separated by 100 yd / 91 m. When you stand by the cairn and look between the snakes in mid summer you observe the Snake in the night sky. (Figure 104)

Figure 104: Ceremonial Stone Landscape astronomical alignment,
San Luis Valley, CO

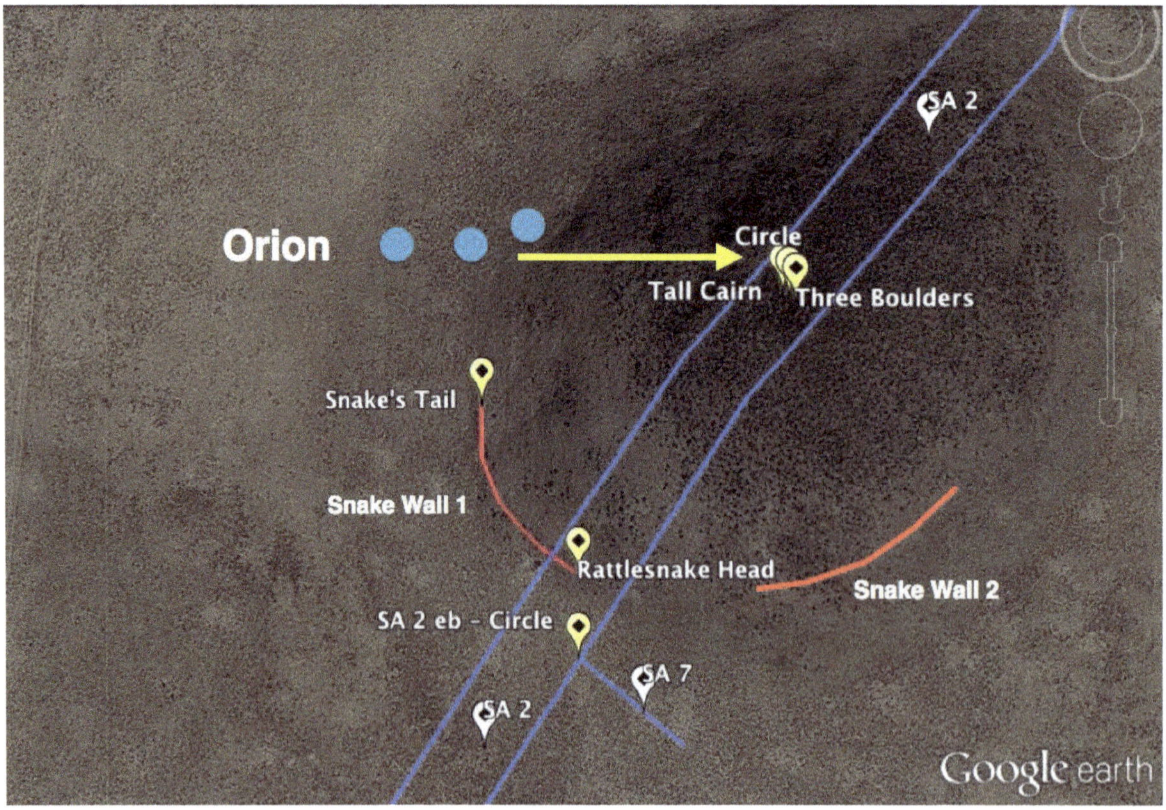

At some sites astronomical alignments may help determine its age. David Gutkowski, independent researcher and member of the New England Antiquities Research Association, has investigated the Council Rock Site in Pennsylvania. The site is a Ceremonial Stone Landscape consisting of low cairns, short low stone walls, circles and large boulders which appear to have been placed in their current position. Two of the boulders have the appearance of a mountain lion and bear's head and the third, a bird. While studying the boulders he observed an alignment with winter solstice sunset, however it was slightly off. (Figure 105) He realized if these features were aligned thousands of years ago, a slight deviation in the alignment when it was first observed could have caused this. He entered his data into NASA's ephemeris calculator, to determine if he could obtain the approximate year the boulders were originally placed there. The alignment dated to 1,825 BC / 3,825 BP and corresponded to winter solstice sunset. In July 2012, I conducted a bind survey with Gutkowski. The site is located along a forested slope and the summer vegetation made it virtually impossible to see more than twenty-five feet away.

Figure 105: Winter solstice sunset, approximately 825 BC / 3,825 BP, Archaic Phase, Council Rock Site, PA

Gutkowski comments "I am most impressed at his finding of three never before noticed stone circles, and that his techniques led him to follow concentrated flows directly to the Council Rocks having no previous knowledge of their location." (Gutkowski 2012, Comments File). Within the area, there are additional stone features which are located on the same area of higher permeability as the three boulders. This strongly suggests they are the same age.

Both natural features, such as mountain peaks, and man-made features, such as walls, have been used for astronomical alignments. While natural features are stationary, the man-made features are flexible. Although the man-made features can be placed anywhere along the desired alignment, our data indicates they were consistently located along areas of higher permeability. Thus, in order to determine the location of a man-made astronomical alignment feature, they determined where areas of higher permeability crossed the desired astronomical alignment and then placed sighting features at those intersections. By aligning these features they could observe the astronomical event and be in alignment with the underworld, present and cosmos.

For example (Figure 106), the location of Pueblo Bonito in Chaco Canyon appears to have been chosen based on the following factors. It is located near the geographical center of the San Juan Basin where most of the groundwater in the "Gallup sandstone formation turns from a northeasterly direction to the northwest where it discharges into the San Juan River in the vicinity of the four corners (Stone 2006)." (Figure 13) Pueblo Bonito is nearly centrally located within the canyon where the most predominate trending fractures and areas of higher permeability are concentrated (Lorenz and Cooper 2003, Schillaci 2003, National Park Service 2012, Johnson 2012). The widest area of higher permeability I located in Chaco Canyon was AR CC 28, 123 ft / 37.5 m wide, and it trends north-south across the center of the structure. The structure's great kivas are located along it. AR CC 5, 67 ft / 20.4 m wide, crosses AR CC 28 at the north end of Pueblo Bonito, where the first rooms were constructed, and continues eastward to the amphitheater and Chetro Ketl. Rooms 32 and 33 are located where AR CC 28 and AR CC 5 intersect. In this area 24,932 turquoise beads, dozens of vessels, 300 ceremonial sticks and two important burials were located (Chaco Research Archives 2012, National Park Service 2012 and Schillaci 2003). Once the site's location was established based on its position in the San Juan Basin and pattern of areas of higher permeability, the astronomical alignments could be established. For example, the western south wall is aligned with equinox sunset (Solstice Project 2012) (Figure 106), and some of the windows provide views of the winter solstice sunrise (Malville 2008). All of the ancestral Native American astronomical alignments I have investigated are located along concentrated flows. Alignments similar to those at Pueblo Bonito have been documented at structures throughout the regions my colleagues and I have researched, as well as other researchers, and strongly suggests they are not coincidental.

Figure 106: Width & trend of areas of higher permeability at Pueblo Bonito

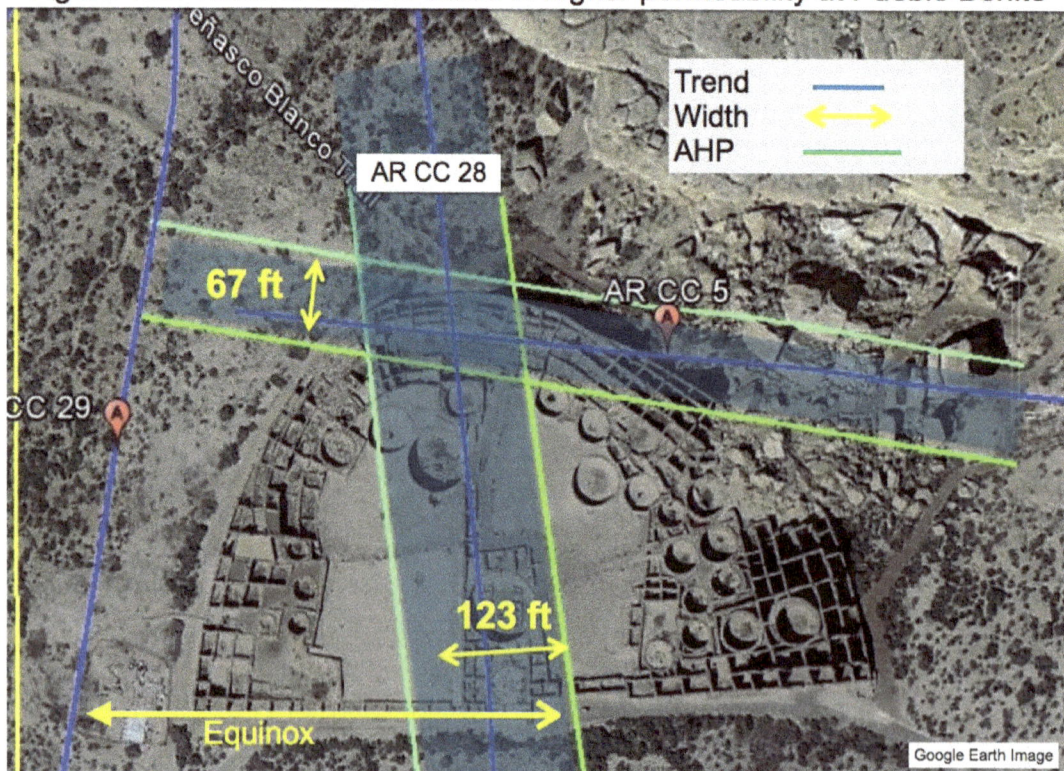

107: Looking from outlier towards the two chimney rocks, Chimney Rock, CO

Figure 108: Chimney Rock outlier & areas of higher permeability, CO

Chimney Rock outlier's location may have been chosen based on an astronomical alignment, especially since its placement near the summit of a narrow ridge line appears to be uncharacteristic of other great houses. Malville suggests observations of the moon standstill between December 1056 and 1076 inspired the construction of the outlier along the crest of the ridge and near the two bedrock features known as the chimneys. From the outlier, moon rise can be observed during the lunar standstill (Malville 2008, p. 91- 93). (Figure 107) When I first observed the site from the park entrance I was doubtful that I would find an area of higher permeability associated with the outlier. However, after dowsing along the trail to the summit, as well as long the base of the ridge, I located two areas of higher permeability, labeled A 3 and A 9, which cross one another where the great house is located. Its two kivas are in alignment with them, as well as some of the walls. (Figure 108) Between Ridge House by the upper parking lot where A 1 and A 2 branch and the outlier, I located three areas of higher permeability which intersect A 3. Within that distance the only area which is wide enough for the outlier structure and viewing the lunar standstill is where A 3 and A 9 cross one another. In addition to the moon standstill, Malville has identified additional astronomical alignments, such as a basin and the north wall of the outlier that are in alignment with June solstice sunrise (Malville 2008, p. 96). The basin is located along A 12 which is below the upper parking lot, and the wall is located along A 3.

At some sites, reflecting pools have been used to observe the night sky, and the ones we have researched have been associated with concentrated flows. For example at Palatki, near Sedona, Arizona, the Grotto Alcove has astronomical seasonal horizon alignments. When you stand in front of the horizon alignment pictograph shown in Figure 109, which is located at the western end of the alcove, it is hard to believe they could observe the entire ridge line as shown in Figure 110. The overhanging bedrock obscures the view. However, when you sit below and in front of the pictograph, and there is a pool of water on the floor, you can see the entire ridge line by using the water as a reflecting pool, which provides a mirror image of the horizon alignment pictograph as shown in Figure 111. When the pictograph and the ridge are compared in Figure 112, the black charcoal mark on the

105

right side indicates the location of winter solstice sunrise and other charcoal mark near the center, equinox sunrise. The left side marks summer solstice sunrise. Since a reflecting pool is used for the observation, the horizon alignment pictograph is a mirror image of the ridge. Considering the importance of this alignment, it is safe to assume the current trees obstructing the view would not have been there at the time of their observations. These features are located where two areas of higher permeability, PR 1 and PR 2, branch from one another. Interestingly, Bear Alcove is adjacent to and west of the Grotto Alcove, and where PR 1 and PR 2 begin to branch, there is a petroglyph mapping the course of these areas of higher permeability which matched my map of these flows. (Figure 8) In Peru, the Inca also used reflecting pools to observe the celestial bodies (Johnson 2009).

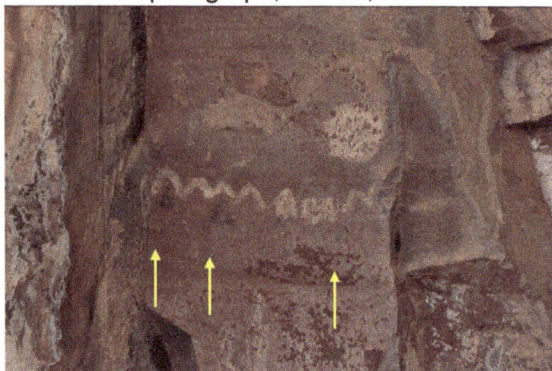

Figure 109: Seasonal horizon alignment pictograph, Palatki, AZ

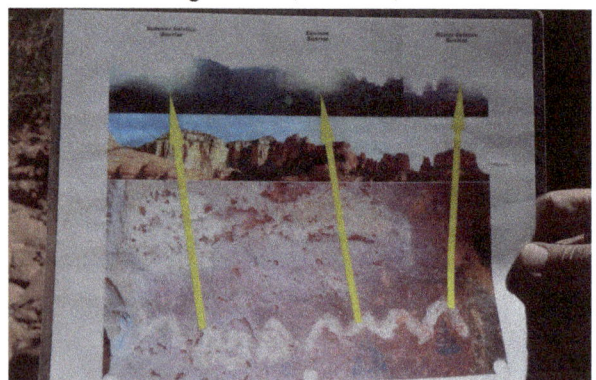

Figure 110: Ridge in line with seasonal horizon alignments, Palatki, AZ

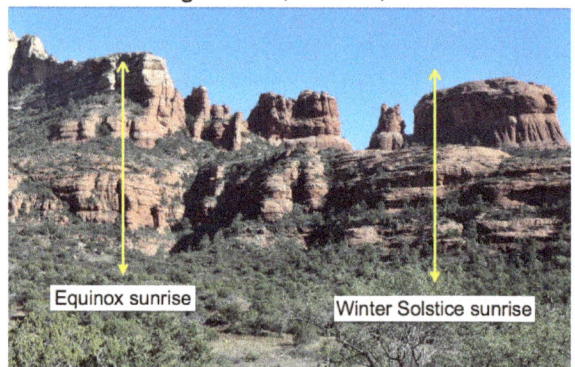

Figure 111: View of horizon in reflecting pool, Palatki, AZ

Figure 112: Pictograph,ridge and seasonal alignments, Palatki, AZ

In addition to these examples, some stone features also function as astronomical alignments. In the northeast, Native American researchers and my colleagues and I have documented numerous turtle cairns where the head is oriented towards winter solstice sunrise.

Artifact Distribution

Our data indicates as much as eighty-five percent or more of the artifact distribution is located along areas of higher permeability. Once you go beyond the width of an area of higher permeability the number of artifacts diminishes to very few. This is especially apparent at sites within the southwest where there is a prolific number of artifacts on the ground surface. (Figure 113) All of the researchers who have

Figure 113: Density of artifacts along area of higher permeability at Chaco great house outlier, NM

conducted site surveys with me agree with this observation. This also indicates ancestral Native Americans were mapping and living on the areas of higher permeability.

Historical Periods

As mentioned above, our data suggests the basic shape of a stone feature / petroglyph remained the same in different regions and during different historical phases, even though it was stylized to meet cultural preferences by different tribes. This can be compared to choosing a font to write with on a computer. For example, an A in Arial, Times and Courier fonts all mean the same, even though they are shaped somewhat differently. The circles in Figures 27, 28 and 29 have the same function in regard to areas of higher permeability even though the style is different.

Thus far, with the exception of one Native American quarry near Lovelock, Nevada, all of the Paleo sites we have surveyed are located on areas of higher permeability. During blind surveys throughout the United States I have locate several Paleo sites by following areas of higher permeability, for example the Crowfield Site shown in Figure 114. Our data also suggests Paleo Indians were locating kill and butchery campsites along areas of higher permeability. Michael Gramly's

Figure 114: Location of a Crowfield Paleo Site along an area of higher permeability, PA

excavations of the Bowser Road and Cedar Fork Creek mastodon sites indicated "Predation took place during the cold season after "ice-up" when mastodons, who require large daily amounts of water, were tethered to dependable flows or places where ice remained thin and water was easily accessible. Springs flowing into ponds were potential water-holes for proboscideans upon their quest for 25-50 gallons per diem." (Gramly 2017 & 2018). In collaboration with Gramly, my survey indicated the springs and butchery campsites at both sites were located along an area of higher permeability, as well as the Bowser mastodon. The Bowser mastodon dated to 11,027+/-54 RCYBP (Gramly 2017). At the time of this publication the Cedar Fork Creek mastodon had not been located. The Stewart's Cattle Guard Site is a Paleo Folsom bison kill-butchery campsite, c.a. 10,800 B.P., located in the San Luis Valley of southern Colorado which was excavated by Margaret Jodry and Dennis Stanford in the 1980's. The location indicated "no evidence of constructed impound or natural trap, apparently it was an ambush strategy" and the animal parts were brought to another site for processing. (Stanford, 1992, pp. 1-11) My survey of the site suggests the ambush site was more spontaneous than planning an entrapment site along a concentrated flow. Therefore, an area of higher permeability was not considered. Thus, to process the animal parts, they moved them to a campsite which was located where two concentrated flows intersect.

However, associating Paleoindians with stone features is complicated since all of the sites I have investigated have been multi-component. For example the site in Figures 15 and 16 contains several stone features, however artifacts date from Paleo to post contact. During the investigation of the Vail Site in Maine, Michael Gramly, associated two oval shaped stone features, labeled "possible cache pits", with a Paleo component dating from 12,400 to 12,900 B.P. (Gramly 2009). Figure 115 shows one of the stone-rimmed cache features in the foreground at the Adkins site, south of the Vail Site in the Magalloway River Valley, Maine. As of this publication, due to the site's remoteness, we have not

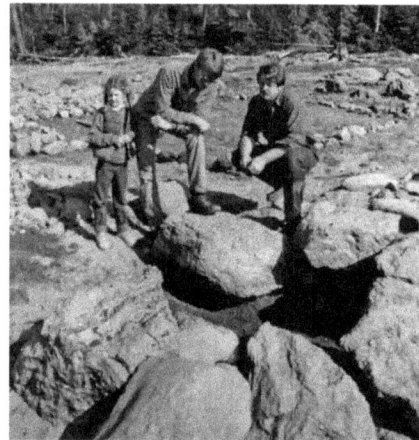

Figure 115: Oval, possible stone-rimmed cache pit, Adkins Site, south of the Vail Site, Maine

Courtesy of Gramly 2016

been able to investigate these features to determine if they are located along one or more areas of higher permeability. I have also documented oval stone features at sites which contain a Paleo component, however they are multi-component, and, as of this publication, the sites have not been thoroughly dated.

Some researchers have associated petroglyphs with the Paleo Period. A new high-tech analysis indicates the oldest known petroglyphs in North America, which are cut into several boulders in western Nevada, date to at least 10,500 B.P. and perhaps even as far back as 14,800 B.P.(Science Daily 2014). Another research team using WRO radiocarbon analysis dated petroglyphs at Little Lake, Coco Range, California to 14,760 YBP, as well as other sites, and "it is clear that substantial evidence exists for Paleoindian rock art manufacture." (Whitley 2014).

Although we have located petroglyphs which appear to be very old on sites containing a Paleoindian component, they have not been dated by procedures like those previously mentioned. One style consists of continuous meandering pecked lines. The patina of the pecking has patinated back to the patina of the host surface. This strongly suggests they are very old and could date to late Paleo or early Archaic

Period. (Figures 116 & 191) They were found along and at intersections of areas of higher permeability. Another form of petroglyphs, which could date to late Paleo or early Archaic, consist of incised, narrow linear lines. (Figure 117) They have also been found along the trend of areas of higher permeability, and where two intersect. They consist of parallel and oblique lines appearing in groups, some groups consisting of seven or thirteen lines. (Figure 188) Their function is not fully understood. They have been centered on and along the margin of areas of higher permeability. Some researchers believe they date to the Archaic Period. One interpretation is the groups of seven are associated with the phases of the moon (seven days each between the new moon, first quarter, full moon and last quarter) and the groupings of 13 as the annual lunar month cycle (13 lunar months in each calendar year). Similar incised lines can be the result of sharping stone tools by rubbing them against an outcrop or boulder.

Figure 116: Possible late Paleo to early Archaic curving line, highlighted in yellow, San Luis Valley, CO

Figure 117: Incised lines possibly late Paleo or early Archaic, Coconino NF, AZ

Like Paleo, all of the Archaic sites I have researched throughout the United States are multi-component. To approximate a stone feature's age, my colleagues and I have based it on its association with diagnostic artifacts and comparing construction styles. For example, in Figure 98 the circle was associated with an Archaic projectile point dating to around 6,000 B.P.. Most of the Archaic projectile points associated with Ceremonial Landscape stone features date from 5,000 BP on. At the Crestone Site two forms of turtle cairns exist next to one another. Although both serve the same function, mapping an area of higher permeability's trend, their construction varies slightly. The turtle in Figure 118 is round with a wide head, while the one in Figure 119 is more conical with a narrower head. It is also possible that Figure 118 is a turtle and Figure 119 is a tortoise. The cairn in Figure 120 was constructed with a mixture of stone shapes creating a rougher surface with wide spacing between the stones. It is located on an area of higher permeability which is equal to its diameter. The site has other stone features associated with it, of which some were used for habitation and projectile points dated to late Archaic, around 1,500 to 2,000 BP. The cairn in Figure 121 was constructed with flat stones creating a smooth round shape and narrow spaces between the stones. It is located along an area of higher permeability, and below the cliff there is evidence of a spring. Cairns like this one have been attributed to the Chaco Culture. This suggests the variances in a stone feature's construction can help determine the historical phase during which it was constructed. Within Ceremonial Landscapes associated with the Archaic Period, stone features coincide with springs, seeps and concentrations of areas of higher permeability. In the southwest habitation structures have been associated with Archaic Ceremonial Landscapes, however in the northeast this is less common.

Figure 118: Turtle cairn, Crestone, CO

Figure 119: Turtle cairn, Crestone, CO

Figure 120: Cairn with large stones & spaces, Archaic Site, CO

Figure 121: Round cairn with flat stone construction, Chaco style, NM

Then, following the Archaic Period, as the population grew and cultures became more complex, in addition to stone features, large roomblocks, great houses and multi structure villages were constructed. In the southwest, Chaco roads, during the Chaco Phase, and racetracks, during the Sinagua Phase, were also added. A very similar pattern evolved in Peru and Chile where geometric shapes mapped the course of areas of higher permeability. In the northeast, stone features, such as cairns and snake walls, mapped the course of areas of higher permeability and have been associated with Native American trails.

In Peru and Chile, we did not investigate any known Paleoindian sites; however, sites containing components of the Sacred Landscape, Ceremonial Landscape and Habitationscapes ranged in age from the Chinchorro Culture dating to 9,000 BP, to the Inca Empire in the 1500s. Sites along one thousand four hundred miles of Peru and Chile's coastline and eastward to the Andes Mountains were researched (Johnson 2009). In North America, our data indicates Paleoindians were locating their sites on areas of higher permeability, and from the Archaic Period to contact with the Europeans, ancestral Native Americans were locating, documenting with stone features and living along concentrated flows. As mentioned above, at this point in time, our data suggests the areas of higher permeability were perceived as a means of aligning the underworld with the physical world, as well as the cosmos.

Benefits Of This Methodology

Ceremonial Landscapes can be large, and when covered with vegetation, it can be difficult to locate all the features. Secondly, some features may be out of sight due to ridges and outcrops. When you follow the areas of higher permeability, they take you to the site's various features whether you can see them or not, and in some cases, considerable distances from the main concentration. During the course of this research we have investigated several sites which had been previously surveyed by other archaeological teams and located additional features which had been missed. Frequently, while mapping areas of higher permeability, we have located archaeological sites which had not been previously documented. As mentioned above, once you know the meaning of the various stone features you can predict which features you will encounter before you get to them while following an area of higher permeability. Conversely, you can predict the direction and width of an area of higher permeability by interpreting the stone features located along it. This methodology expedites a site survey and is more thorough.

Part 2

Features Associated With Areas Of Higher Permeability

Our research has consistently associated the following features with Sacred Landscapes, Ceremonial Landscapes and Habitationscapes. The following lists various features which are associated with these sites and can be used to identify and preserve them. In addition to their description, their association with areas of higher permeability is also presented. This has been separated from Part 1 so that it can be used as a field survey guide.

Amphitheaters - Some sites, such as Chaco Canyon, have large amphitheaters which appear to have been used for large assemblies for various community events. (Figure 122) Often, natural features, such as cliffs, provide acoustics which enable the speaker to project their voice for considerable distances. Areas of higher permeability intersect all the amphitheaters we have investigated. At some locations the natural features have been modified. These

Figure 122: Great house outlier site amphitheater, stone wall outlined in white, NM

modifications could have been done to increase the amplification, accommodate the speaker or, perhaps, align the amphitheater with an area(s) of higher permeability.

Astronomical Observations - Throughout ancient history, astronomical events have been used to predict seasonal cycles and cultural events. Sighting alignments incorporates both natural and man-made features. Thus far, all of the man made ancestral Native American astronomical alignment features we have researched were constructed on areas of higher permeability. The following are examples of these features.

Basins - Man-made basins are different from natural geological kettle holes. Man-made basins are either round or oval and have been pecked or ground into bedrock. (Figure 123) All of the basins we have investigated are located along areas of higher permeability. While many basins have been associated with astronomical alignments, in some cases, basins were also located on each width boundary of a concentrated flow.

Figure 123: Basin associated with Basketmaker and Chaco sites

Constellation Features - At some Ceremonial Stone Landscape sites, great cairns were arranged to replicate a constellation. To accomplish this, the great cairns were located along areas of higher permeability and arranged to represent a constellation. In Figure 124, the position of three boulders replicates Orion's belt. In the winter, when you stand on the small platform at the base of the cairn, you look towards Orion.

Figure 124: Three boulders by cairn represent Orion's belt, San Luis Valley, CO

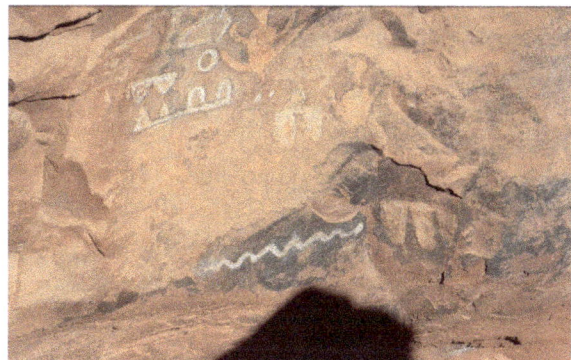

Figure 125: Large pointed boulder's shadow crossing panel 4, Coconino NF, AZ

Pictographs / Petroglyphs - At some sites a stone feature which has been culturally modified can cast a shadow or create a beam of light which passes across various pictographs or petroglyphs at different times during the year, such as solstice and equinox. (Figure 125)

Reflecting Pools - Surface water can be used as a reflecting pool to observe an astronomical event on the horizon or in the sky. For example, in the southwest the astronomical alignment is depicted in a pictograph and / or petroglyph which is in alignment with a reflecting pool and the event on the horizon. Since the reflecting pool functions like a mirror, the pictograph and / or petroglyph image is the opposite of what is observed on the natural horizon. (Figures 111 & 112)

Vertical Stones - Thus far, vertical stones have been associated with astronomical alignments. The alignment stone is usually long and narrow, and has a round or rectangular shape. (Figure 126) They are either embedded in the ground, wedged in a bedrock fracture or supported by a cairn. (Figure 127) Typically, they are within line of sight, thus forming an alignment. Although they are located along a concentrated flow, their alignment is associated with an astronomical alignment and other nearby stone features. If a stone alignment is thousands of years old, the earth's axial precession should be considered for some calculations. For example, the north star five thousand years ago was Thuban, not Polaris. These stone features are very similar to the vertical elongated stones mentioned below under areas of higher permeability width markers, however they perform a different function.

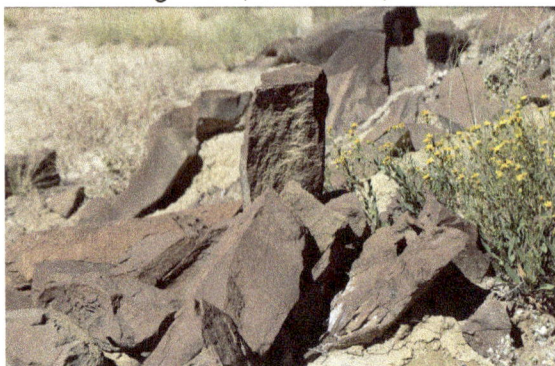

Figure 126: Vertical stone in astronomical alignment, Chaco site, NM

Figure 127: Cairn supporting vertical stone in astronomical alignment, NM

Boulders - In some areas, a large boulder is located on a concentrated flow which crosses the direct alignment between two or more sites which could be several miles apart. These boulders are not perched on other boulders or stones. Some are erected vertically and embedded in the ground to support them. (Figure 128) Others are more round and sit on the ground. The one shown in Figure 129 has cupules and grooves ground into it which indicate where two concentrated flows intersect. Some have been shaped. Either way, they show signs of being placed at a specific location by humans. We have documented them in Peru and Chile, as well as within North America.

Figure 128: Vertical boulder, Spruceton Site, NY

Figure 129: Large boulder with cupules and grooves, NM

Buttes Centered On intersecting Areas Of Higher Permeability - As of this paper, only six of these features have been investigated, and all are located in northern New Mexico. The data strongly suggests they were important features in the vertical and horizontal alignment of the three worlds. All of these buttes are associated with Chaco great houses and outlier sites. Characteristically, several areas of higher permeability intersect the butte, and there is a natural or man-made route to the top where there is a structure. Figures 130 & 31 shows one of these buttes and the route to the top. One of the buttes had five areas of higher permeability intersecting it, and another had eleven. The ray pattern created by

114

the intersecting concentrated flows and the ponding are also associated with line centers, medicine wheels and very large glacier erratics. (Figures 71 - 90)

Figure 130: Footholds to climb butte with structure on top, Gray Hill, Chaco outlier, NM

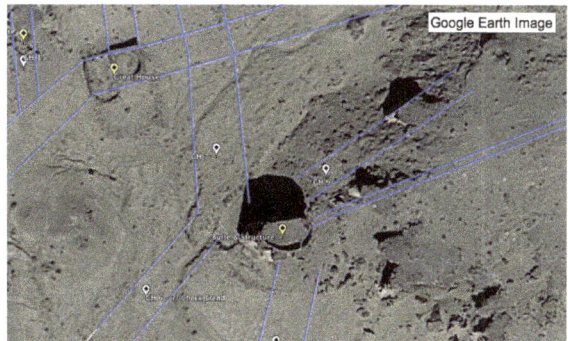

Figure 131: The butte shown in Figure 129, concentrated flows intersecting it, Gray Hill, Chaco outlier, NM

Cairn Types - The diameter and height of different types of cairns can indicate different functions as follows. Also, see turtle and effigy cairns below.

Cairns - They can range in height and diameter from a few feet to a few yards. They can be centered on, along the width boundary and at the intersection of areas of higher permeability. Consistently, they map a concentrated flows course. (Figures 132, 3, 4, 23, 25, 26, 118, 119, 120, 121, 124, 134, 135 & 137) Also, see Width Marker below.

Figure 132: Large cairn, Lewis Hollow Site, NY

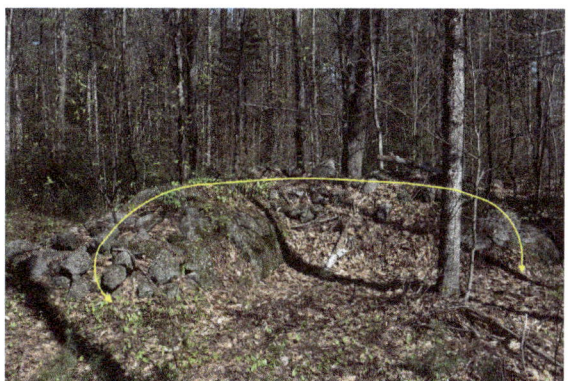

Figure 133: Crescent cairn, NH

Crescent Cairns - In the northeast, they are located at the intersection of two or more areas of higher permeability, and their width is equal to one of the flow's widths. (Figures 133 & 176) They are similar in appearance to herraduras, mentioned below, in the southwest. In the northeast, they have been associated with Native American trails, and Chaco Roads in the southwest. Some are modified to look like effigies. For example, horns added to resemble a buffalo.

115

Great Cairns - Although the minimum size may vary, cairns in the northeast exceeding 15 x 15 x 5 ft / 4.57 x 4.57 x 1.5 m are referred to as great cairns. The largest I documented was 75 x 30 x 12 ft / 22.8 m x 9.14 m x 3.65 m. They are the width of a concentrated flow and often extend along its length. (Figures 134 & 96)

Figure 134: Great cairn, NH

Tall Cairns - In addition to the cairn functions described above, tall cairns can also serve as line of sight markers. (Figures 135, 136, 4, 25 & 26)

Figure 135: Tall cairn, San Luis Valley, CO

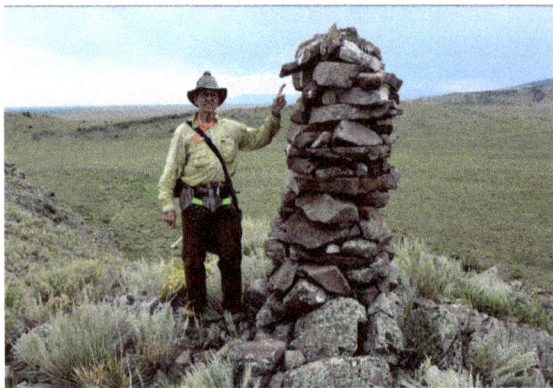
Figure 136: Tall cairn on concentrated flow and line of sight marker, CO

Tall Cairn

Figure 137: Turtle Cairn, Spruceton Valley, NY

Figure 138: Turtle Cairn, Crestone, CO

Turtle / Effigy Cairns - They are shaped like a turtle with a round or oval stone pile for the shell, a stone head with a stone on each side representing front legs, and some have a tail. Some have chambers with a small entrance, while others appear solid. Often, they are the width of an area of higher permeability and located at intersections. When the head points to the left or right, it indicates the concentrated flow is curving in that direction. A turtle cairn can have more than one head. Each head indicates where a concentrated flow intersects the cairn. Some are aligned with astronomical alignments. The southwestern and northeastern turtle cairns are very similar as shown in Figures 137, 138, 23, 118 & 119. Also, some can be very small and appear as if they are emerging from the ground. (Figure 139)

Figure 139: Turtle head emerging on concentrated flow, size 1 ft / .30 m, CO

Ceremonial Stones - In various regions, specific colored stones have been associated with Ceremonial Landscapes, burials and ceremonial sites. For example, in the northeast, quartz stones are commonly located on cairns. In the southwest, red, water worn, rounded stone cobbles have been found in burials and placed on different bedrock features along areas of higher permeability. This suggests they may be associated with sacred sites. (Figures 140 & 141)

Figure 140: Quartz stone on cairn, NH

Figure 141: Red river cobblestone located where two areas of higher permeability intersect, AZ

Chaco Roads - During the first two years, all of the Chaco Roads we investigated were aligned with areas of higher permeability. However, in 2013, as we expanded our investigation further out from Chaco Canyon, we learned this was not always true. This is our current understanding of the correlation between Chaco Roads and areas of higher permeability. (Figures 142 - 145)

Chaco Great Houses And Outliers - When Chaco great houses or outliers are located along one or more areas of higher permeability, and a Chaco Road intersects the site, at least one of the roads follows the trend of a flow which intersects the site. Areas of high permeability can extend from one outlier to another and be associated with a Chaco Road. (Figure 144)

In Dry Areas - In dry areas, such as the northern San Juan Basin north of Pierre's House, Chaco Roads, such as the Great North Road, follow a specific direction and may not align with or cross an area of higher permeability for several miles. However, where the road is aligned with or crosses an area of higher permeability, structures, such as Halfway House, and stone features, such as herraduras, are located along it. (Figure 145)

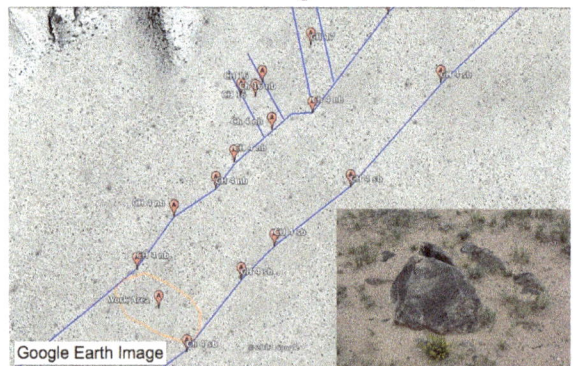

Figure 142: A Chaco Road in Chaco Canyon

Figure 143: Chaco Road, red dots = black basalt boulders along width of flow, NM

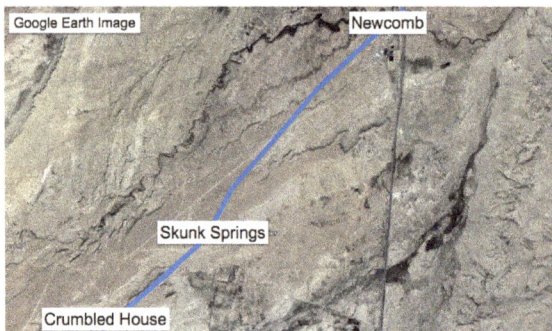

Figure 144: Blue line = continuous concentrated flow & Chaco Road for 5.8 mi & 3 Chaco sites

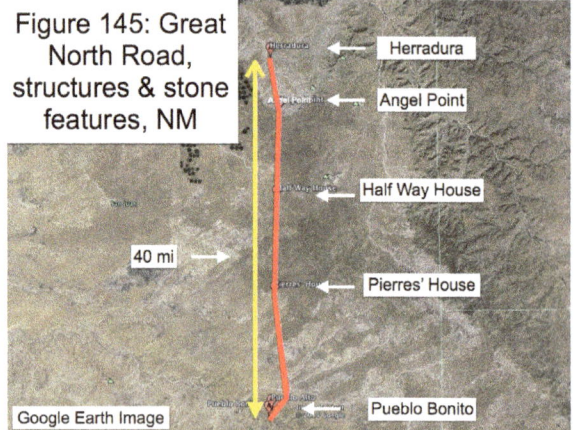

Figure 145: Great North Road, structures & stone features, NM

Circle Types - Circles of various sizes have been associated with areas of higher permeability. Their size and construction is characteristic of different functions.

Large Stone Circles - They consist of medium to large stones and boulders placed in a circle with a diameter 8 ft / 2.4 m or greater where an area of higher permeability turns. Some of the stones may be vertical and, stone features, such as circles, lines and triangles can be located within the circle. The diameter of the circle is equal to the width of one of the areas of higher permeability it is located on. (Figures 146, 67, & 68) This feature has been documented throughout the areas we have researched.

Small Stone Circles - They consist of medium to small stones placed in a circle with a diameter less than 7 ft / 2.1 m. The center can be cleared or contain a few stones. In some cases, some of the stones are vertical. They are located where two or more areas of higher permeability intersect. The circle's diameter may or may not be equal to the width of an area of higher permeability, since they are located on the width boundary of the flow. However, when located on a very narrow concentrated flow, the diameter is equal to the flow's width. (Figures 147, 64)

Figure 146: Large stone circle, CO

Figure 147: 3 ft / 0.9 m stone circle, CO

Ovals - They serve the same function as small circles. They are orientated across one of the areas of higher permeability and equal to its width. (Figures 148 & 115)

Prayer Circles - They consist of a stone circle which may or may not have an entrance. They were used for prayers by an individual or group and are located on a concentrated flow. However, where a large cluster exists, after the area along the concentrated flow is filled up, additional stone circles will be constructed as close as possible, but not on, the flow. (Figure 149)

Figure 148: Oval on area of higher permeability, NM

Teepee Rings - Most teepee rings associated with habitation artifacts are located along an area of higher permeability or where two or more intersect. The diameter of the circle equals the width of one of the concentrated flows. Where large groups of teepee rings exist some of them may be located along side concentrated flow since all the space along the concentrated flow was used up. (Figures 150)

Vision Quest Circle - During this ceremony an individual seeks advice from a guardian spirit. A person can sit in a stone circle for this ceremony. These circles are similar to prayer circles mentioned above. (Figure 149)

Figure 149: Possible prayer circle, MT

Figure 150: Teepee ring with artifacts, MT

Cupule - They are circular pecked depressions on outcrops and boulders. At this point, their function is not fully understood, however they are consistently located along areas of higher permeability. (Figure 151)

Figure 151: Pecked cupules on boulder, Coconino NF, AZ

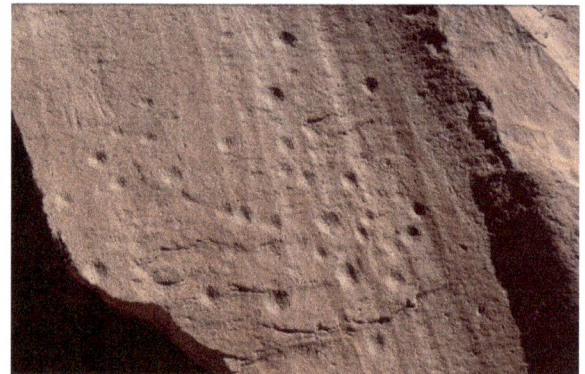

Drive Lines - As of this publication, all of the drive lines I have investigated are located along an area of higher permeability. The cairns and stone piles are along the width boundaries of the concentrated flow they are mapping. They are also connected to other paralleling lines of cairns and stone piles ranging in width from a few feet to 30 ft / 9 m or more feet wide and may intersect one another at oblique angles. (Figures 152, 56 - 60) Many of these lines do not lead to a kill site. Thus, not all single or paralleling stone lines are drive lines. This suggests buffalo and other animal jump sites were not chosen based solely on animal migrations and topography. Even though several other locations along a cliff may have provided the same results, the place where an area of higher permeability intersects it was given priority for a kill site.

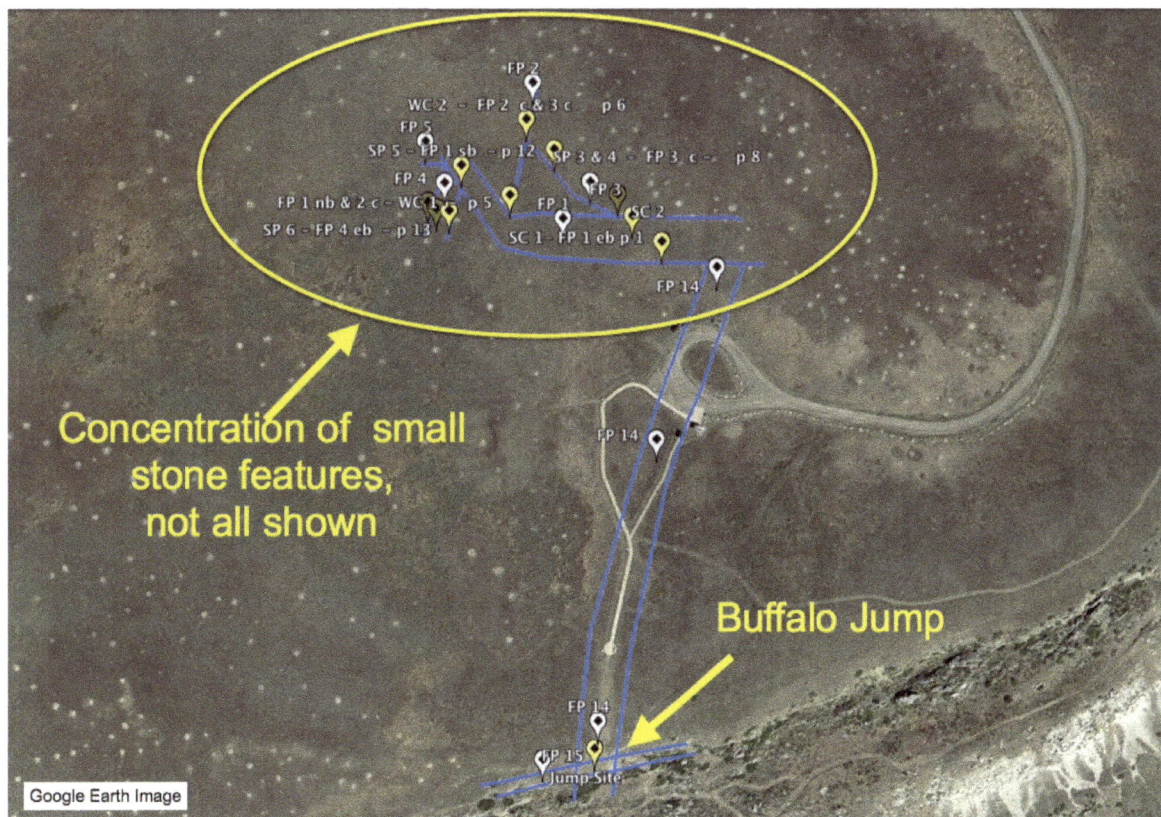

Figure 152: Yellow pins indicate small stone features & blue lines indicate concentrated flows, First People Buffalo Jump, MT

Earthworks - Earthworks in the southwest are similar to great cairns and mounds. Earthworks are located along a concentrated flow or extend across a group of flows. While some earthworks are located along concentrated flows others are not. (Figures 153 & 95)

Figure 153: Chaco earthwork, NM

Effigy Features - They are either naturally formed or culturally modified to appear as an effigy / biomorph. Also, see turtle cairns above.

Effigy Bedrock Features - They are found within bedrock features and can be either naturally occurring or culturally modified. They resemble a biomorphic shape such as an animal, bird, human or plant, to mention a few. These features are commonly associated with Ceremonial Landscapes. While some of the natural effigy bedrock features are located on areas of higher

121

permeability, all of the culturally modified ones are located on concentrated flows. (Figures 154 & 49)

Effigy Mounds - The mound is shaped like a biomorph such as the Great Snake Mound in Ohio. All of the effigy mounds we have investigated are orientated along at least one area of higher permeability. (Figures 155 & 94) Also see mounds below.

Figure 154: Puma head at habitation site, Agua Fria, AZ

Figure 155: Great Snake Mound, OH

Effigy Shapes Etched Into The Ground Surface - In Peru, the Nasca Lines' biomorphs, such as the spider, tree, human and many others, are etched into the floor of the desert. All of the biomorphic features my colleagues and I have surveyed are located along one or more areas of higher permeability. In January 2017 I investigated the Blythe Geoglyphs in California and Arizona and was amazed at how similar they are to the Nasca geoglyphs. (Figure 156) In Figure 157 the hummingbird's beak symbolically touches the broad paralleling lines marking the location of an area of higher permeability in the groundwater as if to drink the water. (Figures 5 & 6)

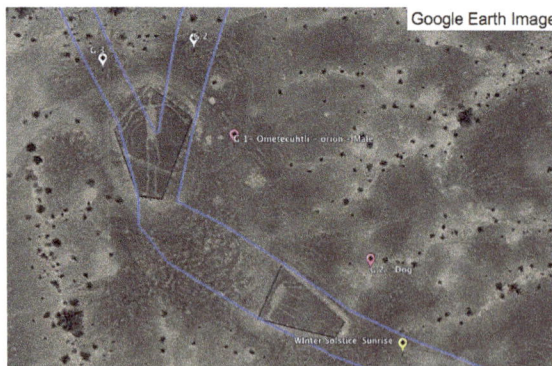
Figure 156: Male / Ometecuhtli / Orion figure & dog with concentrated flows, Blythe, CA

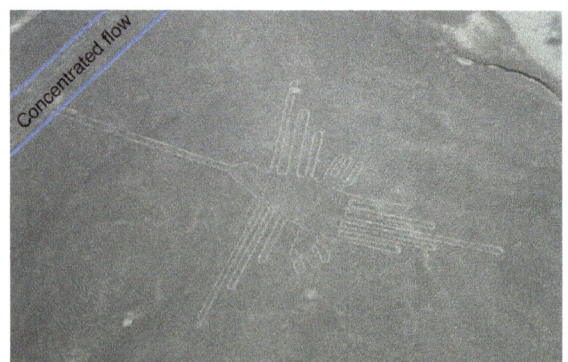
Figure 157: Hummingbird and concentrated flow, Nasca Lines, Peru

122

Effigy Stones / Boulders - These stones are either naturally occurring or culturally modified and resemble a biomorphic shape such as an animal, bird, human or plant, to mention a few. They are commonly associated with Ceremonial Landscapes. While some of the natural effigy stones / boulders are located on areas of higher permeability, all of the culturally modified ones are located on concentrated flows. (Figure 158)

Figure 158: Boulder culturally modified to appear as bear head, Turtle Hill Site, MA

Effigy Stone Piles / Cairns - These features consist of a group of stones shaped like a biomorph. They are located along concentrated flows. For example, turtle cairns, which are discussed above under cairns and shown in Figures 3, 23, 98, 118, 119, 137 & 138.

Figure 159: Nasca Geoglyphs, Peru

.5 mi / .81 km

Google Earth Image

Geoglyph Geometric Shapes - In the Atacama Desert, by removing the darkened surface debris within a shape, such as a trapezoid drawn on the ground, the lighter unoxidized subsurface is exposed, thus highlighting the geoglyph's shape. The debris removed from the interior of the shape was deposited along its borders to accentuate the geoglyph's shape. This technique was also used with the lines that formed the biomorphs. (Figures 159, 5 & 6) All of the geoglyphs we investigated are associated with areas of higher permeability. These features are also associated with the Blythe geoglyphs.

Glacier Erratics - During the course of this research numerous small to large glacier erratics were investigated. Some were on concentrated flows while others were not. However, within Ceremonial Landscapes, glacier erratics that appear to be or are culturally modified were located on concentrated flows. Some very large glacier erratics have the same ray pattern of concentrated flows and ponding that is associated with line centers, buttes and medicine wheels.

Alignment - Where two or more boulders are aligned along a concentrated flow's trend, and the direction points to another site or feature. (Figure 160)

123

Astronomical Alignment - Large erratics were also modified to align with astronomical events. The large erratic in Figure 161 has the appearance of a turtle and is located on a concentrated flow within a large Ceremonial Landscape. The area under it has been cleared of debris. During solstice and equinox sunrise and sunset the sun casts a beam of light on one side or the other of the turtle's head and under it, thus indicating a particular time of year.

Figure 160: Two large boulders on concentrated flow, NY

Figure 161: Turtle Rock, NY

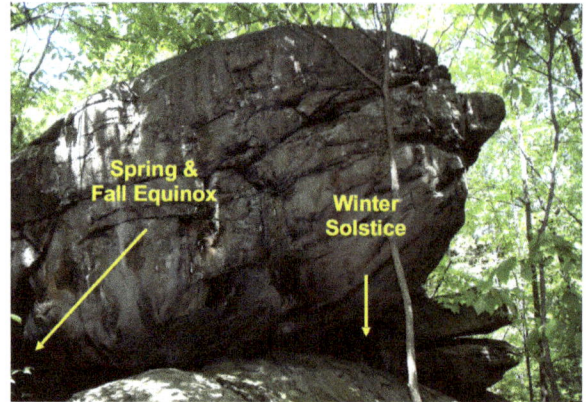

Balanced / Rocking Boulder - A boulder is placed on another boulder along a concentrated flow. It is balanced so it can rocked back and forth making a loud sound. (Figure 162)

Figure 162: Rocking boulder on concentrated flow, NY

Effigy Boulder - All of the culturally modified effigy boulders we documented are located on one or more areas of higher permeability.

Turtle - Some large erratics have been modified to resemble a turtle. In Figures 163 & 161 small boulders extend out from the main boulder to form the neck and head of a turtle, while on each side others form the front legs. Turtles are an important component with many Native American cultures.

Profiles - Some erratics have been shaped to form human or animal shapes, such as a profile. In Figure 164 an erratic is located along a concentrated flow, and the top of the erratic appears as a buffalo's profile.

Figure 163: Great Turtle Rock, NY

Figure 164: Vertical view of buffalo looking towards the sky, Alberta, Canada

Largest Glacier Erratics - Within regions affected by glaciation, the largest glacier erratic is sacred to the local Native American Nations. For example, Big Rock / Okotoks Erratic in Alberta, Canada and Cochegan Rock in Connecticut. I have included this discussion in the section on Intersecting Areas Of Higher Permeability With Ponding. (Figure 165)

Figure 165: Okotoks Glacier Erratic Site, Alberta, Canada

Figure 166: Propped leaning boulder, Turtle Rock Site, NY

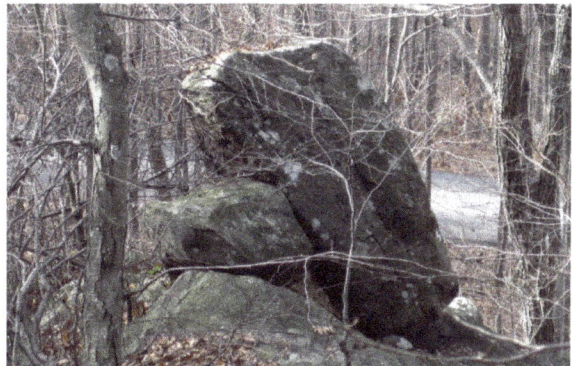

Leaning Propped Boulder - It consists of a boulder leaning up against another boulder. Within Ceremonial Landscapes they are located along a concentrated flow mapping its course. (Figure 166)

Placed Boulder - It is placed on the ground or bedrock and centrally located on an area of higher permeability. The right side of the boulder in Figure 167 looks like a face.

Propped On Single Boulder - When one boulder sets on top of another boulder. Typically the length of the top boulder is aligned with the trend of the concentrated flow. (Figure 168)

Figure 167: Placed boulder on concentrated flow, right side looks like a face, NY

Figure 168: Balanced boulder on another boulder, NY

Tripod Boulder / Propped On Three Rocks - Nearly all of the tripod boulders are supported by three rocks and located along a concentrated flow. Most of the time the supporting stones / boulders form a triangle with the triangle's length aligned with the concentrated flow's trend. This characteristic has been observed throughout the glaciated regions I have researched and appears to be more than coincidental. (Figures 169 & 45)

Vertical Boulder - In this case, an elongated boulder is propped vertically. The one in Figure 170 is located where an area of higher permeability changes course at ninety degrees.

Figure 169:Stones beneath Tripod rock form a triangle & indicate trend of concentrated flow

Figure 170: Glacial erratic where course of concentrated flow turns, NY

Great Houses And Outliers - All of the Chaco great houses and outliers we have investigated are located on one or more areas of higher permeability. (Figures 171, 17, 102, 106, 108 & 180)

Great Kivas - All of the Chaco great kivas we have investigated are located on one or more areas of higher permeability, and their diameter is equal to one of the concentrated flows. (Figures 172, 102 & 106) Also, many of the smaller kivas are also located on the flows.

Figure 171: Red Willow Outlier, NM

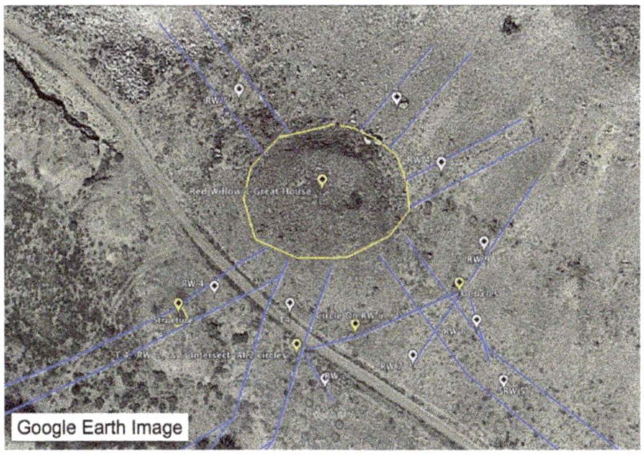

Figure 172: Two concentrated flows intersecting a great kiva, Casa Rinconada, Chaco Canyon

Grooved Meandering Long Lines - They are associated with Chaco Roads and aligned with the trend of an area of higher permeability. (Figure 173)

Habitationscapes - Habitation areas are planned holistically to include components of the underworld, physical world and cosmos both within the community and radiating outward into the landscape. The features within them are aligned with areas of higher permeability. (Figures 174, 10, 15, 16, 17, 69, 78, 79, 91, 95, 101, 103 & 202)

Figure 173: Grooved bedrock along area of higher permeability, NM

Figure 174: Chaco habitationscape, Willow Canyon, NM

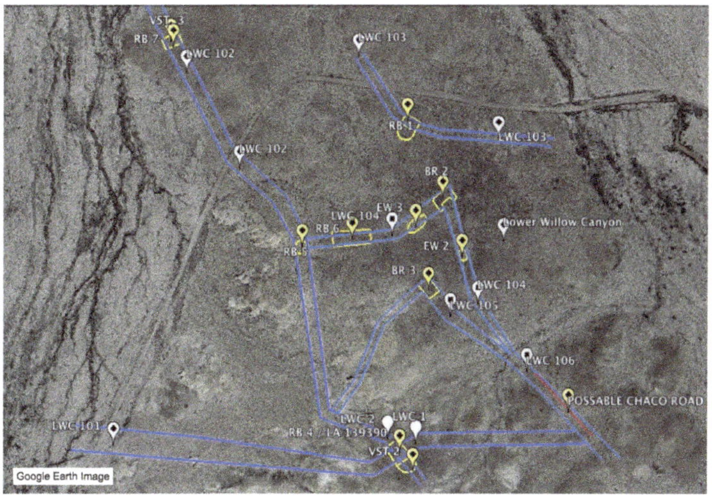

Habitation Structures - They are centered on an area of higher permeability, and often where two or more intersect. Frequently, they are the same width as one of the areas of higher permeability and / or orientated along it. (Figures 175, 106 & 107) Large roomblocks often have several concentrated flows intersecting them. Teepee rings are the diameter of the flow. They include all forms of Native American housing units.

Figure 175: Chaco roomblock, Pueblo Pintado Outlier, NM

Figure 176: Herradura, NM

Herraduras - In the southwest, they are crescent shaped stone features which are associated with late Basketmaker and Chaco Roads. Usually, they are located where two or more areas of higher permeability intersect and are equal to the width of one of the flows. Their construction is very similar to crescent cairns in the northeast which are mentioned above. (Figures 176 & 133)

Line Centers - Within the Nasca Lines and coastal geoglyphs of Peru and Chile, South America, line centers are very similar to the buttes and medicine wheels in North America. Several researchers, including my colleagues and I, have documented line centers which consist of mounds / hills created by a bedrock feature or a point extending from a mountain where several geoglyphs / Nasca Lines intersect (Aveni 1990, Johnson 2009). (Figures 177, 71 & 72) When you stand on the top of the promontory you can see the geoglyphs more clearly. Trapezoids and broad paralleling lines map the trend of areas of higher permeability intersecting this feature. Thus, these geoglyphs indicate where areas of higher permeability intersect the line center.

Figure 177: Line center, blue lines = flows, Nasca Lines, Peru

Medicine Wheels - Of the eight northern plains medicine wheel subgroups defined by Brumley in his book titled Medicine Wheels On The Northern Plains: A Summary And Appraisal, six have spokes radiating out from the center and two are circular without spokes (Brumley 1986). All of the medicine wheels with and without spokes that I have investigated have several areas of higher permeability intersecting them at the center where there is ponding. The rays / spokes indicated the number of concentrated flows intersecting the center. Where a ray intersects the medicine wheel's outer stone circle, its width equals the width of the concentrated flow it is mapping. The inner circle's circumference identifies where subsurface ponding occurs. (Figures 178, 80 & 81)

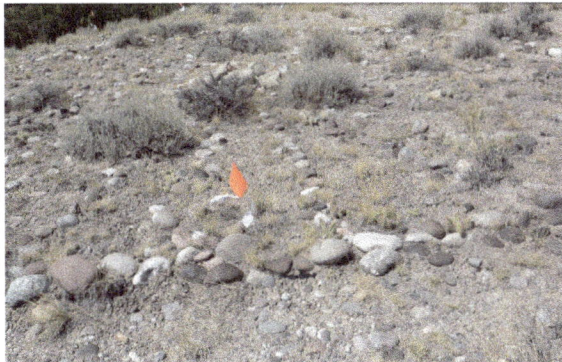

Figure 178: Medicine wheel spokes / rays & center cairn, MT

Figure 179: Mounds along concentrated flow, SD

Mounds - During the course of this research, my colleagues and I have investigated mounds associated with the Adena, Hopewell and Mississippian cultures. All of the mounds we investigated are located on one or more areas of higher permeability. This includes small to large mounds. (Figures 179, 91 - 94)

Effigy Mounds - Figure 155 above.

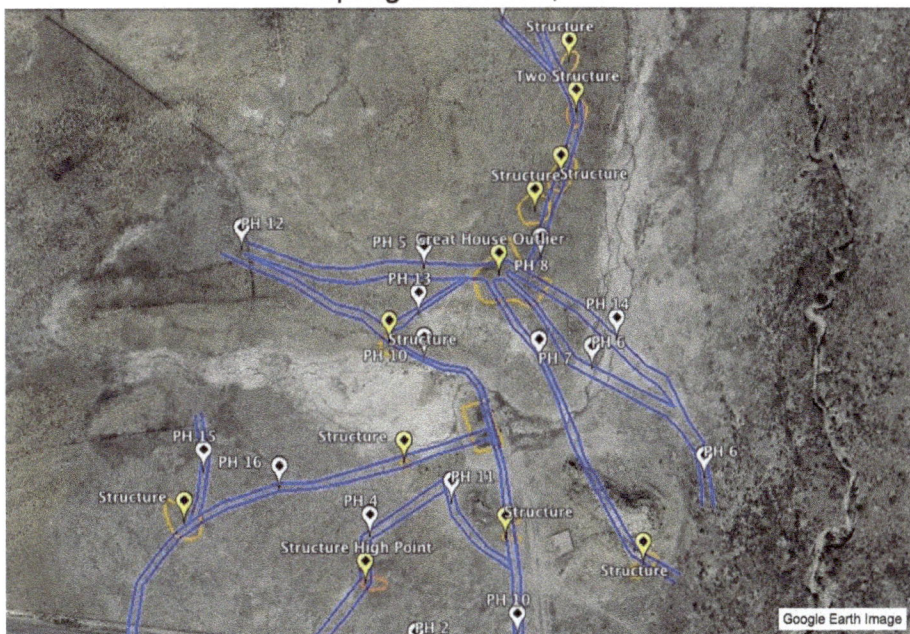

Figure 180: Structures and & areas of higher permeability, Peach Spring Outlier Site, NM

Outlier Sites - This term relates to sites which strongly resemble a larger site that functions as a regional center. (See Chaco great houses above) For example, the focal point for the Chaco / Anasazi culture was located in Chaco Canyon. Within the canyon there are several great houses which resemble one another. As the culture spread outward, additional outlier great houses were constructed several miles from Chaco Canyon which replicate the construction of the great houses within Chaco Canyon. In Figure 180, concentrated flows radiate outward from an outlier. All the other features within the site are connected to it by the interconnected concentrated flows. (Figure 174) Often, large Ceremonial Landscape sites have smaller sites located around them, and the stone features within the outlying sites replicate those found within the main site. Thus, if a large Ceremonial Landscape contains turtle cairns, there is a high probability the smaller sites surrounding it which contain turtle cairns are outlier sites of that site.

Petroglyph And Pictograph Iconography

All of the ancestral Native American petroglyphs and pictographs I have investigated in Peru and Chile, as well as North America, are located along areas of higher permeability. After contact with the Europeans, petroglyphs and pictographs may or may not be associated with a concentrated flow.

Petroglyphs - They are pecked or grooved into a bedrock feature and located along areas of higher permeability. If the flow parallels the cliff, the petroglyphs are located along its length. If it intersects the cliff perpendicularly or at an oblique angle, the petroglyphs are located across its width. Petroglyphs can also be located on flat surfaces. Explanations for various figures are discussed below. (Figure 181)

Pictographs - They are painted on bedrock features and located along areas of higher permeability. If the flow parallels the cliff, the pictographs are located along its length. If it intersects the cliff perpendicularly or at an oblique angle, the pictographs are located across its width or on the margins of the flow indicating its width. Pictographs can also be located on flat surfaces. Explanations for various figures are discussed below. (Figure 182)

Figure 181: Petroglyph panel, AZ

Figure 182-: Pictograph panel, AZ

130

We have associated a variety of symbols with specific characteristics of areas of higher permeability as follows.

Astronomical Alignments - They consist of natural and man made features which align with astronomical events, such as equinox and solstice. They can also consist of culturally modified features which are aligned with a distant natural feature. The culturally modified features are located along areas of higher permeability. (Figure 183)

Astronomical Events - Some of the figures appear to resemble stars, planets and other celestial bodies and document the occurrence of a particular event, such as summer solstice. For example, some researchers refer to the pictograph panel in Figure 184 as the Nova Panel which has been interpreted as showing a super nova, Halley's Comet, moon and hand. They are located along areas of higher permeability.

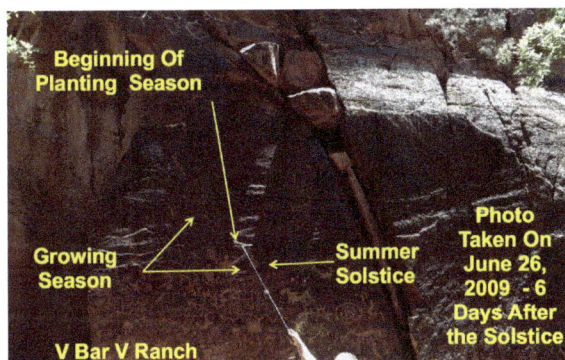

Figure 183: Petroglyph panel indicating seasons & solstices, V Bar V Ranch, AZ

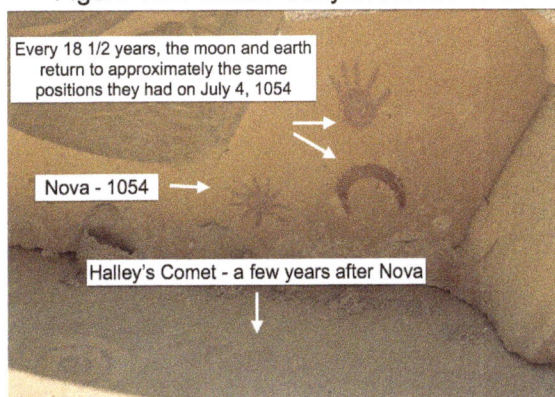

Figure 184: Chaco Canyon Nova Panel

Beliefs - These scenes consist of images related to beliefs, such as creation and birth. They are consistently located on areas of higher permeability. (Figure 185)

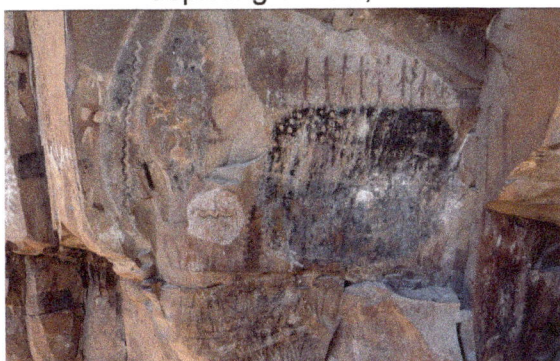

Figure 185: Example of pictographs depicting beliefs, AZ

Figure 186: Turtle pictograph representing the Turtle Clan, AZ

Cultural - They consist of images which are associated with a particular culture, tribe, clan and migrations. They are consistently located on areas of higher permeability. (Figure 186)

Hunting Scenes - They consist of hunting scenes, ambush areas and animal migrations, to mention a few. They are consistently located on areas of higher permeability. (Figure 187)

Figure 187: Hunting scene, Coconino NF, AZ

Incised Lines / Narrow Grooved Linear Lines - They consist of parallel and oblique lines appearing in groups. Some groups consist of seven or thirteen lines. (Figures 188 & 117) Their function is not fully understood. They have been centered on and along the margin of areas of higher permeability. Some researchers believe they date to the Archaic Period. One interpretation is

Figure 188: Incised lines, Coconino NF, AZ

the groups of seven are associated with the phases of the moon (seven days each between the new moon, first quarter, full moon and last quarter) and the groupings of 13 as the annual lunar month cycle (13 lunar months in each calendar year). Similar incised lines can result from sharping stone tools by rubbing them against an outcrop or boulder.

Map Types - In Peru and Chile, several researchers have documented stones which are shaped to resemble structures, sites and irrigation systems. It appears they were used in the planning stage of construction projects. (Figures 189, 7, 8 & 9) We have found petroglyphs in the southwest which map areas of higher permeability within a site. These maps match my map of the concentrated flows in that site.

Maps Of Areas Of Higher Permeability - They consist of pecked lines which document the trend and intersections of areas of higher permeability within the immediate area. In each case, I had completed my survey of the area before we located the petroglyph map. Then, when I compared my map of the flows to the petroglyph map, they corresponded. (Figures 189, 7, 8 & 9) Figure 189 compares my map of areas of higher permeability at El Morro National Monument and a petroglyphs located at the base of the escarpment.

Map / Icon Of Structure - Some images closely resemble those of structures, such as specific great houses, and the number of areas of higher permeability which intersect them. (Figure 190) They are also located on areas of higher permeability.

Figure 189: Areas of higher permeability and petroglyph, El Morro N.M., NM

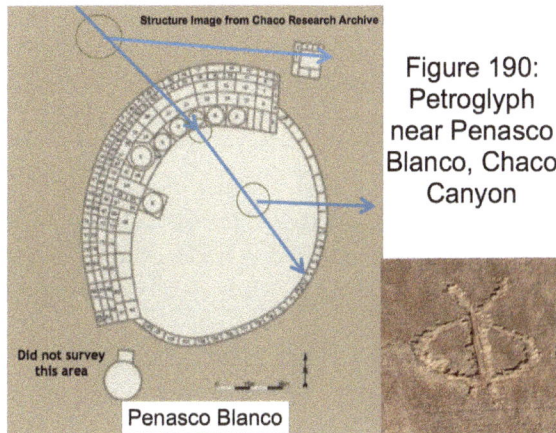

Figure 190: Petroglyph near Penasco Blanco, Chaco Canyon

Meandering Lines - They consist of pecked meandering lines which can also loop. Often the patina of the pecked pattern has basically patinated back to the color of the host bedrock. They are very hard to see. This strongly suggests they are very old and could date to the late Paleo or early Archaic Historical Periods. They are found along areas of higher permeability and at intersections. (Figures 191 and 116)

Figure 191: Meandering line petroglyph, San Luis Valley, CO

Figure 192: Horse & rider on concentrated flow, Coconino NF, AZ

Native Americans Riding A Horse - They are located along areas of higher permeability and may indicate post European contact Native American tribes were still associating with areas of higher permeability, or they simply added these images to older panels. (Figure 192)

Human Figures In Line - A line of human figures have consistently equalled the width of the concentrated flow they are located on. (Figure 193)

Figure 193: The line of people equals width of a concentrated flow, Palatki, AZ

Figure 194: Shaman Figure, Agua Fria NM, AZ

Shaman And Spirit Figures - They are consistently associated with areas of higher permeability. (Figure 194)

Shields - Shields are round with patterns within them and can have rays extending from them. They are located along the width boundaries of areas of higher permeability or centered on narrow widths. (Figure 195)

Spirals - They indicate where the course of areas of higher permeability are curving or turning. (Figure 196)

Figure 195: Shield pictograph,
Coconino NF, AZ

Figure 196: Spiral petroglyph, Agua Fria, AZ

Spirals With Line Extending - The extended line indicates the trend of the area of higher permeability it is located on. (Figure 197)

Sunbursts - They are circular with rays extending from the perimeter. They are found along areas of higher permeability and are similar to shields. (Figure 198)

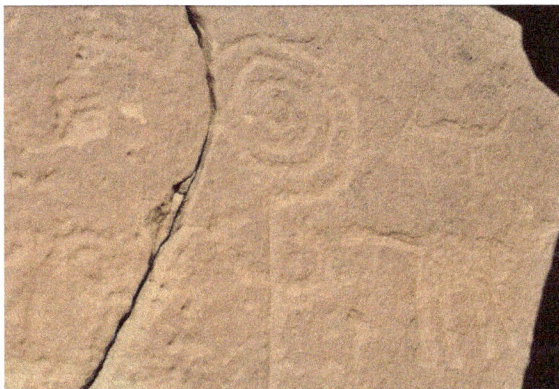
Figure 197: Spiral with line extending, NM

Figure 198: Sunburst, San Luis Valley, CO

Rays From A Central Point - The length of the rays are usually the same length and, if connected, form a circle. They are located along the width boundary of a concentrated flow or centered on it. (Figure 199)

Zigzag Lines - These lines can appear in many styles including zigzag lines, snakes and plants, as well as others. In spite of the style, they indicate the trend of areas of

Figure 199: Rays from a central point,
Shawangunk Mountains, NY

higher permeability, and can be multifunctional, for example, expressing cultural beliefs.

Zigzag Horizontal Lines - They indicate the trend of an area of higher permeability which parallels a cliff. On the ground, they map the trend of the concentrated flow. (Figure 200) Often this symbol has a snake's head.

Zigzag Vertical Lines - They are located along the width boundaries of an area of higher permeability where it intersects a cliff and indicate its width. They can be on vertical and horizontal surfaces. (Figure 201)

Figure 200: Horizontal zigzag lines, Coconino NF, AZ

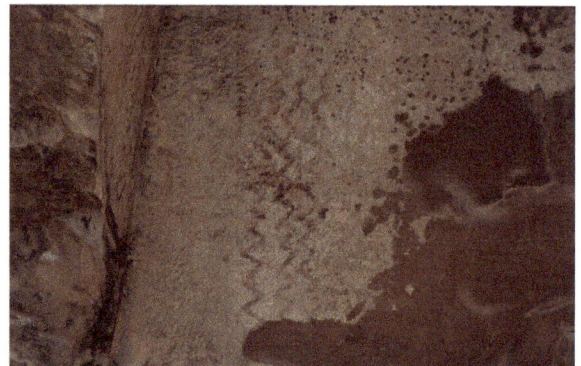

Figure 201: Vertical zigzag lines, Coconino NF, AZ

Plazas - They tend to be centrally located within a Habitationscape. Some have areas of higher permeability radiating outward from them (Figures 202 & 78), while others are bordered by concentrated flows on each side. They are open areas where people gathered.

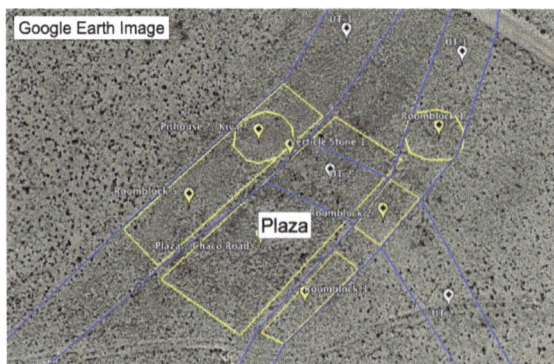

Figure 202: Chaco roomblocks with plaza between them & concentrated flows, NM

Figure 203: Platform above large area for people to gather, CO

Platforms - This feature has been documented throughout all the regions we have investigated. Typically, they consist of a flat, raised, level surface constructed

136

along the slope of a hill or mountain and provide a panoramic view of the area. Some are small enough to accommodate a few people, while others are large enough for a group. Some are located above a large amphitheater within a habitation complex. They appear to have been used for astronomical observations, as well as, ceremonies or celebrations. All of the platforms we have investigated are located along one or more areas of higher permeability. (Figure 203)

Racetracks - They average 30 ft / 9 m wide by fifty or more yards / meters long and are cleared of debris. They appear to have been used at special events such as summer solstice. All of the racetracks I have documented were located during blind surveys and along an area of higher permeability. (Figure 204)

Figure 204: The brown area is a Sinagua race track, AZ

Figure 205: Sipapu, Coconino NF, AZ

Sacred Mountains - These mountains were used to bring people closer to the Great Spirit, and from which they can pray and observe their homeland. The top of the mountain has stone features such as cairns and circles, to mention a few, which map the concentrated flows and serve as prayer and vision quest circles.

Sipapu - It symbolizes the portal through which ancestral Puebloans first emerged from the underworld into the present world. All of the sipapus I have investigated are centrally located on an area of higher permeability. (Figure 205)

Figure 206: Native American stone line / wall, CO

Stone Lines - In the United States, a Native American stone line's length can vary from a few to over a hundred yards / meters long. When they are located along a concentrated flow, they are not straight since they follow the meandering of the flow they are located on. (Figure 206) In some cases, stone lines have been associated with astronomical alignments and are straight since they function as a pointer between two observation points. In Peru, some stone lines are not located along a concentrated flow since they connect features such as line centers with one another. These lines are straight and can extend for a mile / kilometer or more.

Stone Piles - They consist of a group of stones / small boulders placed in piles, however they are not stacked like cairns. They are most commonly found along the width boundaries of an area of higher permeability and centrally located on narrow flows. (Figure 207 & 208) On narrow concentrated flows the diameter can be equal to the width of a concentrated flow.

Figure 207: Stone piles made from basket drops, Nasca Lines, Peru

Figure 208: Stone pile, San Luis Valley, CO

Stone Spirals - They consist of a group of stones / small boulders which are placed to form a spiral. Some of the stones may be vertical and often pointed. They indicate where an area of higher permeability is curving or turning sharply. This feature has been documented throughout the regions we have investigated. Spiral patterns have also been observed within stone piles and turtle cairns. (Figure 209) Also see Figures 196 & 197.

Figure 209: Stone spiral which looks like a coiled snake, San Luis Valley, CO

Stone Triangles - Within the northeastern Ceremonial Landscapes, only a few stone triangles have been documented thus far. The ones we documented were around 30 ft / 9 m wide and 60 ft / 18 m long and located along an area of higher permeability. Since they are hard to see and photograph clearly, I outlined the stone triangle in Figure 210, which is located in Massachusetts. As shown in Figure 211, some triangles are very small and indicate the trend of a concentrated flow. In Peru, triangles can be .5 mi / .80 km or more in length.

Figure 210: Stone triangle, MA

Figure 211: Small triangle & stone circle along trend of concentrated flow, MT

While some are located along an area of higher permeability, others are not, since their function is to point to the source of the concentrated flow in the mountain or where a spring is located in a valley.

Stone Quarry - All of the ancestral Native American stone quarries investigated so far are located along areas of higher permeability. Unfortunately, many have been altered or mostly destroyed by modern mining or construction. However, ancient quarries which are more isolated, and may or may not have stone features associated with them, are located along areas of higher permeability. (Figure 212)

Figure 212: Stone quarry & biface, WY

Trees Culturally Modified - These include peeled and shaped trees which have been documented throughout the United States and are associated with numerous First Nations. Several websites discuss these features. Culturally modified trees are consistently accompanied by stone features, and all of these features have been located along areas of higher permeability. Often, several of these features are grouped together where several areas of higher permeability intersect one another. These trees were multifunctional, for example, some served as trailmarkers, while others indicated burials.

> **Arborglyphs / Message Trees** - Messages or Ute signs were often carved into the bark of a tree and would depict events, such as a tribal fight or hunt. In some cases, they are trailmarkers. For example, Figure 213, the bark contains an image of a person walking towards the left, thus indicating the direction of the trail.

Figure 213: Culturally modified tree with man walking, San Juan Forest, CO

Figure 214: Burial tree,San Luis Valley, CO

Council Trees - As the name implies, these trees indicated the place where meetings were held, often between tribes.

Burial Trees - The Ute burial tree can be either a ponderosa tree with two distinctive 90° bends which point to where the Ute tribal leader is buried, or a cedar tree planted to mark the general location of possibly their honored leader's burial site. (Figure 214)

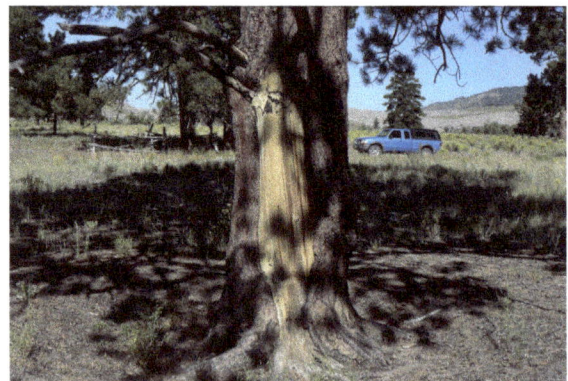

Figure 215: Peeled tree, Sand Dunes NP

Peeled Bark / Medicine Trees - A Ute medicine person would make a small cut on a tree at a spot that matched the site of a person's ailment. A sharp stick would then be inserted into the tree and leveraged upward to peel the bark away. The inner layer of the bark would then be used in a healing ceremony. (Figure 215)

Peeled Bark Trees - They also map the trend of areas of higher permeability. For example, if two peeled trees are located on the same concentrated flow, at least one of the bark peels on each tree will face the other tree, thus indicating the trend of the flow. (Figure 215)

Prophecy Trees - Two trees are grafted together. They are believed to foretell future events. (Figure 216)

Trailmarker Trees - Often they have one 30° bend to the trunk before extending upward. The bend points towards some geological or navigational reference such as a trail, stream, mountain pass or stone feature, to mention few. (Figure 217)

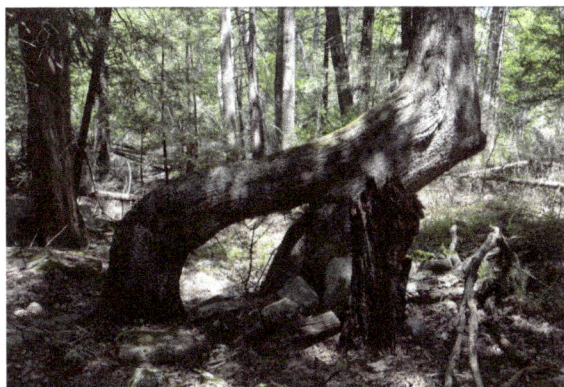
Figure 216: Prophecy tree, NY

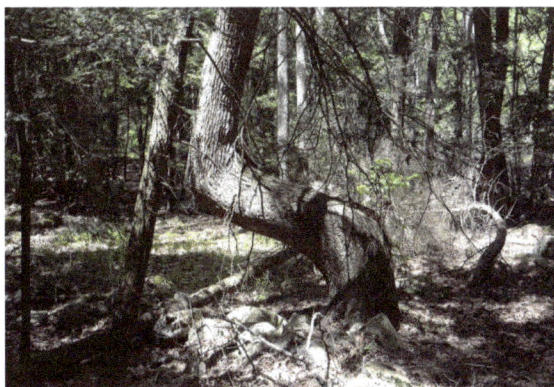
Figure 217: Trailmarker tree, NY

Towers - They are associated with Chaco sites. All of the towers observed thus far were located along or at intersections of areas of higher permeability. One of the towers was aligned with the cardinal points. (Figure 218)

Vertical Stone Slab Structures - They tend to be square or rectangular and vary in size from a few feet to 12 ft / 3.65 m. They are located along areas of higher permeability and at intersections of two or more. Typically, they are equal to the width of one of the concentrated flows. (Figure 219)

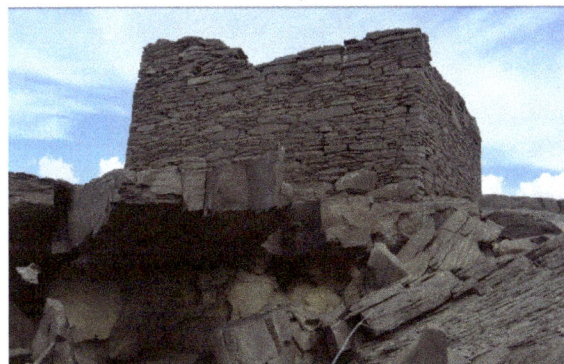
Figure 218: Chaco square tower, by Chaco Outlier, NM

Figure 219: Vertical stone structure, NM

Figure 220: Rectangular stone feature with vertical stone slab along one side, NM

Vertical Stone Slab And Rectangular Feature - This is a rectangular feature with a vertical stone slab along one side. They are located on an area of higher permeability with the vertical stone slab aligned with the trend of the concentrated flow it is located on. (Figure 220)

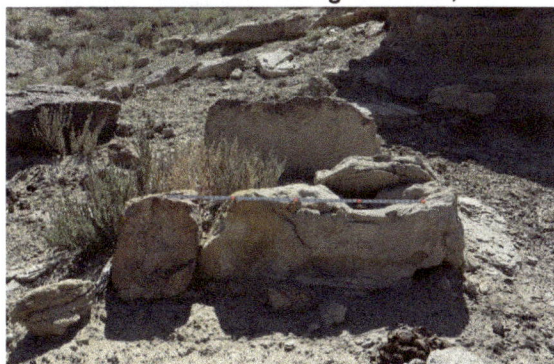

Vertical Wedged Stones - They are intentionally placed in a bedrock fracture or split boulder and located along an area of higher permeability. In the southwest, some are located where they can function as line of sight markers. (Figures 221 and 222) Also see astronomical vertical stones above.

Figure 221: Vertical wedged stone, NM

Figure 222: Vertical wedged stone, Turtle Rock Site, NY

Walls - Various types of stone walls are associated with Ceremonial Landscapes and areas of higher permeability.

Alignment Walls - Some walls located along areas of higher permeability are aligned with the cardinal points and tend to be wider than a typical field wall. Others extend between two features, which, when in alignment, direct one's attention to an astronomical event on the horizon. In Peru, these walls can range from ten to one hundred yards / meters long or more. (Figure 223)

Flat Vertical Slabs Within A Wall - This feature consists of a wall with alternating vertical stone slabs and rounded boulders / stones. The wall is located along the width boundary of an area of higher permeability. (Figure 224)

Figure 223: North south wall along area of higher permeability, NY

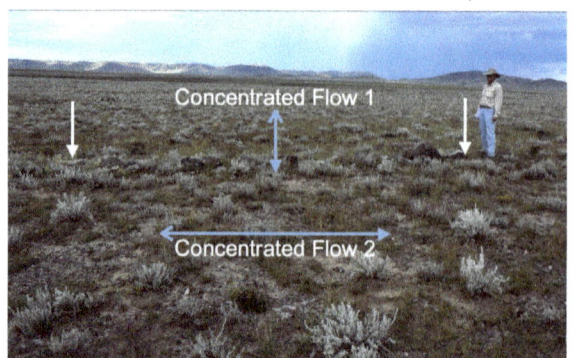

Figure 224: Wall between white arrows with flat vertical slabs and round stones, CO

142

Snake / Serpent Walls - They consist of a meandering wall which does not form an enclosure, and one end may or may not have a boulder(s) which is shaped like a snake's head. Some of these walls intertwine as if two snakes are mating. They are consistently located along areas of higher permeability. (Figure 225)

Stone Lines / Walls - See above.

Figure 225: North snake wall along area of higher permeability, NY

Walls Within Structures - They are often aligned with areas of higher permeability, and parallel walls can indicate the width. (Figures 102 & 106)

Width Markers / Short Walls - Their length is equal to the width of an area of higher permeability. These walls are not very high and often have vertical stones within them. Also see below. (Figure 226)

Features Within Walls - Some walls have features constructed within them which indicate the intersections of two areas of higher permeability, and often the trend. Thus far, the following have been observed at sites in the northeast and southwest.

Figure 226: 22 ft long wall across width of area of higher permeability, NY

Figure 227: Flat stone line and window in snake wall, AZ

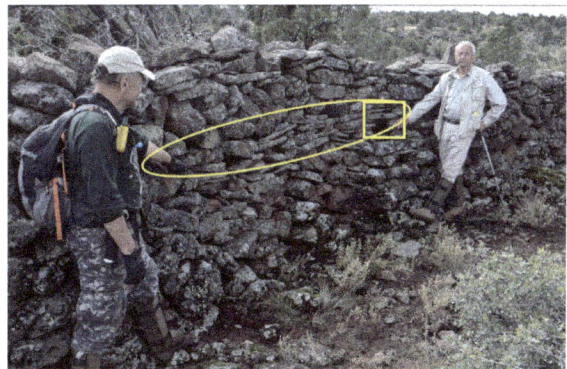

Flat Stone Features Within Walls - They consist of a line of flat stones within a wall which mainly consists of rounder stones and boulders. (Figure 227) The length of the line of flat stones indicates two areas of higher permeability are intersecting, and the width of one of them is indicated by the length of the flat stone line within the wall. Figure 227 also shows one of the windows.

Small Window Like Openings - Within some walls we have noticed small windows which seem to be out of place. Interestingly, we have associated them with the trend of an area of higher permeability which is intersecting another at that location. (Figure 227) If the window passes through the wall at an angle, it indicates one flow is intersecting the other at that angle, which is represented by the window's angle. These small windows are often associated with the flat stone line features mentioned above. Figure 227 also shows one of the flat stone features.

Figure 228: Example of cairn built within a snake wall.

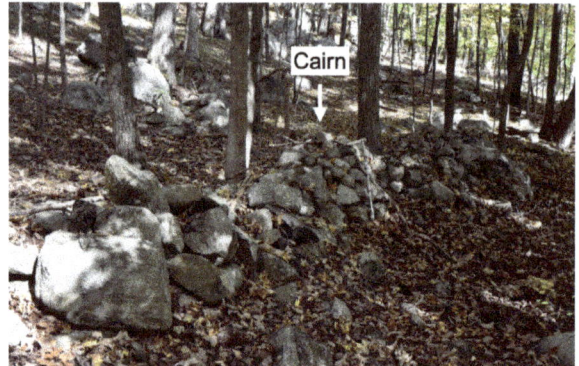

Cairns and Circles - Regardless of their heights, frequently these walls have cairns and circles built within them. In some cases, these features indicate where a secondary concentrated flow intersects the main flow that the wall is associated with. (Figure 228)

Width Markers Of Areas Of Higher Permeability - They consist of stone features which are located along the width boundaries of an area of higher permeability, and often opposite of one another. They consist of a variety of styles as follows.

Cairns - Often, cairns are placed along the width boundaries of an area of higher permeability and opposite of one another. The width between them equals the width of the concentrated flow. If the concentrated flow is narrow, they are centered on it. (Figure 229)

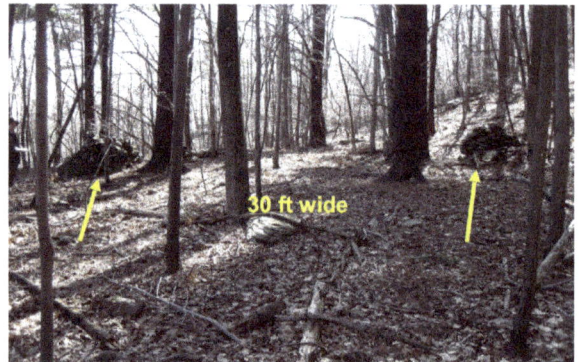

Figure 229: Cairns on width boundaries of concentrated flow, Hudson Valley, NY

Basket Deposits - Along the coast of Peru, the center of geometric geoglyphs, such as trapezoids and triangles, are cleared of debris. The debris was carried in baskets to the perimeter and emptied creating a dotted line of stone piles. (Figures 207 & 208) In the southwest, some stone piles resemble basket deposits and are located along the width boundary of areas of higher permeability.

Flat Stone Features Within Walls - See above Figure 227.

Half Rectangle - Stones are placed along each width boundary and across the width of an area of higher permeability forming half of a rectangle. They function as a width marker. They have been associated with sites in all the regions we have investigated. (Figure 230)

Figure 230: Half rectangle on concentrated flow, NM

Lines Of Boulders - They are located every few yards along the width boundary of an area of higher permeability. Frequently, the boulders are different than the bedrock they are placed on; for example, basalt boulders on a sandstone formation. This indicates they were intentionally brought to this location. (Figure 143)

Stones On Stone - They are located along the width boundary of an area of higher permeability, however they are constructed differently than stone piles and cairns. They consist of stones placed on another larger stone with a flat surface. Often, they have the appearance of a bird's nest. (Figure 231)

Figure 231: Stone on stone, has appearance of a bird's nest, AZ

Figure 232: Vertical stone centered on area of higher permeability & possible astronomical alignment, NM

Vertical Stones - They are elongated and embedded in the ground, to some extent, to support them in a vertical position. They are located along the width boundaries of an area of higher permeability or centered on them, and some are placed in short lines. Others are located where two areas of higher permeability intersect. In some case, they also function as astronomical alignments. (Figures 232, 126 & 127)

Wall - A low to medium high wall runs along one of the width boundaries of an area of higher permeability. Often, other types of features are located on the opposite side. (Figures 233, 206 & 225) Snake wall are very similar.

Work Areas - During the course of our investigation we have located work areas along areas of higher permeability. At each location at least eighty-five percent of the tools and lithic debris were located on the flows. (Figure 234)

Figure 233: Low wall along area of higher permeability, NY

Figure 234: Work area, with large hammer stones on concentrated flow, NM

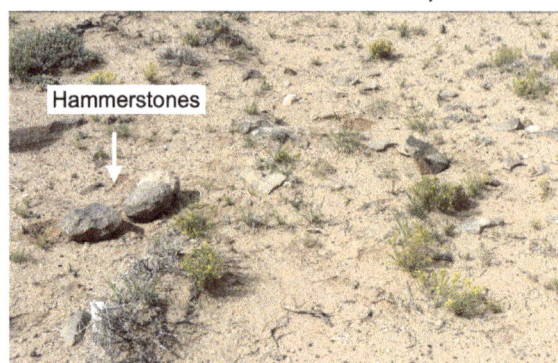

Often, several different types of features are used to map an area of higher permeability. For example, you may find stone piles along the width boundary with tall and turtle cairns, as well as vertical stones centered on them.

Conclusion

Frequently, people ask who were the first to use surface features to map the areas of higher permeability / concentrated flows within the groundwater. Based on the evidence my colleagues and I have gathered thus far, I strongly believe this could have been a universal human trait. Before modern religions developed, ancient cultures around the world associated more closely with Mother Earth. As modern religions developed in other regions of the world, the Western Hemisphere remained more isolated until the sixteenth century. While most modern religions directed human attention away from Mother Earth to a spiritual concept beyond our planet, Native Americans continued to practice their traditional beliefs. Over time, as modern religions developed and spread into other regions, the ancient concepts of associating with the three worlds and their association with concentrated flows within the groundwater was either forgotten or forbidden. This also happened to Native Americans after 1492 as European cultural and religious beliefs spread across the Western Hemisphere. This was augmented by conquest, disease, famine, displacement and laws attempting to force them to accept contemporary European beliefs. During this period, many Native American cultural beliefs were lost, including the meaning of various surface features which were used to map the course of areas of higher permeability within the groundwater, and their association with the Sacred and Ceremonial Landscapes. We may never know who were the first people to conceive this concept, however, it is possible this was a universal human trait. The stone features I investigated in southern England were also located on areas of higher permeability within the groundwater. They are discussed in my book titled

Aligning Megalithic Sites of Southern England and Carnac, France with Groundwater Features.

Often when you conduct an archaeological ground survey, some of the features appear to be associated with one another, while others seem to be randomly placed. However, when you map the areas of higher permeability associated with a site you realize all the features are located on and connected to one another by the subsurface flows. Although we may never know which method(s) ancient people used to map the areas of high permeability within the groundwater, my colleagues and I have consistently demonstrated that we can replicate their documentation of these concentrated flows. By implementing this methodology one can conduct a more efficient and comprehensive investigation of an archaeological site.

Even though Native American oral history, traditions and historical documents support their claim that ancestral Sacred and Ceremonial Landscapes existed prior to 1492, many non-native archaeologists have neglected them. Throughout our research of these landscapes and Habitationscapes in Peru, Chile, Canada and the United States, various fundamentals remain the same among Native American First Nations during different historical periods and in diverse environments. To understand these concepts and the features they contain, researchers need to use an interdisciplinary approach and examine them holistically. Each feature discussed above is intimately associated with one another and each feature's function(s) cannot be fully understood when it is studied individually. Combined, the features functioned as a universal written language for Native Americans. By combining Native American oral history and traditions with a more thorough understanding of the physical components of the Sacred and Ceremonial Landscapes and Habitationscapes, both non-native, as well as Native Americans, can develop a more comprehensive understanding of their ancient past. For example:

During an investigation of a site near Tohatchi, New Mexico, Tamara Billie, Senior Archaeologist, and Tim Begay, Navajo Cultural Specialist, Navajo Historic Preservation Office, informed me about a nearby Chaco site that I was not aware of and suggested that I investigate it. During the weekend when no one from the Historic Preservation Office could accompany me, I decided to survey this site. A few days later Kelley Francis, Navajo Cultural Specialist, Navajo Historic Preservation Office, and I investigated roomblock 3 at the Tohatchi Butte site. Roomblock 3 is located on a hill and provides a panoramic view of several sites within the ancient Tohatchi complex. Francis and I were discussing various sites when Francis pointed to the site Billie and Begay had mentioned to me and said it is associated with a coyote in a Navajo traditional chant (story), however he was not sure why. Knowing what was there, I asked Francis if he has seen anything associated with a coyote at the site, and he said he had not. Then I told Francis I had located a section of a bedrock outcrop which looks like the profile of a coyote's head at that site. (Figure 235) The feature appears to be natural, however it could have been culturally modified to some extent. Interestingly, the feature is not obvious when casually examining the site. I located it as I was mapping the course of the areas of higher permeability associated with the site. As I followed a concentrated flow across the site I located where another branches from it. At the intersection, a roomblock extends along the length of a second area of higher permeability and towards the north end of the outcrop where the coyote profile is located. When you are standing at the intersection of the two areas of higher permeability and looking at the outcrop, you can clearly

Figure 235: The coyote profile, Navajo Nation

see a coyote head profiled; however, if you are off by a few feet in either direction, it is not as noticeable. Therefore, it can easily be missed. By applying my methodology at this site, a coyote's profile was located which confirmed a Navajo traditional chant's (story) description of the site. Following submission of the report to the Navajo Nation Historic Preservation Department, Billie commented to me, "You are supporting our efforts to connect the prehistoric landscape to the present."

Since 1492, Native American Sacred and Ceremonial Landscapes have been destroyed throughout the United States and Canada. Thus, the remaining sites represent a small percentage of those that existed in the past, and they need to be preserved as an important component of their ancestral, as well as contemporary, cultural and spiritual beliefs. This book is dedicated to the preservation of Native American Sacred and Ceremonial Landscapes throughout the Western Hemisphere, as well as similar sites throughout the world. Collectively, they help us develop a more comprehensive understanding of our past.

Part 3

David Johnson's Dowsing Methodology

Site And Stone Feature Analysis

As discussed in Part 1, it is important to consider the following. When researchers learn that dowsing is included in my methodology, they conclude that this is the only method I use to reach my conclusions. Actually, this is not the case. In addition to dowsing, geological, hydrological, archaeological and ethnographic studies are included. Within each region, Native American First Nation archaeological, spiritual, cultural and elder authorities are consulted and collaborate with this research. All of these diverse disciplines are considered prior to writing a final report.

This section discusses my dowsing methodology since many researchers are not familiar with it or have simply dismissed it as unscientific. However, once they apply this methodology they tell me it changed the way they analyze archaeological sites. By adding another layer, the areas of higher permeability within the groundwater, to their investigation the placement of various features becomes more clear, as well as their association with one another.

Johnson's Dowsing Methodology

I developed the following methodology over the course of twenty years beginning with my research on the Nasca Lines and other coastal geoglyphs in Peru and Chile, South America, and the Native Americans' Ceremonial Landscapes throughout North America. Consistently, the same methodology was used for each site.

Johnson's Methodology

*AHP = Areas of Higher Permeability
A. **Tools**

   1.   Dowsing rods
   2.   GPS unit
   3.   Compass
   4.   Notebook
   5.   Measuring devices for both long and short distances.
   6.   When possible, use satellite images of the site to assist in mapping it.
   7.   It helps if you have one or two people helping you.

B. Using Dowsing Rods

1. Dowsing Rod Description

a. Various types of dowsing can be used to obtain the same results. My methodology uses two right angle metal rods which are 12 in / 30.4 cm by 5 in / 12.7 cm. The short end is inserted into a plastic tube. My hands hold the plastic tubes and do not touch the rods. This allows the rods to swing freely. (Figure 235)

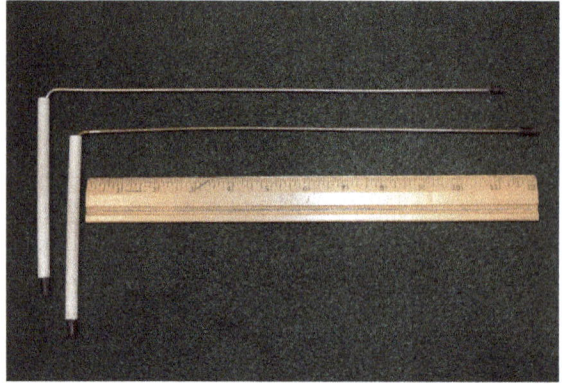

Figure 235: Johnson's dowsing rods

If you are learning to use metal rods, it is advisable to begin by practicing on known concentrated flows first, such as water pipes.

2. Man Made Features Can Influence The Rods

a. When passing under or over electrical lines the dowsing rods will cross. If the electrical line is a single cable, the rods will cross briefly as you walk over or under it. If it is a major power line the rods will cross while you are under it and indicate the width of the power lines above you.

b. When crossing over or under water or oil pipes the dowsing rods will cross. The pipes are usually less than 3 ft / .914 m wide.

3. Natural Features Can Influence The Rods

a. Recent precipitation, both rain and snow, can soak into the ground and create ponding or flows near surface which the rods will detect. This water tends to dry up in a few days. Therefore, it is wise to wait until the ground dries out.

b. The rods will cross wherever snow covers the surface. Wait until it melts and the ground dries out.

c. Magnetite deposits will cause the rods to cross. If this happens the rods will cross over a broad area, and you will have difficulty locating the AHPs.

C. Procedure For Conducting A Site Survey

1. Documentation

a. Flag, label and GPS every point of interest during the survey

b. Take detailed notes

c. Thoroughly document the areas of higher permeability

d. Describe each surface feature and measure it

e. Determine if the feature is associated with the width or trend of an AHP

2. Surface Flows Versus Subterranean Flows

a. Observing surface flows while dowsing can mislead you. When mapping AHPs using dowsing, it is important to ignore the topography. Most of the time the AHPs within the groundwater do not correspond to surface features which can conduct water, such as streams and rivers.

b. Once you complete mapping the AHPs, compare their flow pattern to surface flows. If they are similar, both may be following the same geological feature.

c. Also, compare them to geological features which may be visible at the site.

3. Beginning A Site Survey

a. Whenever possible, establish a grid line along two sides of the site. For example, the south and east sides of a site.

b. Dowse along each grid line and flag the width of each concentrated flow intersecting it.

c. From the grid lines follow each area of higher permeability across the site while flagging the width boundaries frequently, as well as where other concentrated flows intersect it. Also flag any archaeological features observed along the AHP.

d. Flag where two AHPs intersect or cross one another, however continue to document the one you are currently following. Then once it is completed, document the other AHPs one at a time.

4. Interpreting The Dowsing Rods

a. **Locating AHP near you**
   1. **If you are not following a grid line**

a. Stand still while keeping the rods parallel and perpendicular to one another and watch which way the rods turn, left, right, straight forward or back towards you. This indicates the direction you should walk to locate the AHP.

b. While walking towards the AHP, the rods will not swing back and forth until you are close to the AHP. The closer you get to the AHP, the more the rods will swing back and forth. If the rods swing slowly it usually indicates a narrow AHP, and if they swing rapidly it indicates a wide AHP.

c. When the rods stop moving and remain crossed you are standing above an AHP.

2. If you are following a grid line

a. Follow the grid line. When the rods cross, document both width boundaries of the AHP.

3. Interpreting the rods when crossed

a. Rate of flow

1. The rate of flow is the number of gallons / liters per minute an AHP conducts. The geology of an area affects the rate of flow. Therefore, it is difficult to determine the rate of flow using dowsing within a given location without researching the scientific geological and hydrological data.

2. If there are wells with high capacity pumps within the area which operate regularly, they can affect the rate of flow by drawing large amounts of groundwater from the water table and / or AHPs.

3. Barely cross - weak rate of flow and could also indicate near surface water, usually from recent precipitation.

4. Middle cross - moderate rate of flow.

5. Complete cross - high rate of flow.

6. Just because an AHP is wide, for example 100 ft / 30.48 m, it does not mean the rate of flow is high.

b. Determining the width and trend of an AHP

1. The trend of an AHP can meander, and its width can vary.

2. To obtain the best results, map an AHP completely across a site to determine its average width and trend.

3. When you encounter an AHP, flag the width boundary.

4. Then, follow that width boundary for at least 50 ft / 15.24 m, and flag it frequently. The line of flags indicates the trend of the concentrated flow.

5. When you stand on a width boundary of an AHP, the rods will point away from each other. This also indicates the trend of the flow at that location.

6. Go back to the first flag and then cross the AHP perpendicular to the trend. Then, flag the opposite width boundary. The distance between them is the width of the AHP at that location.

7. The trend of some AHPs can change abruptly. For example, when one fault intersects another at a right angle, the AHP can change course by 90 degrees.

8. If two AHPs intersect one another, move off the flows and dowse around the intersection to determine if they merge or cross one another.

9. If they merge or branch from one another, they will not cross one another.

10. If they cross one another and their width and trend are the same on both sides of the intersection, it indicates they are located at different depths within the ground.

11. If two cross, their trends can be the same on both sides of the intersection, however its width may be narrower on one side. This usually indicates one of the concentrated flows is either loosing or gaining water to the other AHP.

c. Dowsing while riding in a vehicle

1. Once you master dowsing while walking, it is possible to use this technique while riding in a vehicle.

2. While someone else drives, sit in the passenger seat and hold the rods as if you were walking with them.

3. Make sure there are no water bottles under the rods.

4. Operate the rods as if you are walking.

5. On very rough roads it is difficult to hold the rods parallel and perpendicular.

d. Determining the depth of an AHP

1. Based on my experience, it is very difficult to learn how to determine the depth of an AHP. With that said, here is the procedure I was taught by another dowser.

2. This works best for AHPs wider than 15 ft / 4.57 m and have a high rate of flow as indicated when the rods crossed completely.

3. Stand in the middle of the AHP with the rods crossed and walk in a circle within the width boundaries of the concentrated flow.

4. Then, walk away from the flow at a right angle.

5. The rods will try to turn back toward the AHP.

6. To prevent this, tilt the ends of the rods slightly downward to keep them from turning back.

7. Continue walking until the rods turn back even though they are tilted downward.

8. Measure the distance from the point where they turned back to where you started.

9. This should be the approximate depth to the AHP.

10. Warning: If you cross another AHP, water pipe or electrical line, this procedure will not work.

D. Feature Identification

These features include culturally modified trees, petroglyphs, pictographs, structures and stone formations, for example, cairns, circles, crescent shaped cairns and snake walls .

1. Johnson's book titled <u>Native Americans' Sacred And Ceremonial Landscape's Correlation With Groundwater</u> can assist in identifying the features associated with North American and South American sites. The book titled Megalith Features of Southern England and Groundwater can assist you in identifying the features in England.

2. GPS the location of each feature.

3. If they are large, such as large roomblocks, GPS each corner.

4. Determine if a structure's walls and features are aligned with the width and / or trend of one or more AHPs that intersect or cross it.

5. For circular structures, GPS the diameter on two opposite sides of the perimeter and compare its diameter with the width of the AHP. Frequently they are the same.

6. For square or rectangular structures, GPS each corner, measure the width and length. Compare the structure's width and length with the AHP. Often, the structure's width or length is equal to the width of the AHP.

E. Artifacts Documentation

1. At some sites the sheer number of artifacts, such as pottery shards, makes it impossible to document every item, however their distribution is important in relation to the AHP. Our data strongly suggests 85% or more of all the artifacts are located along the AHPs.

2. GPS the location of projectile points and tools to determine if they are located along an AHP.

3. For large accumulations of artifacts, such as pottery shards, estimate the percentage of artifacts on and off the AHP.

F. Hydrological Features Associated With The Site

1. Once you complete mapping the AHPs, document the hydrological features present.

   a. **Springs**

1. Estimate the rate of flow.

2. If possible, ask local residents or the area's water department for data on the spring. For example, rate of flow and seasonal changes.

3. In some cases, springs have been drilled and a pump installed.

4. In some cases, springs have been drilled, however they do not require a pump since they are artesian.

5. Also keep in mind that some springs have dried up.

b. **Wells**

1. If possible, obtain when it was dug / drilled, well depth, depth to water and seasonal changes.

2. For wells with pumps, obtain the pump's capacity, average rate of flow, pipe diameter and seasonal changes.

3. If there are two or more wells close together, they can affect each other's rate of flow.

4. In some cases, wells do not require a pump since they are artesian.

5. Research USGS hydrological maps of the area.

G. Geological Features Associated With The Site

1. Some of the features which can conduct AHP include faults, bedrock fractures, dikes, contact zones between two different bedrock types and alluvial deposits which have larger grains concentrated within smaller grain deposits.

2. Document the geological features.

3. Research USGS geological maps of the area.

H. Entering Mapping Data

1. Enter the GPS points into your mapping program.

2. Categorize the features, use a different icon for each category and consecutively number each feature within that group.

3. I use blue lines to indicate each width boundary of an AHP wider than 15 ft / 4.57 m and a single line for the narrower ones.

I. **Final Site Map**

1. Once all the data is mapped, you should be able to determine the following:

   a. How many AHPs bring water into the site.

   b. How many AHPs are located within the site.

   c. The correlation between the AHPs' trends and widths to the location and size of stone features and structures.

   d. Percent of features on and off AHPs.

   e. Artifact distribution on and off AHPs.

Conclusion

My colleagues and I have used this methodology throughout the regions we have researched. Consistently, ancestral Native American archaeological features are located along the areas of higher permeability within the groundwater that we have mapped. This strongly suggests they were mapping the concentrated flows and locating their habitation, ceremonial and sacred sites along them to achieve a vertical alignment of the three worlds. By implementing this methodology, we can conduct a more efficient and comprehensive investigation of an archaeological site. Researchers who are applying this methodology and I agree that this procedure is paramount in understanding the placement of ancestral Native American archaeological features.

Bibliography

Adams, Charles
  1991 *The Origin and Development of the Pueblo Katsina Cult*, University of Arizona Press.

Agenbroad, L. and J. Mead
  1992 *Quaternary paleontology and paleoenvironmental research in National Parks on the Colorado Plateau, Park Science* 12: 13-14. http://cpluhna.nau.edu/index.htm

Akins, Nancy J.
  1986 "A Bicultural Approach To Human Burials From Chaco Canyon, New Mexico", *Reports of the Chaco Center*, Number Nine, Branch Of Cultural Research, U.S. Department of the Interior, National Park Service. http://www.chacoarchive.org/media/pdf/002164.pdf

Albertini, Arn
  2009 "Airport Expansion at Turner's Falls Defeated", January 7, 2009, *Recorder,* Turner's Falls, MA, accessed November 3, 2014, http:rockpiles.blogspot.com/2009/01/airport-expansion-at-turners-falls,hlml

Anderson, John W.
  2015 *Ute Indian Prayer Trees of the Pikes Peak Region*, Old Colorado City Historical Society, Colorado Springs, Colorado.

Anthropology Laboratories of Northern Arizona University
  2012 *The Sinagua*, http://jan.ucc.nau.edu/d-antlab/Soutwestern%20Arch/Sinagua/sinagua.htm

Archaeology Southwest Magazine
  2000 Volume 14, Number 1, Winter 2000, http://www.archaeologysouthwest.org/pdf/arch-sw-v14-no1.pdf

Arizona Department of Water Resources
  2012 *Verde Valley River Basin,* http://www.azwater.gov/azdwr/StatewidePlanning/RuralPrograms/OutsideAMAs_PDFs_for_web/documents/verde_river.pdf

Aveni, Anthony
  1990 *The Lines of Nasca*, edited by Anthony Aveni. Memoirs of the American Philosophical Society, vol. 183, pp.1-40. The American Philosophical Society, Philadelphia.

Ayers, Steve
  2012 "Big Chino: The big water bank", *Verde Valley News*, http://verdenews.com/
        main.asp?SectionID=1&subsectionID=1&articleID=30964

Beers, F.W.
  1878 *The History of Montgomery County and Fulton Counties, NY*, F. W. Beers
        & Co., accessed November 13, 2014, http://rootsweb.com/~nymontgo/
        charleston/charfeature.html

Benson, Larry, Linda Cordell, Kirk Vincent, Howard Taylor, John Steins, G.Lang
        Farmer and Kiyoto Futa
  2002 "Ancient Maize from Chacoan Great Houses: Where was it Grown?",
        PNAS, October 28, 2003, Vol. 100, No. 22, 13115, http://www.pnas.org/
        content/100/22/13111.full.pdf

Berger, W.H. Ph.D.
  2009 "On The Climate History Of Chaco Canyon, Noted on Chaco Canyon
        history in connection with the presentation Drought Cycles in Anasazi
        Land – Sun, Moon, and Ocean Oscillations", at the *PACLIM Conference* in
        Asilomar, California, in April 2009. http://www.escholarship.org/uc/item/
        1qv786mc

Bingham, John Pratt
  2010 *God and dreams : is there a connection?*, Eugene, Oregon: Resource
        Publications. pp. 65—66. ISBN 9781606086674

Bjorndahl, Ryland
  2018 *Geologic Controls on the Distribution of Springs in the Ica Valley,* research
        paper, Geoscience Department, University of Calgary, Alberta, Canada.

Bostwick, Todd W.
  2008 *Beneath The Runways – Archaeology of Sky Harbor International Airport,*
        Pueblo Grande Museum Parks and Recreation Department and Aviation
        Department, City of Phoenix, Arizona.

Brinton, Daniel G.
  1905 *The Myths Of The New World A Treatise on the Symbolism and Mythology
        of the Red Race Of America*, David McKay, Publisher, Philadelphia,
        Digitized by the Internet, archivehttps://archive.org/stream/
        mythsofnewworldt00briniala#page/n5/mode/2up/search/writing

Brumley, John H.
  1986 *Medicine Wheels On The Northern Plains: A Summary and Appraisal,*
        Ethos Consultants Ltd. for The Archaeological Survey of Alberta, Canada,

Bureau of Land Management web site for Colorado
2014   Accessed October 29, 2014, http://www.blm.gov/co/st/en/nm/canm.html

Bureau of Land Management
2016 *Definitions*,U.S. Department Of The Interior, Bureau Of Land Management, Wyoming, viewed October 10, 2016, ww.blm.gov/wy/st/en/programs/ Cultural_Resources/definitions

Cahokia State Official Website
2014   *Cahokia*, viewed November 3, 2014, http://www.cahokiamounds.org/learn/

Cassells, Steve
1983   *The Archaeology Of Colorado*, Johnson Books, Boulder, Colorado.
1997   *The Archaeology Of Colorado*, Johnson Books, Boulder, Colorado.

Chaco Canyon
2012   *The Past is Alive*, http://chaco.malpurposed.net/index.html

Chaco Culture National Historical Park
2012   http://www.nps.gov/chcu/index.htm

Chaco Research Archive
2012   http://www.chacoarchive.org/cra/

De Pastino, Blake
2014   "Ceremonial 'Axis' Road Discovered in Heart of Ancient City of Cahokia", *Western Digs*, May 19, 2014, viewed December 18, 2016, http:// westerndigs.org/ceremonial-axis-road-discovered-in-heart-of-ancient-city- of-cahokia/

Desert Rock Energy Project, Draft EIS
2007 *Affected Environment*, Chapter 3, May 2007, http://teeic.anl.gov/ documents/docs/library/DesertRockDraftEIS_Chapter3.pdf

Doxtater, Dennis
2012   *A Report on Geopatterns Softwear: describing and analyzing large-scale geometry between Anasazi and natural sites in the SW U.S.*, accessed October, 2014, http://cala.arizona.edu/sites/default/files/faculty_papers/ Doxtater%20-%20A%20Report%20on%20Geopattern%20Software.pdf
2013   *Landscape alignments among 21 natural features and 61 Anasazi great kiva sites on the Southern Colorado Plateau: a comparison with random patterns*, accessed October, 2014, http://cala.arizona.edu/sites/default/ files/faculty_papers/LANDSCAPE%20ALIGNMENTS%20(doxtater) %209-12-12.pdf
2017   *The Great North Road As Anasazi Origin Ritual: Chaco and Totah in context with triadic plateau structures*, accessed December 2016, http://

architecture.arizona.edu/sites/default/files/faculty_papers/
Great%20North%20Road%20as%20Origin%20Ritual.pdf

Ellis, Captain Franklin
    1878 *History of Columbia County, New York, Land Grants-Purchases From Indians*, Chapter III, pp. 15 to 2, Published by Everts & Ensign, Philadelphia, PA, http://usgennet.org/usa/ny/county/columbia/genhistcolco/chapt3_1878_hist.htm

Fast, Natalie
    2011 "How Great Were Cedar Mesa Great House Communities?", *SAA 2011,Cedar Mesa Symposium*, Washington State University Research Exchange

Feininger, Tomas
    1978 "The Extraordinary Striated Outcrop at Saqsaywamàn, Peru", *Geological Society of America Bulletin*, v.89, P. 494-503, April 1978, doc. No. 80402.

Fewkes, Jesse Walter
    1971 *Archeological Expedition to Arizona in 1895*, First edition from which this edition was reproduced was supplied by International Bookfinders, Inc., Beverly Hills, California, A Rio Grande Classic, First published in 1898, A paper extracted from the Seventeenth Annual Report of the Bureau of American Ethnology, 1895-19896, Part II, by J. W. Powell.

Friends of the Well
    2012 *Montezuma Well*, http://www.friends-of-the-well.org/news.html

First People - The Legends
    2016 *Spider Rock - A Navajo Legend*, accessed November 7, 2016,http://www.firstpeople.us/FP-Html-Legends/SpiderRock-Navajo.html

Fisher, Richard D.
    2012 *Ancient Knowledge of the Chaco Canyon Anasazi*, Internet, http://www.canyonsworldwide.com/chaco/images/ChacoCanyonAnasaziPaper.pdf

Florissant Fossil Beds National Monument
    2017 *Culturally Modified Trees*, National Park Service, Accessed January 15, 2017, Culturally%20Modified%20Trees%20-%20Florissant%20Fossil%20Beds%20National%20Monument%20(U.S.%20National%20Park %20Service).webarchive

Fowles, Severin M.
    2009 "The Enshrined Pueblo: Villagescapes And Cosmos In The Northern Rio Grande", *American Antiquity*, 73(3). 2009. pp. 448-466, The Society for American Archaeology.

Frances, Julie E. and Lawrence L. Loendore
    2002 *Ancient Visions - Petroglyphs and Pictographs of the Wind River in Bighorn Country, Wyoming and Montana*, University of Utah Press.

Fritts, Harold C.
    1992 "Dendrochronological Modeling Of The Effects Of Climatic Change On The Tree-Ring Width Chronologies From The Chaco Canyon Area, Southwestern United States", *Tree-Ring Bulletin*, vol. 52, 1992. http://www.treeringsociety.org/TRBTRR/TRBvol52_31-58.pdf

Funk, Robert E.
    1976 *Recent Contributions To Hudson Valley Prehistory*, The University of the State of New York, The State Education Department, Albany, New York, 12234.

Gage, James and, Mary Gage
    2015 *Stone Structures of Northeastern United States*, stonestructures.org Committee on Interior and Insular Affairs 1992, pp. 243 and F. W. Beers 1878

German Archaeological Institute
    2007 *Archaeological Project Nasca-Palpa, Peru*, www.dainst.org/index_593_en.htm#

Glowacka, Maria D.
    1999 "The Concept of Hikwsi in Traditional Hopi Philosophy", *American Indian Culture and Research Journal*, 23:2, (1999), p.p. 137-143.

Glynn, Frank
    1973 "Excavation of the Pilot's Point Stone Heaps," *Bulletin of the Archaeological Society of Connecticut* No. 38 1973. pp. 77 - 89

Grahame, John D. and Thomas D. Sisk, ed.
    2002 *Canyons, Cultures and Environmental Change: An introduction to the land-use history of the Colorado Plateau,* 12/2/12 <http://www.cpluhna.nau.edu/>.

Gramly, Richard Michael
    2009 *Paleo-American and Paleo-Environment at the Vail Site, Maine*, Persimmon Press, North Andover, Massachusetts, pp. 13.

2017   *Archaeological Recovery of the Bowser Road Mastodon, Orange County, New York*, ASAA/Persimmon Press, North Andover, Massachusetts.

2018   "Cedar Fork Creek: A Man-Mastodon Association in North-Central Ohio", presented at the 85th Annual Meeting of the Eastern States Archaeological Federation Conference, October 1-4, 2018.

Grissino-Mayer, Henri and Christopher H. Baisan

1998   *A Multicentury Reconstruction of Precipitation for Great Sand Dunes National Monument, Southwestern Colorado,* Thomas W. Swetnam Laboratory of Tree-Ring Research, The University of Arizona Tucson, Submitted July 20, 1998 to the Mid-continent Ecological Science Center, U.S. Department of the Interior, National Park Service, Great Sand Dunes National Monument, accessed November 20, 2014, http://web.utk.edu/~grissino/downloads/GSD%20Finalreport.pdf

Gulliford,Andrew

2017   "Secrets of the Saquache stone snakes", *Durango Herald*, February 9, 2017, Durango, Colorado

.

Gwinn, Vivian, R. and Bruce Hilpert

1990   *The Chaco Handbook: An Encyclopedia Guide*, University of Utah Press, Salt Lake City

Hahman, Richard W., Sr. and Alice Campbell

1980   "Preliminary Geothermal Assessment of the Verde Valley, Arizona", *Arizona Geological Survey,* Open-File Report 80-12, April, 1980, http://www.azgs.az.gov/publications_online/ofr/ofr8012.pdf

Hall, S.A.,

1977   "Late Quaternary Sedimentation and Paleoecologic History of Chaco Canyon, New Mexico", *Geological Society of America Bulletin*, v. 88, p. 1593-1618.

Heitman, Carrie

2010   *Hierarchy and Social Inequality in the American Southwest, A.D. 800–1200*, Department of Anthropology, University of Virginia, Charlottesville, VA, http://www.ncbi.nlm.nih.gov/pubmed/21059921

Henderson, Charles

1947   "Map of Ouilmette Reservations 1828–1844 With its Indian Reminders". *Wilmette Life* , September 1947, Wilmette, IL.

Holtz, Jeff

2007   "Mohegans Buy Rock Sacred To Tribe", *New York Times*, accessed July 8, 2007, https://www.nytimes.com/2007/07/08/nyregion/nyregionspecial2/08noticedct.html

Hovenweep National Monument
  1999 *Canadian Journal of Earth Sciences*. 36 (8): 1347–1356. doi:10.1139/
      cjes-36-8-1347. Archived from the original on 2005-05-13.
  2004 Geologic Resource Evaluation Report, *National Resource Report NPS/
      NRPC/GRD/NRR-2004/002*, Geologic Resources Division, Natural
      Resource Program Center, Denver, Colorado, http://www.nature.nps.gov/
      geology/inventory/publications/reports/hove_gre_rpt_print_body_high.pdf

Jackson, Lionel E., Jr., Elizabeth R. Leboe, Edward C. Little, Philip J. Holme,
Stephen R. Hicock & Kazuharu Shimamura
  1999 "CANQUA 99 Guidebook: Late Quaternary Geology of the Foothills, from
      Calgary to the Alberta–Montana Border" (PDF).

Jackson, Lionel E., Elizabeth R. Leboe, Edward C.Little, Phillip J. Holme, Stephen R.
Hicock, Kazuharu Shimamura, Faye E. Nelson
  2008 "Quaternary stratigraphy and geology of the Rocky Mountain Foothills,
      southwestern Alberta". *Geological Survey of Canada Bulletin 583*.
      doi:10.4095/224301.

Jefferson, Dr. James
  2012 - 2018   Personal conversations and site surveys.

Johnson, David W.
  1998 "The Water Lines of Nasca", *Rumbos* 3(11): 50-56. Lima.
  1999 "The Correlation Between the Lines of Nasca and Water Resources", pp.
      157-164, in *Geheimnisvolle Zeichen im Alten Peru*, edited by
      Herausgegeben von Judith Rickenback, Rietberg Museum, Zurich,
      Switzerland
  2000   "The Lines of Nasca: Clues To The Origin Of Groundwater In Southern
      Peru", in *Geological Society of America*, November 2000, Dr. Steve
      Mabee, Dr. Donald Proulx, David Johnson and Janna Levin co-authors.
  2002   "The Correlation Between Geoglyphs and Subterranean Water Resources
      in the Rio Grande de Nasca Drainage", (with Donald Proulx and Stephen
      B. Mabee) in *Andean Archaeology II – Art, Landscape and Society,* edited
      by Helaine Silverman and William H. Isbell, pp. 307-332, Oxford: Kluwer
      Academic/Plenum Publishers.
  2003   "The Nasca Lines: Geoglyphs Reveal An Ancient Water Map", in
      Permaculture Activist, Winter 2003-04, No. 51,"
  2009 *Beneath The Nasca Lines and other Coastal Geoglyphs of Peru and Chile*,
      Global Learning Inc, Poughkeepsie, NY
  2017   "The Ancestral Native Americans' Sacred Landscape and Features
      Associated with Areas of Higher Permeability Within the Groundwater",
      Occasional Papers Number IV, 27 - 95, The Incorporated Orange County
      Chapter Of The New York State Archaeological Association, Goshen, N.Y.

2018 "The Ancestral Native Americans' Sacred Landscape", in *Spirits In Stone: The Secrets on Megalithic America*, Chapter 10, edited by Glenn Kreisberg, Bear & Company, Rochester, Vermont.

2018 Papers on Ceremonial Landscapes, No. 2018-14, National Anthropological Archives, Smithsonian Institution, Washington, D.C.

2020 *Native Americans' Sacred and Ceremonial Landscapes Correlation with Groundwater*, Hudson House Publishing, Poughkeepsie, New York.

2020 *Aligning Megalithic Sites of Southern England and Carnac, France with Groundwater Features*, Hudson House Publishing, Poughkeepsie, New York.

Johnson, Raymond H., Ed DeWitt, Laurie Wirt, L. Rick Arnold, and John D. Horton

2011 "Water and Rock Geochemistry, Geologic Cross Sections, Geochemical Modeling, and Groundwater Flow Modeling for Identifying the Source of Groundwater to Montezuma Well, a Natural Spring in Central Arizona", In cooperation with the *National Park Service, Open-File Report 2011–1063* , U.S., In cooperation with the National Park Service, U.S. Department of the Interior U.S. Geological Survey, http://pubs.usgs.gov/of/2011/1063/ and http://pubs.usgs.gov/of/2011/1063/pdf/OF11-1063.pdf

Judge, James W.

2004 "Chaco's Golden Century", *In Search of Chaco – New Approaches to an Archaeological Enigma*, edited by David Grant Noble, pp. 1-7. School of American Research Press, Santa Fe, New Mexico.

Kari, James and Ben A. Potter

2010 "The Dene-Yeniseian Connection: Bridging Asian and North America", In *The Dene–Yeniseian Connection,* ed. by J. Kari and B. Potter, 1–24. Anthropological Papers of the University of Alaska, new series, vol. 5. Fairbanks: University of Alaska Fairbanks, Department of Anthropology.

Kantner, John

1996 *Chaco Roads, Evaluating Models of Chaco*, A Virtual Conference, University of Colorado, http://www.colorado.edu/Conferences/chaco/open.htm

1997 "Ancient Roads, Modern Mapping Evaluating Chaco Anasazi Roadways Using GIS Technology", *Expedition*, Volume 39, No. 3 (1997), pages 49 to 61, http://www.penn.museum/documents/publications/expedition/PDFs/39-3/Ancient.pdf

Kehoe, Thomas F.

1958 "Tipi Rings: The 'Direct Ethnological' Approach Applied to an Archeological Problem", *American Anthropologist*. 60 (5): 861.

Kincaid, Chris
    1983 *Chaco Roads Project, Phase 1: A Reappraisal of Prehistoric Roads in the San Juan Basin*, Albuquerque, Bureau of Land Management.

Konieczkl A.D. and S.A. Leake
    1997 *Hydrogeology and Water Chemistry of Montezuma Well in Montezuma Castle National Monument and Surrounding Area, Arizona*, U.S. Geological Survey, prepared in cooperation with the National Park Service, http://pubs.usgs.gov/wri/1997/4156/report.pdf

Kreisberg, Glenn M.
    2010 *Serpent of the North the Overlook Mountain / Draco Correlation*, New England Antiquities Research Association (NEARA)
    2018 *Spirits In Stone: The Secrets on Megalithic America*, edited by Glenn Kreisberg, Bear & Company, Rochester, Vermont.

Laity, Julie E. and Michael C. Malin
    2002 "Sapping processes and the development of theater-headed valley networks on the Colorado Plateau", *The Geological Society of America Bulletin, v. 96, no.2, pp. 203-217.*
    http://www.google.com/hws/search?br=&client=dell-usuk&channel=news-psp&safe=high&adsafe=high&hl=en&ie=UTF-8&oe=UTF-8&q=Sapping Processes and the development of theater - headed valley networks on the Colorado plateau

Lambers, Karsten
    2004 *The Geoglyphs of Palpa, Peru – Documentation, Analysis and Interpretation*, Dissertation, University of Zurich, Switzerland: 97, 137, 147, and 100 – 111.

Langenberg, Cruden W. and RC Paulen
    2003 "Geology of the Frank Slide and southwestern Alberta", *Edmonton Geological Society* – Geological Association of Canada annual field trip celebrating the 100th anniversary of the Frank Slide Disaster, Edmonton, Alberta, Edmonton Geological Society, 34 pp.

Leonard, Edward
    2011 "Archaeologist Claims 12,000-Year-Old Solstice Site In Clarke County", *Clarke Daily News*, Virginia, October 23, 2011, http://www.clarkedailynews.com/archaeologist-claims-12000-year-old-solstice-site-in-clarke-county/25889

Limbrunner, James, Daniel Sheer, Matthew Heberger, Michael Cohen, Jim Henderson and Bob Raucher

2011 *Policy Options for Water Management in the Verde Valley, Arizona*, prepared for The Nature Conservancy, http://www.pacinst.org/reports/verde_river/verde_river.pdf

Lipe, William D. and Mark D. Varien
1999 "Colorado Prehistory: A Context for the Southern Colorado River Basin", *Colorado Council of Professional Archaeologists*, chapter 8. http://www.woodscanyon.net/museum/Pueblo%202/PII.pdf

Lorenz, John C. and Scott P. Cooper
2001 *Tectonic Setting and Characteristics of Natural Fractures in Mesaverde and Dakota Reservoirs of the San Juan Basin, New Mexico and Colorado*, Sand 2001-0054, Unlimited Release, Printed January 2001,
2003 "Tectonic Setting and Characteristics of Natural Fractures in Mesaverde and Dakota Reservoirs of the San Juan Basin", *New Mexico Geology*, February 2003. Volume 25, Number 1. http://geoinfo.nmt.edu/publications/periodicals/nmg/downloads/25/n1/nmg_v25_n1_p3.pdf

Love, David W.
1977 "Dynamics of Sedimentation and Geomorphic History of Chaco Canyon National Monument, New Mexico", *New Mexico Geological Society Guidebook*, 28th Field Conference, San Juan Basin III, 1977, p. 291, http://nmgs.nmt.edu/publications/guidebooks/downloads/28/28_p0291_p0300.pdf
2011 "Geomorphology,Hydrology and Alluvial Stratigraphy in lower Chaco Canyon do not Support the Possible Existence of Prehistoric Sand-Dammed Ephemeral Lakes", *New Mexico Geology*, November 2011, Volume 33, Number 4.

Lucero, Jose
2002 *Cultural Water Study of the Rio Grande*, unpublished paper, May, 20, 2002.

Lusky, Terry
2001 "Where did the Ojibwe dream catcher come from?" *Sweetgrass*, Volume 8 Issue 4 2001, Edmonton, Canada, http://www.ammsa.com/publications/alberta-sweetgrass/where-did-ojibwe-dream-catcher-come-0

Malotki, Ekkehart and Michael Lomatuway'ma
1987 *A Hopi Legend of the Sunset Crater Eruption-Earth Fire*, Northland Press, Flagstaff, Arizona.

Malakoff, David
2015 "Celestial Timekeeping", *American Archaeology,* a quarterly publication of The Archaeological Conservancy, Spring, Vol. 19 No.1, pp. 32-38.

Malouf, Carlin
    1961 "The Tipi Rings of the High Plains", *American Antiquity*, 26 (3): 381 - 389.

Malville, J, McKim
    2008 *Guide to Prehistoric Astronomy in the Southwest,* Johnson Books, Boulder, Colorado.

Marshall, Anne
    2002 Anasazi Great Houses, *Idaho University,* http://www.webpages.uidaho.edu/chaco/index.htm

Martin, Larry
    2005 "A General Description of the Hydrogeology, Water Supply Wells, Groundwater Monitoring, and Potential Threats to Groundwater Resources of Chaco Culture National Historical Park, New Mexico", *Technical Report NPS/NRWRD/NRTR-2—5/325,* Water Resources Division, Fort Collins, Colorado, http://www.nature.nps.gov/water/technicalReports/Intermountain/chcu.pdf

Mavor, James W. and Byron E. Dix
    1989 *The Sacred Landscape of New England's Native Civilization Manitou,* Inner Traditions International, Rochester, Vermont, p.72

Maxson, Thomas F.
    2009 *Mount Nimham: The Ridge Of Patriots*, Kent, New York: Rangerville Press, 2009.

Mayers, Patrick
    2014 National Park Service, *Great Sand Dunes National Park web site*, accessed November 18, 2014, http://www.nps.gov/grsa/historyculture/index.htm

McCluskey, Stephen and Chamberlain Von Del
    2010 *Case Study 4.1:Navajo Star Ceilings,USA*, http://www.astronomicalheritage.org/images/content/astroherit/WHC-internal/ch04cs1.pdf

McGaa, Ed
    1990 *Mother Earth Spirituality - Native American Paths to Healing Ourselves and Our World*, Harpers, San Francisco.

Mythology Dictionary
    2016 "A Creator-goddess of the Hopi. Daughter of Sotuknang", accessed November 5, 2016, http://www.mythologydictionary.com/kokyangwuti-mythology.html

New Mexico Office of the State Engineer / Interstate Stream Commission
2014   http://www.ose.state.nm.us/index.php

Mindeliff, Cosmo
1891-92 "Aboriginal Remains in Verde Valley, Arizona", *Thirteenth Annual Report of the Bureau of Ethnology to the Secretary of the Smithsonian Institution*, http://www.manybooks.net/titles/mindeleffc1996119961-8.html.

Moulton, Gary E.
2001   *The Journals of the Lewis and Clark Expedition*, edited by Gary E. Moulton, 13 vols. (Lincoln: University of Nebraska Press, 1983-2001) Discovering Lewis and Clark, Bison in the Journals, accessed November 7, 2016, http://www.lewis-clark.org/article/443

Morrow, Baker H. and V.B.Price
1997   "Anasazi Architecture and American Design", University of New Mexico Press, *The Chacoan Roads*, Marshall, Michael, 62, National Park Service.
2010   *Montezuma Castle National Monument*, http:/www.nps.gov/moca/historyculture.index.htm

Mullett G.M.
1979   *Spider Woman Stories*, published by The University of Arizona Press,Tucson, Arizona, 1979, ISBN 0-8165-0621-3

NASA
2012   http://www.ghcc.msfc.nasa.gov/archeology/chaco_compare.html

Nash, Stephen E.
2014   "Southwestern (U.S.A.) Archaeological Tree-Ring Dating: 1930-1942Laboratory of Tree-Ring Research", *Bulletin of the History of Archaeology*,The University of Arizona, Tucson, Arizona.http://www.archaeologybulletin.org/article/download/bha.07202/344

National Geographic
2017   *Underwater Archaeologist: Dr. Guillermo de Anda*, accessed November 29, 2017, https://www.nationalgeographic.org/news/real-world-geography-guillermo-de-anda/
2017   *Secret Passageway Discovered Underneath Mayan Snake God Temple*, accessed November 29, 2017, http://www.ibtimes.com/secret-passageway-discovered-underneath-mayan-snake-god-temple-2614377

National Park Service, Great Sand Dunes National Park
2014   "Alden Narango, Southern Ute tribal historian", *National Park Service*, Great Sand Dunes National Park web site, accessed November 11, 2014.
2014   *Geology*, accessed October 29, 2014, file:///Users/DJohnson/Desktop/Reports%20Southwest%20Fall%202014/NPS:

169

%20Nature%20&%20Science»%20Geology%20Resources%20Division.w
ebarchive

National Park Service
  2007 *Montezuma Castle & Tuzigoot*, U.S. Department of the Interior, Montezuma
       Castle National Monument and Tuzigoot National Monument, http://
       www.nps.gov/tuzi/planyourvisit/upload/Verde-Valley-Geology_2007.pdf
  2012 *Chaco Culture, Master Plan, Chaco Canyon National Monument*, New
       Mexico, http://www.nps.gov/history/history/online_books/chcu/
       master_plan/sec2.htm
  2012 *Groundwater Study Helps Protect Montezuma Well, National Park Service*,
       C:\A - Arizona & New Mexico 2012\A - YOUR Reports for 2012\A - You
       September - October Reports\Article for Conference\Reports on area\NPS
       Explore Nature » Water » Montezuma Well.htm

Native American Encyclopedia
  2014 *Water Symbol*, accessed November 15, 2014,
       http://nativeamericanencyclopedia.com/meaning-the-water-symbol/
       accessed November 23, 2014

Native American Languages
  2016 *Legendary Native American Figures: Spider Woman*, *Native languages of
       the Americas Website*, copyright 1998-2015, accessed November 7, 2016,
       http://www.native-languages.org/spider-woman.htm

Native Stones
  2014 *Native Stones*, accessed November 12, 2014,
       http://www.nativestones.com/cairns.htm

Niles,Susan
  1992 "Inca Architecture and the Sacred Landscape: in The Ancient Americas",
       Art from Sacred Landscapes, edited by Richard Townsend. The Art
       Institute of Chicago, 1992. P. 357.

Noble, David Grant (editor)
  2004 *In Search Of Chaco New Approaches to an Archaeological Enigma*,
       School of American Research Press, Santa Fe, New Mexico.

Oak Creek Watershed Council
  2012 *Water Sources Oak Creek Canyon*, Oak Creek Canyon, Arizona, http://
       oakcreekcanyontaskforce.org/WatershedBasedPlan_05.php

Ojibaw
  2015 "Sacred Landscape", *Native American Netroots*, posted September 9,
       2013,http://nativeamericannetroots.net/diary/1559.entry-header

Ortiz, Alfonso
    1969 *The Tewa World*, University of Chicago Press, Chicago

Patterson, Alex
    1992 *A Field Guide to Rock Art Symbols*, Johnson Books, Boulder, Colorado.

Patterson, Carol - Rudolph
    1997 *On the Trail of Spider Woman - Petroglyphs, Pictographs, and Myths of the Southwest*, Smith, Gibbs Publisher

Pierce, Greg, Dr.
    2014 *State Archaeologist Reports On His Research At Vore Buffalo Jump*, Vore Buffalo jump website, accessed February 17, 2017, http://www.vorebuffalojump.org/pdf/VBJ-Pierce-article.pdf

Plog, Stephen
    2010 "Hierarchy and Social Inequality in the American Southwest, A.D. 800-1200", *Proceedings of the National Academy of Science of the United States of America*, vol. 107, no. 46. http://www.pnas.org/content/107/46/19619.full

Powell, Eric A.
    2014 "The Buffalo Chasers", *Archaeology*, November / December 2014, Volume 67, Number 6, pp. 53 - 56 & 64.

Powell J. W.
    1901-1902 *Twenty-Third Annual Report of the Bureau of American Ethnology to the Secretary of the Smithsonian Institution*, Washington, Government Printing Office, 1904, Digitized by the Internet Archive, https://archive.org/stream/thezueniindians00stevrich#page/n53/mode/2up

Powers, Robert P., William B. Gillespie, Stephen H. Lekson
    1983 *The Outlier Survey A Regional View Of Settlement In The San Juan Basin*, Division Of Cultural Research, National Park Service, U.S. Department of the Interior, Albuquerque, New Mexico, Internet Archive, http:/archive.org/stream/outliersurveyreg00powe/outliersurvey00powe_djvu.txt

Powers, Robert P., William B. Gillespie, Stephen H. Lekson
    1983 *A REPORT ON GEOPATTERNS SOFTWARE: describing and analyzing large-scale geometry between Anasazi and natural sites in the SW U.S.*, Division of Cultural Research, National Park Service, U. S. Department of the Interior, National Park Service, Albuquerque, New Mexico, http://www.chacoarchive.org/media/pdf/002161.pdf

Reed, Paul F.
    2006 "Salmon Pueblo: Chacoan Outlier and Thirteenth-Century Middle San Juan Community Center", *Archaeology Southwest Magazine,* Volume 20, Number 3, Summer 2006, Center for Desert Archaeology, http://www.archaeologysouthwest.org/pdf/arch-sw-v20-no3.pdf

Ritchie, William A.
    1958 "An Introduction To Hudson Valley Prehistory", *The New York State Museum And Science Service Bulletin,* Number 367, The University of the State of New York, The State Education Department, Albany, New York.
    1961 "A Topology and Nomenclature for New York Projectile Points", *The New York State Museum And Science Service Bulletin,* Number 384, The University of the State of New York, The State Education Department, Albany, New York.
    1965 *The Archaeology Of New York State*, The American Museum Of Natural History, The Natural History Press, Garden City, New York.

Rock Piles
    2010 *USET Resolution 2007:037*, Rock Piles, Tuesday, November 11, 2010, accessed November 12, 2014, http://rockpiles.blogspot.com?2010/11/uset-resolution-2007037.hyml

Rosenberry,Donald
    2012 *Ground-water Sapping and the Generation of Natural Amphitheaters,* Geography Department, University of Colorado, Boulder, Colorado, http://www.colorado.edu/geography/geomorph/rosenberry/

Proulx, Donald A.
    2006 *A Sourcebook of Nasca Ceramic Iconography Reading a Culture Through Its Art*, University of Iowa Press, Iowa City, Iowa.

Sanford, Dennis J. and Jane S. Day
    1992 *Ice Age Hunters Of The Rockies*, Denver Museum Of Nature and Science and University Press Of Colorado, Boulder, Colorado.

Schillaci, Michael A. and Christopher M. Stojanowski
    2003 "Postmarital Residence and Biological Variation at Pueblo Bonito", *American Journal Of Physical Anthropology,*120:1-15 (2003) https://tspace.library.utoronto.ca/bitstream/1807/2316/2/Schillaci1.pdf

Schroeder, Albert H.
    1960 "The Hohokam, Sinagua and the Hakataya", No. 5, *Society for American Archaeologgy and the University of Wisconsin Pres*s, 1960, http://digital.library.wisc.edu/1711.dl/EcoNatRes.ArchivesArch5

Science Daily
    2013 "Dating oldest known petroglyphs in North America", University of Colorado at Boulder. Dating oldest known petroglyphs in North America. *Science Daily*, 13 August 2013, www.sciencedaily.com/releases/2013/08/130813121622.htm>.

Schnorenberg, Megan and Gene Gade
    2005 *Geology Of The Vore Buffalo Jump*, Vore Buffalo Jump website, accessed February 17, 2017, http://www.vorebuffalojump.org/pdf/VBJ%20Geology.pdf

Sebastian, Lynne and Jeffrey H. Altschul
    2016 *An Archaeological Survey of the Additions to Chaco Culture National Historical Park, Settlement Pattern, Site Typology, and Demographic Analyses: The Anasazi, Archaic, and Unknown Sites*, Chaco Research Archive, chacoarchive.org.

Sering, Ron
    2013 "Along Ancient Trails - Archaeology In The San Luis Valley", *Colorado Central*, September 2013. No. 232, pp. 14-16.

Slifer, Dennis
    1998 *Signs of Life - Rock Art of the Upper Rio Grande*, Ancient City Press, Santa Fe, New Mexico.

Slifer, Dennis and James Duffield
    1994 *Flute Player Images In Rock Art - Kokopelli*, Ancient City Press, Santa Fe, New Mexico.

Silverman, Helaine
    1988 "Nasca 8: A Reassessment of its Chronological Placement and Cultural Significance": *in Vitzthum, V.J., ed., Studies in Andean Anthropology*, Ann Arbor, Michigan: Discussions in Anthropology, v.8, pp.23-41.
    1990 "Beyond the Pampa: The Geoglyphs in the Valleys of Nazca": *National Geographic Research* 6(4): 435-456.
    1993 *Cahuachi in the Ancient Nasca World,* Iowa City: University of Iowa Press.

Silverman, Helaine and Proulx, Donald A.
    2002 *The Nasca,* Blackwell Publishers Inc, Malden, Massachusetts.

Sofaer, Anna and Sinclair, Rolf M.
    1983 "Astronomical Markings at Three Sites on Fajada Butte", *Astronomy and Ceremony in the Prehistoric Southwest*, John B. Carlson and W. James Judge, editors, Maxwell Museum of Anthropology, Anthropological Paper, Papers, No 2, 1983, See solsticeproject.org.

2010 *"The Primary Architecture of the Chacoan Culture: A Cosmological Expression, Solstice Project of Chaco Canyon"*, Appeared in *Anasazi Architecture and American Design*, edited by Baker H. Morrow and V.B. Price, Albuquerque, NM: University of New Mexico Press, 1997. http://www.solsticeproject.org/primarch.htm

Solstice Project, Research
2012 http://www.solsticeproject.org/primarch.htm

Springer, A.E. and M.C. Fry
2005 "Report for 2005AZ89B: Big Chino Basin 3-D Digital Hydrogeologic Framework Model", Conference Proceedings: o. 2005. 3-D Visualization of Aquifers of Arizona Using the GeoWall. Annual meeting of the *Arizona Hydrological Society*, September 22-25, Flagstaff, AZ.

Stalker, A Mac S.
1975 "The Big Rock", In *Structural Geology of the Foothills Between Savanna Creek and Panther River, S.W. Alberta, Canada*, May 23, 1975, H.J. Evers and J. E. Thorpe, eds., pp. 9-11, Calgary, Alberta, Canada: Canadian Society of Petroleum Geologists.

Stevenson Matilda Coxe
???? *The Sia*, Smithsonian Institution - Bureau Of Ethnology, Digitized by the Internet Archive,
https://archive.org/stream/siasmithsonian00stevuoft#page/n1/mode/2up

Stone, William J.
2006 *Hydrogeology of the Gallup Sandstone, San Juan Basin*, Northwest New Mexico, online. http://info.ngwa.org/gwol/pdf/810600286.PDF

Strahler, A.
1065 *Introduction to Physical Geology*, Wiley and Sons, Inc., p. 363, 375-379.

Stryd, Arnoud H.
1998 *Culturally modified trees of British Columbia*, Prepared by Archaeology Branch B.C. Ministry of Small Business, Tourism and Culture for the Resources Resources Inventory Committee, British Columbia Ministry of Forests, 1998, 2001, https://www.for.gov.bc.ca/ftp/archaeology/external/!publish/web/professionals/cmthandbook.pdf

Trento, Salvatore Michael
1978 *The Search For Lost America – Mysteries Of The Stone Ruins In The United States*, Penguin Books, New York, NY.

Tuzigoot National Monument
  2012 Clarkdale, Arizona, visited November 4, 2014,   http://www.nps.gov/nr/
        travel/culture_diverity/Tuzigoot_National_Monument.html

Twenter F.R.
  2012 "Rocks and Water in Verde Valley, Arizona", *NEW MEXICO GEOLOGICAL
        SOCIETY,* Thirteenth Field Conference, US Geological Survey, Iowa City,
        Iowa.

United South and Eastern Tribes, Inc.
  2001 *Ceremonial Landscapes*, visited November 4, 2014,
        http:www.indian.senate.gov/sites/default/files/upload/files/Michell-Hicks-
        testimony.pdf

United States Geological Survey
  2012 "Boundary Descriptions and Names of Regions, Subregions, Accounting
        Units and Cataloging Units", *U.S. Geological Survey*, http://
        water.usgs.gov/GIS/huc_name.html.

United States. Congress. House. Committee on Interior and Insular Affairs
  1992 Subcommittee on National Parks and Public Lands, *Proposed additions to
        the national wild and scenic rivers system: hearings before the
        Subcommittee on National Parks and Public Lands of the Committee on
        Interior and Insular Affairs*, House of Representatives, One Hundred First
        Congress, second session ...Washington : U.S. G.P.O. : For sale by the
        U.S. G.P.O., Supt. of Docs., Congressional Sales Office, 1992, Editorial
        Note: Letter from Elwood H. Miller, Jr., Chairman, The Klamath Tribe
        [Oregon], dated 6/5/1990 to Representative Bruce Vento

United States Geological Survey
  2012 *Map View of the Nation*, Internet

Urton, Gary
  1985 "Animal Metaphors and the Life cycle in an Andean Community", in *Animal
        Myths and Metaphors in South America*, edited by Gary Urton. University
        of Utah Press, Salt Lake City, 1985. P. 251-284.
  1990 "Andean Social Organization and the Maintenance of the Nasca Lines", *In
        The Lines of Nasca*, edited by Anthony Aveni. Memoirs of the American
        Philosophical Society, Vol. 183 pp. 173-206. The American Philosophical
        Society, Paris.

USGS
  2012 *Possible Effects of Groundwater Pumping on Surface Water in the Verde
        Valley, Arizona*, USGS, http://pubs.usgs.gov/fs/2010/3108/fs2010-3108.pdf

2014   *Geophysics of the Rio Grande Basins*, San Luis Basin Geophysics, visited November 3, 2014, http://crustal.usgs.gov/projects/rgb/SanLuisBasin/index.html

Vore Buffalo Jump
2016   *History*, accessed February 17, 2017, http://www.vorebuffalojump.org/content/history/

Van Dyke, Ruth M.
2004   "Chaco's Sacred Geography", *In Search of Chaco – New Approaches to an Archaeological Enigma*, edited by David Grant Noble, pp. 78-85, 2013Several Papers, http://binghamton.academia.edu/RuthVanDyke

Wahkpa Chu'gn Buffalo Site
2016   *History*, http://buffalojump.org/index2.htmWall, Steve and Harvey Arden 1990, *Wisdomkeepers - Meeting With Native American Spiritual Elders*, Beyond Words Publishing Inc.

Welch, A.B.
2014   *Beliefs of the Sioux Nation*, accessed November 14, 2014,http://www.welchdakotapapers.com/2011/12/sacred-stones-and-holy-places/

Wells, Don
2016   *Trail Tree Newsletter*, January 2015

Wells, D. and D. Wells
2011   *Mystery of the Trees: Native American Markers of a Cultural Way of Life that May Soon Be Gone*, Mountain Stewards Publishing, Jasper, GA.

Whitley, David S., Ronald I. Dorn, Julei Francis, Lawrence L. Loendorf, Thomas Holcomb, Russel Tanner and Joseph Bozovich
1996   "Recent Advances In Petroglyph Dating And Their Implications For The Pre-Clovis Occupation Of North America", *Proceedings of the Society for California Archaeology*, 1996, Vol.9, pp. 92-103.http://www.scahome.org/publications/proceedings/Proceedings.09Whitley.pdf

Wikipedia
2014   *Ceremonial Stone Landscape*, accessed November 11, 2014, http://en.wikipedia.org/wiki/Ceremonial_Stone_landscapes
2014   *Culturally Modified Trees*, accessed November 20, 2014, http://en.wikipedia.org/wiki/Ceremonial_Stone_landscapes
2014   *Long Walk of the Navajo*, accessed November 14, 2014, http://en.wik/ the navajohttp://en.wikipedia.org/wiki/ Long_Walk_of_the_Navajo
2014   *Saksaywaman*, accessed November 10, 2014, http://en.wikipedia.org/wiki/Saksaywaman

2014   *Trail Trees*, accessed October 29, 2014, http://en.wikipedia.org/wiki/
        Trail_trees

2015   *Isla del Sol*, accessed November 5, 2015, http://en.wikipedia

2016   *Medicine Wheel*, accessed November 7, 2016, https://en.wikipedia.org/
        wiki/Medicine_wheel#cite_ref-royalalbertamuseum.ca_1-2

2016   *Spider Grandmother*, accessed November 7, 2016, https://
        en.wikipedia.org/wiki/Spider_Grandmother#cite_ref-6

2017   *Athabaskan languages*, accessed July 16, 2017, https://en.wikipedia.org/
        wikiAthabaskan_languages

2017   *Glacier Erratic*, accessed November 29, 2017, https://en.wikipedia.org/wiki/
        Glacial_erratic

2017   *Tipi Ring*, accessed October 17, 2017, https://en.wikipedia.org/wiki/
        Tipi_ring

2018   *Big Rock (glacial erratic) Okotoks*, Alberta Canada, Accessed 6-25-18,
        https://en.wikipedia.org/wiki/Big_Rock_(glacial_erratic)

2018   *Mohegan Tribe*, Accessed 6-25-18, https://en.wikipedia.org/wiki/Mohegan

Wilcox, David R.

2005   *Plateau The Land and People of the Colorado Plateau*, Spring/Summer
        2005, Volume 2, number 1, Museum Of Northern Arizona, Flagstaff,
        Arizona.

Whittall James P. II

1948   "Hunt's Hill Ste-Souterrain, Montville, Connecticut," *Bulletin of Early
        Sites Research Society 11* (no. 1, 1984): 7-12.

Wolley, Anne M. and Timothy Shilling

2013   "Native American culture and prehistoric bison hunting in the Black Hills",
        Park Science, Vol. 30, No. 2, Fall 2013, National Park Service, viewed on
        October 12, 2016, http://www.nature.nps.gov/parkscience/Archive/PDF/
        Article_PDFs/ParkScience30(2)Fall2013_26-29_VawserSchilling_3663.pdf

Wood, John Edwin

1978   *Sun, Moon and Standing Stones*, Oxford University Press, Oxford,
        England, Zuidema, R. T.

1964   The *Ceque System of Cusco: The Social Organization of the Capital of the
        Inca*, Brill, Leiden.

Zoll, Kenneth J.

2008   *Sinagua Sunwatchers – An Archaeoastronomy Survey of the Sacred
        Mountain Basin*, Sunwatcher Publishing, Sedona, Arizona

2011   *Understanding the Rock Art of Sedona and the Verde Valley*, Verde Valley
        Archaeology Center, Inc., Camp Verde, Arizona

Site Report Archival Files

The following agencies have archived Johnson's site reports for their jurisdiction.

Bureau Of Land Management

Agua Fria National Monument
Park Archaeologist
21605 N. 7th Avene
Phoenix, Arizona 85027-2929
Phone - 623-580-5507 or 5565

Bureau Of Land Management Montana State Office
Chief, Branch of Social and Cultural Resources
5001 Southgate Drive
Billings, Montana 59101- 4669
Phone - 406-896-5214

Bureau Of Land Management Yuma Field Office / Lake Havasu Field Office
Park Archaeologist
7341 A E 30th St
Yuma, Arizona 85365
(928) 317-3312

Costilla County, Colorado
Chief Administrative Officer
Board of County Commissioners
Costilla County
P.O. Box 100
352 Main Street
San Luis, CO 81152
Office 719-672-9226

La Garita Ranch, Colorado
5609 County Road 41.2
Del Norte, CO 81132
Phone - (710) 580-2486

Lewis Hollow Site, New York
Overlook Mountain Center
Phone - 845-417-8384
https://www.overlookmountain.org

National Forest Service

Coconino National Forest
Forest Archaeologist
1824 South Thompson Street
Flagstaff, AZ 86001
Phone - 928-527-3476

National Park Service

Chaco Culture National Historical Park
Chief of Cultural Resources
1808 County Rd. 7950
Nageezi, NM 87037
505-786-7014, ext. 226

Great Sand Dunes National Park
Park Research Coordinator
11500 Highway 150
Mosca, CO 81146-9798
Phone: 719-378-6361

Montezuma Castle National Monument
Chief of Cultural Resources
P. O. Box 219
Camp Verde, AZ 86322
Phone number - 1-928-649-6195, ex 225

Navajo Nation
Senior Archaeologist
Cultural Resources Compliance Section, Historic Preservation Department
P.O. Box 4950
Window Rock, Arizona 86515
928-871-7198

New York State Archaeologist's Office
State Archaeologist and Director
Cultural Resource Survey Program, New York State Museum
Division of Research and Collections
Cultural Education Center 3122
Albany, NY 12230
Phone - 518-402-5975

New York State Palisades Interstate Park Commission
Bear Mountain, NY 10911
(845) 786-2701 ext 263

Ramapough Lunaape Nation
Chief
189 Stag Hill Rd.
Mahwah, NJ 07430
Phone - 201-529-1171

Salmon Ruins Museum
Executive Director
Salmon Ruins Museum
6131 US Highway 64
P. O. Box 125
Bloomfield, New Mexico 87413
Phone - 505-632-2013
www.salmonruins.com

Smithsonian Institution
National Anthropologic and Archaeological Library,Washington, D.C.
    File Reference:
    David Johnson
        2018   Papers on Ceremonial Landscapes, No. 2014-14, National
                Anthropological Archives, Smithsonian Institution, Washington, D.C.

Tsuut'ina Nation Tribal Office
9911 Chiila Blvd.
Tsuut'ina, AB T2W 6H6
Phone - (403) 281-4455

Zapata Site Report
Zapata Homeowners Association
Board of Directors
PO Box 1282,
Alamosa, CO 8110

Acknowledgments

My colleagues and I are very grateful to the following agencies who granted us research permits within their jurisdiction and shared their knowledge with us.

Athna Nation
Chief Gary Harrison
Angela Wade, Cultural ANA SEDS Project Manager

Bureau Of Land Management
Gary Smith, Chief, Branch of Social and Cultural Resources, Montana State Office
Jessica Han, Archaeologist, Yuma Field Office / Lake Havasu Field Office
Dan Haas, Colorado State Archaeologist, Lowry Great House Outlier
Tim Watkins, Park Archaeologist, Agua Fria National Monument
John Park, Retired BLM archaeologist

Costilla County, Colorado
Ben Doon, Chief Administrative Officer, Costilla County Board of Commissioners

Blackfoot Nation
Virgil Edwards, Historic Preservation Department

National Forest Service
Wendy Sutton, Archaeologist, Chimney Rock National Monument
Lindsey Smith, Archaeologist, Chimney Rock National Monument
Peter Pilles, Forest Archaeologist, Coconino National Forest
Walter Gosart, Archaeologist, Coconino National Forest
Travis Bone, District Archaeologist, Coconino National Forest
Terri Lynn Green, Palatki and Honanki manager, Coconino National Forest

National Park Service
Dabney Ford, Chief of Cultural Resources, Chaco Culture National Historical Park
Aron Adams, Chief of Cultural Resources, Chaco Culture National Historical Park
Roger Moore, Assistant Archaeologist, Chaco Culture National Historical Park
Fred Bunch, Chief of Cultural Resources, Great Sand Dunes National Park
Andrew Valdez, Geologist, Great Sand Dunes National Park
Matthew Guebard, Chief of Cultural Resources, Montezuma Castle National Monument
Melissa Philibeck, Assistant Archaeologist, Montezuma Castle National Monuments
As well as several of their staff.

Navajo Nation Archaeologists, Navajo Nation Historic Preservation Department, Cultural Resource Compliance Section
Ronald Maldonado

Ettie Anderson
Tamara Billie
Tim Begay
Kelley Francis
And several of their staff.

New York State Archaeology Department
    Christina B. Rieth, Ph.D., State Archaeologist and Director, Cultural Resource
        Survey Program, New York State Museum

Northern Arapaho Nation Directors, Historic Preservation Office
    Yufna Soldierwolf
    Devin Oldman

New York State Palisades Interstate Park Commission
    Ed McGowan, Director of Science and Trailside Museums and Zoo
    Jesse Jaycox, Regional Supervisor
    Eric Humphrey, Park Director, Minnewaska State Park
    Michael Mcelroy , Park Director, Sterling Forest State Park
    John Burley, Park Director, Harriman State Park
    Michael Cahill, Park Forest Ranger, Highland Lakes and Goosepond Mountain
        State Parks
    Evan Thompson, Clarence Fahnestock Memorial State Park
    Declan Hennelly, Clarence Fahnestock Memorial State Park

Hopi Nation
    Terry Morgart, Hopi Cultural Preservation Officer
    Max Taylor, Water Resources Technician, Hopi Department of Water Resources

Montana State Parks
    Sara Scott, Director, Montana State Parks Cultural Resources
    David Andrus, Park Manager, Madison Buffalo Jump
    Jarret Kostrba, Park Manager, Pictograph Cave
    Rick Thompson, Park Manager, First Peoples Buffalo Jump

Tsuut'ina Nation
    Chief Lee Crowchild
    James Big Plume, Specific Claims and Research Director
    David Onespot, Senior Indigenous Field Assessor
    Declan Starlight
    Justin Onespot

Salmon Ruins Museum
    Larry Baker, Executive Director

Vore Buffalo Jump
Jacqueline Wyatt, President of Board of Directors
Ted Vore

Wahkpa Chu'gn Buffalo Jump
John and Anna Brumley

Zapata Homeowners Association
Jack Zeman, President, Board of Directors

The following people were instrumental in contributing to the data discussed within this text. Without their support, knowledge and contributions I would not have been able to conduct this research or develop a more in-depth understanding of ancestral Native Americans Ceremonial Landscapes.

La Cuma de Aztlan Sacred Sites Protection Circle
Alfredo Figueroa, Elder
and several of their committee members

Narragansett Nation
Doug Harris, Deputy Tribal Historic Preservation Officer

New England Antiquities Research Association
Harvey Buford
Glenn Kreisberg
Donna Thompson
Bill Sharp
Doug Schwartz
and several members

Orange County Chapter of the New York State Archaeological Association
Howard Banney
Donald Bayne
Thomas Brannan
Dr. Ned Doucet
Wayne Knapp
Clifton Patrick
Kathleen Pemble
Dr. Gregory Sohrweide
and several members of this chapter

Ramapough Lunaape Nation
Chief Dwaine Perry
Two Clouds

Ute Nation
Dr. James Jefferson, Elder

Verde Valley Archaeological Association
Linda Krumrie
Richard Henderson
Kenneth Zoll
and several other members

The following people assisted with documenting and analyzing the sites.

Priscilla Johnson, David Johnson's wife
Dr. Philip LaPorta, Archaeologist & Geologist
Carl Niemann from Germany assisted me in Peru, as well as in Arizona.
Dr. Dennis Stanford, Archaeologist, Smithsonian Institution
Tom Maxson, historian

Arizona
Nelson Avery
Glenn Waltrip
Michael Chappell

Colorado
Ken Frye
Alva Hibbs
Mark Jones
Dr. Forrest Ketchin, Anthropologist
Jose Lucero
Barbara Maat
John McEvoy
Thomas Peay
Wayne Ross
Mike Spearman
Danny Temple
Shane Temple
Don Wells
Daniel Wallich

New Mexico
Brooks Marshall
Richard Friedman, Geologist and archaeologist,
Todd Myers, Manager of Soda Springs Ranch
Scott Cooper, Geologist

Index

www.ingramcontent.com/pod-product-compliance
Lightning Source LLC
Chambersburg PA
CBHW061233270326
41929CB00030B/3475